The Robot Factory

Joseph Ganem

The Robot Factory

Pseudoscience in Education
and Its Threat to American
Democracy

 Springer

Joseph Ganem
Loyola University Maryland
Baltimore, MD, USA

ISBN 978-3-319-77859-4   ISBN 978-3-319-77860-0 (eBook)
https://doi.org/10.1007/978-3-319-77860-0

Library of Congress Control Number: 2018936525

Cover illustration by Charlie Love

Printed on acid-free paper

This Springer imprint is published by the registered company Springer International Publishing AG part of Springer Nature.
The registered company address is: Gewerbestrasse 11, 6330 Cham, Switzerland

For Sharon
and our children
Thomas, Katherine, and Claire

Preface

I have spent my entire life in school. During this time—over half a century—schools have been in a constant state of reform. We just can't seem to get Education as a service right. And yet *education*, as an experience, is undeniably uplifting; we are all students at one time or another, and most of us also teach at one time or another, even if teaching is not our profession.

I began teaching soon after I started first grade. My mother tells a story of how I played "school" with my younger siblings and, unbeknownst to her, taught my three-year-old brother how to read and write his name. When my brother arrived at preschool, his teacher expressed anger at my mother for teaching him how to write his name before he started preschool, a skill she had planned on teaching. My mother, apologizing, explained that she had no idea how he learned to write his name. Later, my brother fessed up that he and I "played school" and "Joe was the teacher."

That began my career as an educator, and I have been fascinated with the processes of learning and teaching ever since. Although "to learn" and "to teach" are separate verbs with different meanings, the two processes are intimately intertwined. A teacher will learn a great deal through the act of teaching, and a learner will eventually need to teach him or herself the material. Learning is always a collaborative process. The teacher cannot simply transfer knowledge and understanding to a student.

Through my lifelong development as a teacher and learner, I have reflected on many of the pressing issues in education. I am also a scientist, and I recognize how education reformers and innovators often couch their proposals with the language and trappings of science. In recent years, I have become deeply troubled by the agenda of the education reform movement and its misuse of science, a misuse so widespread and prevalent that I think it warrants being called pseudoscience. Pseudoscience is a set of false beliefs and assumptions camouflaged with meaningless jargon, data, and statistics to give an appearance of scientific validity. Unfortunately, pseudoscience can therefore blend in with a great deal of legitimate science on education.

As pseudoscience, education reform—with its mandated standards, high-stakes tests, accountability metrics, and focus on "college and career readiness"—lacks scientific validity, and is in fact, not about science or education. Instead, education is now a program to train skilled, compliant workers who will accept what they are told and do what they are asked. It is a program to create robots.

It is ironic that we are training children to submit to authority, while at the same time we are telling them that the path to future success lies in the fields of science, technology, engineering, and math (or STEM to use the ubiquitous acronym). Unquestioned acceptance of authority is the opposite of science. This irony extends into the public sphere: science as a method of acquiring knowledge, a body of knowledge, and an occupation is under attack by many politicians and corporate leaders. Many of the same people who run our government and business institutions and who depend on science for their power, influence, and wealth routinely denounce science and scientists for uncovering truths that threaten and inconvenience their self-interests. Yet these same political and corporate leaders want to invoke science whenever it suits their interests, particularly in regard to "data-driven" education reform.

The assertion that education is in a state of "crisis" that threatens our country's political and economic future has been fashionable for many decades now, and this crisis narrative is routinely supported by data derived from student tests. I argue in this book that there is indeed a crisis in education, but the crisis is not what we think it is and it has nothing to do with test scores or other data-driven accountability metrics used to judge student achievements and the effectiveness of teachers and schools. In fact, the education crisis we are facing extends far beyond classrooms and schools, and the "solutions" will exacerbate the crisis, not fix it. I argue that the "solutions" being forced on schools are an intentional attack on our democracy by a political and corporate class that does not actually want an educated and informed citizenry.

The real educational crisis we face is twofold: a denial by the reform movement and many others in positions of power of the essential attributes of an authentic education and the concurrent creation of a system designed to authentically educate only a few, select, chosen students. Authentic education, with attributes that include critical thinking, exposure to diverse ideas, peoples, and cultures, and the skills of asking relevant questions and collaboratively solving meaningful problems, is no longer a priority for most of our "educational" institutions. I argue that authentic education is essential for doing real science and for participating in and maintaining American democracy.

The consequences are pronounced and profound. We are witnessing an unprecedented breakdown of our political and economic systems. Our democracy has evolved into a plutocracy. Unchecked market forces have produced extreme levels of economic inequality. Education is being "reformed" in such a way that it is now an enabler of these breakdowns, rather than a bulwark to guard against them. All this is happening while STEM fields are being promoted in educational settings. However, closer examination reveals that it is STEM *skills* that reformers want students to acquire, not a STEM *education*. As I explain in this book, an education in the STEM fields, particularly in math and science, is fundamentally also a liberal arts education. And like the professional practice of science today, the liberal arts is also under attack.

I find it bizarre that many of the same people who disparage science are also vocal advocates for urging more students to enter STEM fields. This simultaneous debasement and advocacy of science results in a kind of cognitive dissonance. Reformers actively undermine their stated goals by modeling the exact opposite of the predilections and behaviors inherent in the scientific method that they claim to value. Such cognitive dissonance results in an epidemic of what I call "willful ignorance" in the education reform movement. Indeed, this epidemic—a return to the kind of magical, wishful thinking that the modern scientific method was supposed to banish—has infested many institutions in our society, especially in the political and corporate arenas that set education policies.

It is not my intent to impugn the motives of all those who are involved in education reform movements, many of whom I believe to be sincere and well-meaning in their desire to improve educational practices and outcomes. However, I am deeply suspicious of many reforms seemingly being driven by political and corporate interests. The willful ignorance I observe is often from politicians and corporations who routinely use the language of science to advance beliefs and self-serving agendas that upon closer scrutiny not only have no scientific basis, but are in fact detrimental to education. The public is presented with false choices; these false choices are amplified in a media echo chamber that repeats catch phrases and sound bites, but does a poor job of evaluating evidence and questioning assertions. Make a claim often and loud enough and it becomes conventional wisdom, even if that claim rests on thin evidence or logical fallacies.

Organization of *The Robot Factory*

The Robot Factory begins with the observation of an introductory lesson in a third-grade math class. Any observer will intuitively understand this lesson as deeply flawed. After the introduction, *The Robot Factory* is divided into four parts of expanding scope beginning with why the approach to education observed in this third-grade class is flawed and yet still persists, and concluding with the broader implications for our society that result from deep misunderstandings of what it means to educate and be educated.

Part I of *The Robot Factory* explains how many of the data-driven approaches to evaluating student achievement and the effectiveness of schools, teachers, and educational programs have more in common with pseudoscience than real science. I begin by articulating essential attributes of real science, and distinguishing how pseudoscientific studies are always missing at least one and often more than one of these essential attributes. I then examine some widely used approaches to evaluating educational outcomes and demonstrate how each lacks one or more of the essential attributes of real science.

Despite deep flaws in the use of data and logic, these pseudoscientific explanations remain compelling because they rely on emotionally engaging narratives that offer simple solutions to complex problems. People want to believe the narratives, despite the bogus statistics and logical fallacies; therefore, pseudoscientific explanations are attractive and continue to propagate.

Part II of *The Robot Factory* is an exposé on the misunderstanding of math and science in educational settings. I show that our education system fails to properly teach these disciplines. These subjects are difficult for students and teachers in part because of the inherent difficulty of these disciplines, but also because the K-12 curriculum often misrepresents the motives and methods of professional practitioners. Coupled with the alluring pseudoscientific narratives I debunk in Part I, this failure to teach math and science results in a population of citizens unable to use math and science. The result: an abounding prevalence of pseudoscience in public discourse.

The issues raised in Parts I and Parts II of *The Robot Factory*—the use of pseudoscience in education and failure to provide an adequate education in math and science—are inextricably linked. When flawed math and science methodologies are used to advance destructive educational agendas, it is little wonder that our children fail to learn these subjects. To use math and science correctly in any context, education or otherwise, we need to provide a solid and accurate education in these subjects.

Part III of *The Robot Factory* goes beyond classrooms and schools to examine education and science in the broader context of contemporary American society. I examine how pseudoscientific narratives are constructed and the paralysis of false choice that they impose. Because of widespread beliefs in the pseudoscientific narratives surrounding education (as well as many other pressing issues), we are unable to solve communal problems. This is a threat to American democracy.

Educational institutions cannot be separated from the society and culture in which they operate. Moreover, it is not reasonable to expect that these institutions can instill the same values in our children that are overtly scorned by adults. In the promulgation of pseudoscientific narratives, we see "educated" adults rationalizing all kinds of intellectual dishonesty—even outright lies—in pursuit of "higher" purposes (albeit purposes that somehow "coincidentally" align exactly with their self-interests and often narrow beliefs and rigid ideologies).

One such pseudoscientific narrative that I examine in detail in Part III of *The Robot Factory* is what I call the "tautology of the market." A tautology is a circular argument, an assertion that is true by definition because the conclusion of the argument is deemed true from the onset and then used as evidence to support the argument. I show that the assertion that educational outcomes can be improved by allowing market forces to operate freely is a tautological argument. In fact, market forces are already too prevalent in education; market forces are undermining education and have become a driver of inequality that threatens our democracy.

Part IV of *The Robot Factory* is a rethinking of what it means to educate and be educated in the 21st century. I view education through an even wider lens and examine its relationship to society in a historical context. We live in a paradoxical time, in which knowledge is abundant and free and yet education has become more valuable than ever. I argue that we need to move away from mandated educational standards and outcomes; instead, we need to think in terms of the change effected in individuals by the educational process, a process of ongoing development that will extend over a lifetime and be unique for each individual.

In the last chapter in Part IV of *The Robot Factory*, I argue that our standards-based approach to education is not only obsolete, but, more importantly, is also a denial of our essential humanity. I argue that education today treats children as robots to be programmed rather than as autonomous human beings. The dehumanization of education is a trend that must be reversed or ultimately it will destroy our relatedness with one another, and with that our ability to collectively face impending challenges that threaten our future, challenges in which the stakes are already high and are continuing to escalate.

My Fundamental Beliefs

Before delving into the details of my arguments, allow me to share some of the fundamental beliefs that shape how I conduct, observe, and write about education.

• **Context is important—and is often overlooked.** Each school is a unique institution situated in a specific environment. What works in an impoverished urban area will be very different than what works in an affluent suburb. The current trend toward standardization does not account for these differences. It assumes that what works in affluent schools should work everywhere if only the educators would cooperate. This is a fantasy world created by politicians and corporations. It is simply not reality.

The fantasy is enticing because of its simplicity and the absolution it grants to our political leaders. In the fantasy narrative, society mirrors the schools—meaning that good schools will result in a moral and productive citizenry. To achieve prosperity, all that needs to be done is fix the schools. But the reality is that it's the other way around—schools mirror the society.

Currently, our society is experiencing an enormous growth in income and wealth inequality, and that inequality is reflected back in schools that provide vastly different experiences and outcomes depending on the economic background of their students. Politicians of both parties do not want to face that reality because they would then also have to deal with the structural economic issues that they have created through tax codes and policies that exacerbate income inequality. It is far easier for politicians to say that all would be well if the schools were up to standard. It is also a convenient misdirection that diverts attention away from their failure to govern effectively and their slavish devotion to corporate interests.

• **When people are inclined to avoid responsibility, they will often neglect to see the forest for the trees.** Effort is spent on the trivial, and then we try to convince ourselves that somehow the trivial is important. In the context of education, this is especially true for the current fad of "data-driven" accountability. As I demonstrate, data-driven reform is more akin to a pseudoscience than a real science; if enough data is collected it can be used to support just about any narrative. In many cases of dysfunctional schools or programs, an experienced educator simply could use professional judgment to recommend changes and improvements. Unfortunately, instead these failing schools are presented as mysteries only to be solved through massive data collection and sophisticated statistical analysis.

Such data collection is often part of a ruse to avoid accountability and to advance narratives of convenience rather than to face harsh truths. The goal is to avoid using professional judgment because that would require true accountability. Other variations of this behavior include "zero tolerance" policies. Authorities simply declare that they will have zero tolerance for any kind of drug, or any object that could be construed as a weapon, or sexting, or some other trending behavior fueling a media-induced panic, and they expel or suspend students regardless of circumstances. These kinds of policies also conveniently absolve the authority figures from responsibility of employing professional judgment or discretion.

• **Human development and brain development are biological processes that cannot be sped up.** Education is fundamentally a biological process. Neural circuits in the brain must be formed, and this only happens through active engagement, repetition, and reflection by the learner. Teachers do not possess magic words or strategies that implant knowledge into a student. This fact is easy to see for physical activities. No one would expect to be able to learn how to dance, play the piano, or golf from reading a book and listening to a teacher. But for cognitive activities like math and reading, we somehow think teachers can just transfer the knowledge to the student without the student exerting the same kind of struggle and practice required for learning physical activities. Authentic expertise, whether it is for physical or cognitive activities, must be developed and that rate of development is different for every individual.

Additionally, human development is a lifelong process that cannot be sped up. To go from birth to full adult takes over 20 years, and that timescale cannot be changed simply because we wish it to go faster. For example, consider your average five-year-old. His brain is working hard on developing social skills, and he lacks the ability to focus for extended periods of time. Therefore, a developmentally appropriate kindergarten would give him ample opportunity to learn socialization skills through unstructured play, rather than rote reading and math skills through highly structured lessons. On the other hand, a developmentally appropriate high school would expect its students to take much more responsibility for structuring their time and learning than adults today are willing to grant them.

As it currently exists, our educational system fosters a bizarre schism in how we treat our children's development. We expect children in third grade to learn algebraic concepts that would challenge many adult learners. At the same time, we infantilize young adults in regard to many aspects of their personal development—such as sexuality, drinking, and time management—and thus also deny their fundamental agency as human beings. The result is innumerable stressed-out youth who are unprepared for the adult world both socially and academically.

• **If we want more people trained in math and science, we should look at how mathematicians and scientists actually conduct their work.** Scientific work is different than presented in school and very different than what many people imagine. Science is not about amassing reams of data, looking for correlations in the data, and then debating their statistical significance. Science is about uncovering the underlying causes for effects so that these effects can be controlled and reproduced. I observe many instances in which no attempt is made to understand causation. This results in the mistake of confusing correlation with causation; even more troubling, it is often an intentional method of advancing whatever goals the claimant is making. Reproducibility is never even examined. In our hyper-partisan society, in which "winning" is valued more than solving problems, science is politicized and corrupted to the point where it is no longer recognizable to scientists.

My anger at the misuse of science to achieve political goals in regard to education reform in part fuels the motivation for writing this book. But I am equally distressed by the corruption of the scientific method to advance self-serving agendas in other policy debates. Climate change is a prominent example. I hope that in writing this book, and in explaining both science education and the misuse of science in education, readers will be better able to evaluate and weigh completing claims when scientific authority is invoked in other policy debates.

• **Most of the pitched ideological battles on educational practices present false choices.** Real experts employ multiple strategies to solve problems and check the results of their solutions. Fluent readers employ phonics and whole language strategies to decode and comprehend text. People skilled in math possess conceptual understanding and computational prowess. To become a scientist, you must engage in hands-on experiential activities and commit a great deal of facts to memory. However, ideologues who argue vehemently for one side over the other on these issues often ignore how people with real expertise perform these activities. Experts do indeed think differently than nonexperts, but expert thought processes are hardly ever rigid and linear. In the act of learning any subject, one need not take one particular pathway to achieve understanding; indeed, the *deep understanding* that characterizes expert thinking is usually arrived at through multiple pathways, not either/or choices.

But false choice is a problem with more than just teaching methodologies. In fact, false choice has become a defining characteristic of public discourse in 21st century America. Policy advocates of all persuasions use emotionally engaging narratives with heroes and villains to advance self-serving agendas, instead of dispassionately assessing all the available evidence when considering the pros and cons of various options. Whether the issue is education reform, healthcare, climate change, or any other complex issue, our leaders routinely bombard us with false choices rather than carefully thought out plans and recommendations. Rather than seek the truth, people are asked to choose sides in a battle.

• **Schools are not cultural islands.** It is not possible for adults to expect schools and children to live by a set of values that these same adults are unwilling to model. We expect educators to instill in our youth cultural mores that are an antithesis to the values of hyper-partisanship and consumer consumption that define early 21st century America. Consider, for example, the value of responsibility. Our political and corporate leaders spend enormous effort avoiding responsibility, but at the same time demand it from children and teachers. The same can be said for the value of intellectual honesty.

Indeed, I would argue that the erosion of our children's agency is a means of masking this values hypocrisy. We do this because we are in denial ourselves as to the extent that young people are perceptive of the vast gulf between our stated values and our actions. This "do as I say, not as I do" attitude saturates all public spaces today through ubiquitous advertising across all media platforms and the public pronouncements of our political leadership. We prefer to be willfully ignorant of the fact that our youth are fully aware of the dishonest, self-serving rhetoric from the adults around them.

• **There are no easy answers for improving education and you should not believe anyone who claims to have them.** Education reform is rife with ideologues—people who claim that a particular method, approach, organizational structure, management practice, or funding source will solve all of the problems. The old adage "If it seems too good to be true, then it probably is," applies to the acquisition of anything of value, especially educational achievement. Education is valued because it is difficult to attain.

While there are no magic bullets for education, neither is the process mysterious. We have at our disposal a vast, peer-reviewed, scientifically valid literature on human development and effective developmentally appropriate educational practices. My hope is that this book will help readers distinguish the real science on educational practices from the pseudoscience. We *know* how to educate our children. What we lack is the willingness to devote the necessary political and financial resources to make it happen for everyone— not just a lucky chosen few.

• **Our relationships are what make us human, and ultimately all human activity, whether it is family, social, or in education, business, or government, is about relatedness.** Healthy human beings have an innate desire to connect to others and to be part of something bigger than just the individual. Humans are not widgets; relationships matter. Any organization that refuses to acknowledge this fact will be inherently dysfunctional. A factory model for education that imposes rigid standards and behaviors might be convenient for the management, but it will never produce the desired results.

The crisis we face in education originates from a deeper crisis in our society—a breakdown in relatedness with each other, with our institutions, with our history, with our environment. We cannot fix education by elevating test scores or even by closing achievement gaps between the various ethnic and socioeconomic groups that make up American society. We can only do it by improving our relatedness to each other, reducing the inequalities that are tearing at our social fabric, embracing our shared histories, and coming together to meet the immense environmental challenges that threaten our collective future.

These beliefs are the themes that I expand on throughout *The Robot Factory*. To begin, let us go back to third grade and enter a classroom. Let us visit a third-grade math class in which the students are programmed, rather than taught.

Baltimore, MD, USA   Joseph Ganem

Acknowledgments

This book originated from a number of blog posts and opinion pieces that I wrote and were published in *APS News*, the *Baltimore Sun*, and the *Daily Riff*. Some portions of this book's text have appeared in different forms in these publications, and I thank their editors for giving me a public platform that generated the feedback necessary for me to expand on and refine my thoughts and ideas on education.

Most significantly, I thank Cathy J. Westerberg, editor of the *Daily Riff*. I spent many hours on the phone with her in engaging discussions on education issues and brainstorming topics to write about. She has been an enthusiastic supporter of this book project throughout its long road. She read early drafts of the manuscript and provided thoughtful and extremely helpful feedback.

My colleague at Loyola University Maryland, Lisa Zimmerelli, head of Loyola's writing center, had a substantial role in shaping this book. Through written comments and thought-provoking conversations, she provided essential editorial guidance for structuring the book, and I greatly appreciate her thoughtful, careful, and enthusiastic editing of the entire manuscript.

I thank Gregory Derry, Jacqueline Ganem, Ingeborg Heyer, Charles Murn, and Wendy Smith, for reading the manuscript and providing thoughtful feedback, comments, suggestions, and corrections.

I thank Graham Van Dixhorn of *Write to Your Market.com* for consultations on marketing and book cover writing.

I greatly appreciate the work of my editors—Christopher Coughlin and Ho Ying Fan—at Springer. They enthusiastically embraced the project and provided useful help and advice.

My family has been essential for this project. Some of the observations and insights I recount in the book are from my own children—Thomas Ganem, Katherine (Katie) Ganem, and Claire Ganem—and their experiences navigating the K-12 public school system in Baltimore County.

Most importantly, my wife, Sharon Baldwin, has been a constant source of support. She has been my sounding board for many of the ideas in this book. She is also a teacher in the public schools and I remain in awe of her unflagging commitment and daily struggle to provide a public education to the most vulnerable among us—preschool children with special needs.

Introduction

Why I Would Fail Third Grade Math

During American Education Week one year, I visited my daughter's third grade math class. The teacher was going over problems on a test she had just given, reading each problem out loud.

"If Johnny has $88 and spends $32 on clothes, write a number sentence that shows how much money Johnny has left." She then wrote on the board the following:

$$\$88 - \$32 \ = \$56$$

Then she turned to the class and asked, "Is that a number sentence?"

At this point, five minutes in, I realized that I would be in trouble in this class. I had no idea how to answer her question. In my line of work, this kind of expression is called an "equation." The class, however, came through. In unison they yelled, "Yes." The teacher wrote a second equation on the board:

$$\$88$$
$$- \$32$$
$$= \$56$$

"Is this a number sentence?"

Again, I had no idea, but the class in unison yelled, "No."

The teacher continued. "All of you know what a number sentence is. The directions on the test were to write a number sentence. But I just looked at the papers, and 10 out of 28 of you wrote this." She pointed to the second, column method of subtraction on the board. "That is not a number sentence so I had to mark all of those papers wrong."

A child raised his hand. "But I got the right answer."

"I know you got the right answer, but you didn't follow directions. The directions were to write a number sentence."

A second child raised her hand. "But I got the right answer."

"I know you can do the problem. But when we take the state exam in the spring, they won't know that you can do the problem. The graders will want to see a number sentence. It's important that you follow directions because we want to show them what smart students we have at our school."

A third child raised her hand. "But I got the right answer."

"But, I just explained. You didn't write a number sentence. If I mark that correct now, you will do that again in the spring. The people grading the state exam want to see a number sentence. They won't know that you know how to do the problem."

None of the children looked convinced. More hands went up. Exasperated, she cut off further discussion with an old parental standby: "It's for your own good."

A Multitude of Problems in One Brief Lesson

This brief exchange between a third-grade teacher and her students that day illustrates multiple problems with our approach to education in the United States. When I tell this story, the initial reaction from most people is outrage. They say: "She's teaching to the test." But that is not actually the underlying problem with this lesson. In addition, the phrase "teaching to the test" is a misnomer. She can't be "teaching to the test" because she is not actually teaching. She is programming these children to do what they are told and not ask questions. The goal of this lesson is to produce automatons, not independent thinkers.

The deeper underlying problem with this lesson is that it is happening to begin with, *even though all the participants know that it is wrong.* The observer-parent and all the children know that it is wrong, which means that it is hard for me to believe that the teacher doesn't know that it is wrong. I suspect that many of the school administrators overseeing this lesson also know that it is wrong. Yet, all the participants—students, teachers, administrators, and parents—are all acting in good faith. They all love the students, want them to learn, and want them to develop into competent adults.

However, all the participants are playing a part that has been scripted for them. They sense that their actions are misguided, and yet all have been convinced that following the script is necessary in order to achieve success. High scores on the state test will be "scientific" proof of success so every action that might possibly maximize those test scores must be taken. But let us briefly review some of these actions and their implications.

• **Manipulating Test Data** As I stated, the phrase "teaching to the test" is a misnomer; I am a teacher and I give tests. I only test what I teach. To do otherwise would be unfair to the students and not informative to me. What I witnessed in my daughter's classroom—and is occurring in so many classrooms today across the country—is manipulation. Once the teachers begin manipulating student behaviors to achieve the desired testing outcomes, the data that results will have no scientific validity. This is just one of many examples of pseudoscience in education that I expose in Part I.

• **Misrepresenting the Discipline of Math** Math problems have single correct answers, but usually *not* single correct solutions. There are usually multiple methods for arriving at correct solutions to math problems—some more elegant, creative, and even surprising than others. It is this attribute of math that imbues it with richness, allows for creativity, and makes it an attractive discipline to pursue. Instilling in children the belief that math is a repetitive, formulaic, robotic activity will squelch their intellectual curiosity for math.

The misrepresentation of the disciplines of math and science is a serious deficit in our educational system discussed at length in Part II. We encourage children to pursue STEM (Science, Technology, Engineering, Math) fields, while at the same time discourage them with a curriculum that fails to provide compelling motivations for entering these fields.

• **Impeding Parental Involvement** The use of unnecessary jargon—e.g., "number sentence"—impedes parental involvement in the education of their children. The English language has a perfectly good word for "number sentence"—equation—that most people know and is in fact in universal use by professional practitioners of math and science. But the jargon serves a purpose. It prevents parents from following the lesson and possibly questioning the efficacy of this curriculum. A parent, such as myself, might have the knowledge and ability to assist my children with third-grade math, but I can't actually teach this lesson because I don't know the unnecessary jargon.

Parental involvement is a key ingredient for educational success. Parents with high incomes and levels of education will overcome these barriers and stay involved. But these barriers will isolate parents in more stressful circumstances from full participation in their children's education. Erecting barriers such as these to parental involvement exacerbates educational inequalities, which drives economic inequality—a destructive spiral discussed in Part III.

• **Emphasizing Being "Smart" Rather Than Accomplishing the Task** The teacher exhorted her students to follow directions so that they could show the test graders how smart they all are. The ethic that "being smart" matters more than real accomplishment is part of the pervasive testing culture in American education, and it does a great disservice to our children. The adult world rewards the establishment and attainment of worthy goals. No one is paid for being smart; employers and customers only pay for results with tangible value. Even people synonymous with being smart—such as Einstein—are remembered because of their accomplishments.

Being "smart" isn't even a definable attribute because all populations have a diversity of aptitudes, interests, and abilities. We should celebrate this diversity; not attempt to erase it. Standardizing and then idealizing the attribute of "smart" by mandating defined educational outcomes for all dehumanizes all and undermines our relatedness as human beings. As I will conclude in Part IV, ultimately the destruction of our relatedness is the crisis we are facing in education and in our larger society.

I suspect that all of the participants in this third-grade math lesson are aware of at least some of these issues that I have articulated, yet they persist in their actions because of the veneer of "scientific" authority that the test provides. So let us begin by examining what science is and is not.

Contents

Part I   Pseudoscience in Education   1

1   What Science Is and Is Not   3
     Doing Real Science: Essential Elements   4
     The Magical Thinking Behind Pseudoscience   11
     References   12

2   Data-Driven Education Reform: A New Pseudoscience   15
     The "Mathematical Intimidation" of Teachers   16
     The Statistical Impossibility of Adequate Yearly Progress in Schools 23
     The SAT: Promoting Equal Opportunity or Perpetuating
     a Hierarchy?   29
     Assessing Colleges: Self-Selected Data   33
     Facts Versus Stories   37
     References   41

3   The Complexity Myth: The Opposite of Science   45
     The Quest for the Perfect Teacher   46
     The Teacher-Student Relationship   48
     Teachers Are Real Human Beings (Not Idealized Fantasy People)   53
     Impossible Expectations = Teacher Shortages   58
     Across Time and Space: The Complex Web of Human Relatedness   63
     References   64

Part II   Misunderstanding Math and Science Education   67

4   **Why Our Kids Don't Get Math**   69
    The Widening Gap Between High School and College Math   71
    The Disconnect Between the Math Curriculum and Professional
    Practitioners   78
    Making Math Relevant: Assessing Reading Comprehension or
    Math?   81
    The "Chinese Room"   87
    References   88

5   **Misunderstanding Science Education**   91
    Why Science Is Hard   94
    Science as a Noun   99
    Science as a Question   104
    Science as a Conversation   105
    Science as a Guide   108
    Science as a Verb   113
    The Limits of Science   116
    Having it Both Ways   121
    References   124

Part III   The Threat to American Democracy   127

6   **False Choice: Pseudoscientific Narrative**   129
    The Dark Side of Storytelling   131
    Schools Are Not Cultural Islands   140
    Dismembering Literature to Avoid its Truths   144
    References   148

7   **School Choice: The Tautology of the Market**   151
    Free Markets: An Untestable Hypothesis   152
    Markets: Meaning, Politics, and Morality   155
    Education Markets: The Higher-Ed Debacle   160
    The Charter School Movement   163
    The Logical Fallacies Embedded in the "Business Model"   170
    The Paradox of Wealth   176
    References   181

Part IV   Rethinking Education 185

8   The Paradox of Education in the 21st Century 187
Back to the Future 188
Change-Focused Education 195
Beyond the "Business Model" 200
Rethinking College: Preparing for the Unimagined 203
The Expectations Trap 207
The Limits of Education 211
The Necessity of Purpose and Meaning 214
References 219

9   The Robot Factory 221
Performing Versus Understanding 224
Do Robots Understand? 227
Willful Ignorance in the Classroom 230
Relatedness 234
Authentic Education 235
The Use of Pseudoscience in Education 237
The Real Crisis 240
A Call to Action 241
References 244

Index 247

About the Author

Joseph Ganem, Ph.D. is a Professor of Physics at Loyola University Maryland. He is an author on numerous scientific papers in the fields of optical materials, lasers, and magnetic resonance, and has received grants from Research Corporation, the Petroleum Research Fund, and the National Science Foundation for his research on solid-state laser materials. He has taught physics in the classroom for more than 20 years and has served on the Maryland State Advisory Council for Gifted and Talented Education.

Dr. Ganem is the author of the award-winning book *The Two Headed Quarter: How to See Through Deceptive Numbers and Save Money on Everything You Buy*. He speaks and writes frequently on science, consumer, and education issues, and has been a contributor of articles on these topics to the *Baltimore Sun* newspaper. For its 2017 "Best of Baltimore" awards, *Baltimore* magazine named him one the "Best Baltimoreans" in its people in the media section for the category "Best Defense of Science."

Dr. Ganem earned a Ph.D. from Washington University in Saint Louis, a M.S. from the University of Wisconsin-Madison, and a B.S. from the University of Rochester. He did postdoctoral work at the University of Georgia-Athens and at the United States Naval Research Laboratory in Washington, DC.

For more information visit www.JosephGanem.com.

Part I

Pseudoscience in Education

1

What Science Is and Is Not

All participants in the education process—teachers, admissions counselors, administrators, politicians, and policymakers—want to give their practices a scientific justification based on objective, evidence-based criteria and demand "proven results" based on "data." This is a laudable goal, but most don't actually understand science, the how and why of scientific measurement, data interpretation, and conclusions. As we shall see, many of the "data-driven" education policies and reforms thus resemble what is called "pseudoscience" more than real science.

Distinguishing real scientific claims from pseudoscientific ones can be difficult because it is the basis for the claims being made that needs to be evaluated, not the plausibility of the claims themselves. Both scientists and charlatans can make fantastic sounding claims and assertions. In many cases the claims of the charlatans are more believable. Consider the following sales pitches:

- I have a small device that you can carry in your pocket and it will insure that you never get lost. It knows at all times exactly where you are and it will give you precise directions to any place you need to go. Just state the location out loud and follow its spoken commands.
- I have a medicine that will prevent and cure migraine headaches. It uses all-natural plant-based ingredients diluted in water and has no side effects. Trained homeopathic doctors have prescribed this medication for over a hundred years and tens of thousands of patients have attested to its effectiveness.

© Springer International Publishing AG, part of Springer Nature 2018
J. Ganem, *The Robot Factory*, https://doi.org/10.1007/978-3-319-77860-0_1

With no prior knowledge, the latter claim is much more plausible than the former. However, the scientific understanding of nature that allows us to carry GPS enabled smartphones is legitimate; these devices really do work. But homeopathy is dismissed in the mainstream medical community as a pseudo-science. What is the difference?

After all, not all science is as reliable as a smartphone, and these devices too will make errors. Scientists, being human, also make errors, are wrong some-times, and succumb to the same human foibles as everyone else—especially when it comes to denial and wishful thinking. In addition, the body of human knowledge collectively referred to as "science" evolves in time, and scientific beliefs in one era might be rejected at a later time. To further con-found matters, the reliability of our scientific knowledge appears to exist along a spectrum, with some branches of science universally accepted and undisputed—e. g. Newton's laws of motion—and other branches considered speculative and subject to debate—e. g. string theory.

What makes knowledge "scientific" is the *process* by which it was obtained. This process has identifiable elements, some or most of which are missing in pseudoscientific works. Differentiating science from pseudoscience is an extensive topic, with a significant philosophical literature, as well as book-length treatments for general audiences [1–3]. However, we do have general consensus on a number of elements considered essential to the scientific method. After identifying and exploring the essential elements of a scientific approach to obtaining knowledge, I discuss examples of pseudoscience in education, Later, in Chapter 5, I go into more detail on the workings of the scientific process, but let's begin with the essentials.

Doing Real Science: Essential Elements

The scientific method, as it is articulated at the K-12 level, teaches students a rigid series of steps: ask a testable question (the hypothesis), design a con-trolled experiment, collect data from the experiment, analyze the data, and infer whether the data supports or refutes the hypothesis. This simplified sum-mary of the scientific method does contain some of its essential elements: Experiments must be designed to answer specific questions, and for data to be useful it must be acquired and analyzed in a way that relates to the hypothesis. However, this is a gross oversimplification of the conduct of actual science—a topic discussed later in Chapter 5. Science isn't that straightforward. Often major discoveries result from observations made outside of the stated hypothesis.

Moreover, this simplified view of science focuses mostly on the activities of measurement and data collection, which by themselves have almost no meaning. As a practicing scientist I am constantly faced with the "measurement problem"; when I walk into my lab, there are literally an infinite number of measurements I can choose to make, and I must decide what to measure and then interpret what that measurement means. Therefore I need to have a reason—*a motivation*—for a particular action. The reasons can be varied: testing equipment, obtaining preliminary results, collecting publishable data, or attempting to reproduce data. Acquiring lots of data for its own sake is not synonymous with doing science.

For an investigation to be *scientific* one must consider all of the critical elements of the scientific method, including those on the front and back ends of the measurement and data collection processes. These elements include:

1. The question posed must be relevant.
2. The question posed must be falsifiable.
3. The data collection must be systematic and consistent.
4. Causal explanations for observed effects must be provided.
5. The explanations must offer a simplified understanding of natural processes.
6. The explanations must avoid "over-fitting" the data.
7. The experiments must be reproducible by other researchers.
8. The understanding of nature that results must allow for the correct prediction, and if possible, control of future events.

Let's elaborate on each of these elements:

1. A relevant question. Before beginning an investigation, there must be a motivation—that is, a researcher must pose a question that is interesting, relevant, and whose answer will lead to further insights. Science is not testing the composition and hardness of every rock found on the ground. Science is not describing in elaborate detail every plant and animal species in a field. Science is not, as the Beatles' song puts it, counting the "four thousand holes in Blackburn, Lancashire," in order to "know how many holes it takes to fill the Albert Hall." *To be science,* an investigation cannot just be an elaborate exercise in data collection; rather, to be science, an investigation must be organized and systematized in such a way that it serves to motivate the research and researcher by addressing a relevant question.

If we go back to the third grade class I visited, the practice of testing all the children in math is not scientific unless the tests are designed and administered in a way that addresses specific relevant questions on the teaching methods used (pedagogies) and student learning outcomes (achievements). Having a "standardized" test isn't science if the only question at stake is to find out which students score higher than others, and which schools have higher overall test scores. A ranked list of test scores for students and schools with no other context provided is just trivia, because unless it relates to relevant questions, it has no inherent meaning. A scientific investigation must be motivated by scientifically valid questions of significance, not by questions of minutiae and trivialities.

2. The question posed must also be falsifiable. This means that it must be possible to prove the hypothesis wrong, because otherwise an experimental test of the hypothesis would not be possible [4]. You cannot construct hypotheses that are tautologies—that is, statements that are always true—because this results in circular arguments. When a hypothesis is a tautology, the hypothesis is deemed true from the onset and becomes evidence for its own support. Such a hypothesis can never be falsified. For example, the statement that the Earth and all life on it are creations of God is a tautology because in Christian theology God is the creator of the universe. Creationism is not a science because it can never be falsified. This might be a valid belief system, but it is not a valid scientific hypothesis.

Likewise, saying that a good third grade math teacher has students that all do well on the state exam is a tautology. This statement cannot be falsified because by definition any class of students that does well on the state exam had a good teacher. Finding a class with high-scoring students and a bad teacher is not possible if this is the definition of a good teacher. If your hypothesis is that good teachers produce students with high test scores, then the attributes and actions of a "good" teacher must be defined independently of the test scores in order for it to be testable. A scientific hypothesis cannot be a tautology because it must be a statement that is either refutable or verifiable by experimentation, not true from the onset.

3. Systematic and consistent data collection. Procedures for data collection cannot be manipulated to support the self-interest of particular groups of people. Pharmaceutical companies are not doing science when they report only the trials that show efficacy of a new drug, while they dismiss the failed trials as some kind of aberration resulting from an elaborate set of required conditions that weren't quite right. Energy companies are not doing science when they commission environmental studies and declare the results proprietary, releasing only data that shows them in a favorable light. In both of these examples, self-selecting data is a form of manipulation that invalidates the science.

The "teaching to the test" I observed in third grade math, as I explained, is also a form of manipulation. Such actions by the teacher render the test data meaningless for scientific purposes. When data has been manipulated to produce the desired results, then no valid scientific conclusions can be drawn.

4. Causal explanations must be provided. In analyzing the experimental data, the scientist must propose *causal* explanations for the observed effects. After conducting an experiment, simply stating that the data either supports or refutes the hypotheses is not acceptable science. An investigator might not be able to prove a chain of causes, but if unproven, there must be further investigations possible to test the proposed causes. Without causal explanations, it becomes possible to fall into the logical trap of mistaking correlations for causes. For example, a perfect (100%) correlation exists between incidents of prostate cancer and being male. Of course, being male is not a cause of the disease; simply—and obviously—it is correlated because only men have prostates [5]. In contrast: there is a strong but less than perfect correlation between being a smoker and developing lung cancer. However, smoking is a proven cause of lung cancer. Establishing the causal chain of events of how smoking results in lung cancer in some (but not all) smokers was not easy and took numerous studies and decades of scientific work. The causal pathways were not obvious even though the correlation was.

In the third grade math class I visited, the students were exhorted to show how "smart" they are. But, while being "smart"—assuming that a working definition can be made—might be correlated with student achievement, it is not causal. Simply having a class of smart students will not cause them to learn or cause teachers to be effective. Administering a test and then concluding from the results that all the students are "smart" is not a scientifically valid insight.

5. The causal explanations must offer a simplified understanding of natural processes. Indeed, the point of science is to find simpler underlying principles for complex phenomena that allow for predictions of future events. Every experimental outcome cannot be assigned a unique explanation, and data that refutes a hypothesis cannot be ignored as a "special case" because neither practice results in a simplified understanding of nature, or makes predictions possible. If we deem the outcome of every experiment in a study a special case that needs a unique, complex, narrative in order to explain it, then we gain zero scientific insights.

"Anecdotal evidence" is the term used for narrative explanations of events and such evidence abounds in our everyday interactions with one another. You hear your neighbor say: "My best friend felt much more energetic after taking the homeopathic medicine for migraines." But you know that your uncle tried the same medication and he felt the same afterwards. Therefore, since the homeopathic medicine cured your neighbor's best friend it must work, and your uncle must have a different illness. This kind of reasoning from anecdotes is commonplace. However, it does not simplify our understanding of how to treat migraine headaches because these stories are unique to the individuals involved, and, therefore, no underlying principle can be articulated.

Likewise, if test scores go up in Mrs. Smith's class after a new math curriculum is introduced, but go down in Mr. Jones' class after introduction of the same curriculum, concluding that the new curriculum is an improvement and that there is a problem with Mr. Jones' teaching is neither valid nor helpful for informing Mrs. Hart on whether she should adopt the new curriculum. We don't gain from these narratives any simplified understanding of what makes a better math curriculum if every teacher has a different story to tell about their experiences.

6. Science avoids over-fitting the data. "Over-fitting" is a term used in statistics that refers to using a model to make predictions that has much more complexity than the available data can support [6]. No data set is ever perfect. There is always a level of randomness present in any set of measurements—what statisticians refer to as the "noise." But if a model with enough complexity is used, patterns will be found in the noise that the model can then "explain."

For example, media pundits seem to have a hobby of over-fitting sports data in order to "predict" the outcomes of such things as election winners and stock market returns. If the Super Bowl winner is an NFC team it foreshadows a bullish year in the stock market, while if the winning team is from the AFC it portends a bearish year [7]. There is the "Redskins rule" that states that if the Washington Redskins football team wins their last home game the incumbent party will win the election that year, while a loss in their last home game means that the incumbent party will lose [8]. My personal favorite for this kind of analysis is the "ex-Cub factor," which posits that the World Series will be won by the team with the fewest former Chicago Cubs as players [9]. At least this model uses a baseball statistic to predict a baseball outcome.

If your predictive model is so complex that it includes all available sports data, then given the literally millions of sports statistics accumulating in databases every year, it will always be possible to sift through them and find particular statistics that are perfectly correlated with low-frequency events such as World Series winners, or year-end closes of the Dow Jones Industrial Average, or outcomes of biannual elections. Of course, all of these correlations are spurious and fail to predict anything. The "Redskins rule" has failed to "predict" the last two presidential elections and the Chicago Cubs recently won a World Series. A signature of over-fitting is when a model fits past events but fails to predict future ones.

Even the pundits will admit that these correlations are spurious, and in fact their articles are usually meant to be humorous. Less humorous are the highly complex statistical models for evaluating teachers that have become widespread. In Chapters 2 and 3 we will examine models used for evaluating teaching effectiveness that use dozens of inputs to "predict" low-frequency outcomes such as their students' gains in math scores at the end of the year. These models are classic examples of over-fitting; however, in contrast to the humorous articles over-fitting sports statistics to make "predictions," these teaching evaluation models are taken seriously.

7. The results must be reproducible by other investigators. Reproducibility of results in future experiments by other investigators is an essential part of the scientific method. It is how science self-corrects. If causes for an effect cannot be identified, then it will not be possible to reproduce the effect or control future outcomes.

In the late 1980s, scientists announced unexpected discoveries in physics and chemistry with profound implications for energy technology. One was "cold fusion"—energy production from nuclear reactions that power the sun, but at low Earth-like temperatures—and the other was high-temperature superconductivity—materials that offer no electrical resistance at temperatures much higher than previously believed possible. Investigators could not reproduce cold fusion and the work was ultimately discredited [10]. However, investigators from all over the world could reproduce high-temperature superconductors [11]. Thus, the latter was scientifically valid because others were able to reproduce the findings.

Reproducibility is a serious problem in much of the data-driven education reform movement. Part of this problem is that reproducing the exact conditions in an educational setting year after year is rarely possible. Education always takes place in a cultural context, with each new generation of students growing up in what is essentially a different culture. The American culture of the 1960s when I went to third grade was radically different in many ways from the American culture of the 2000s when my daughter went to third grade.

However, human development does not change as much as many educators think that it does, or wish that it would. In addition, the basic facts of math have also not changed. That means that it should be possible to replicate successful methods for teaching math. Yet policymakers keep altering the math curriculum, pushing more and more advanced concepts into younger grades without any reproducible evidence that the new methods are effective. As a result, ineffective, developmentally inappropriate math instruction is now a serious problem throughout the K-12 curriculum.

8. Science should have the power to predict and, when possible, control the future. The benefit to society that comes from doing science is in obtaining knowledge of how *significant* events can be *predicted*, and if possible *controlled in the future*.

The National Weather Service does not collect enormous amounts of weather data from all over the world just to keep its staff busy and employed. It is using this data to build models that will predict future weather events. While weather cannot be controlled, just being able to reliably predict weather can save lives and enormous amounts of money by giving people a chance to prepare. Likewise, medical researchers are not investing enormous amounts of time and money developing imaging techniques such as MRIs, PET scans, and CAT scans because they like to look at the pictures. They want to predict if a patient is developing cancer and learn to control the spread of the disease.

In educational settings, articulating, assessing, and documenting learning outcomes isn't inherently useful. The goal should be to use the data to build models for student learning that can predict outcomes. In fact, numerous valid research studies across many disciplines strive to use test data to predict the outcomes resulting from different teaching methods in order to identify best educational practices. However, a great deal of the test data collected by the state and the federal government is not used for this purpose. Instead it is used to harass, threaten, and intimidate schools and teachers. Using the test data to predict educational outcomes and then provide guidance on interventions to change them is rarely a priority for politicians.

These essential elements of science—relevant, falsifiable questions, systematic and consistent data collection, causal explanations, simplified understanding of natural processes, avoidance of over-fitting, reproducibility, predictability, and control—must be present in any study claiming to be scientific. Science ought to be powerfully in the service of education and yet much of the real science on education and human development is ignored in favor of "evidence-based" reports and "data-driven" practices that are missing at least one, or in many cases several, of these essential elements.

The Magical Thinking Behind Pseudoscience

The stunning success of modern science has not resulted in the extermination of supernatural explanations, or what I call "magical thinking." Supernatural explanations for events such as demons, witches, astrological signs, and so on, have prevailed for most of human history. Only in the last few hundred years has scientific thinking and methodology profoundly changed how humans interact with and predict occurrences in the natural world. However, magical thinking still persists, and indeed is reincarnated as "pseudoscience" with all the trappings of real science.

Belief systems such as creationism, homeopathy, alien astronauts, astrology, positive thinking, and ESP are some examples. All of these belief systems come with scientific-sounding claims. All offer causal explanations of phenomena with supporting evidence. All offer statistics to back up their claims. But on closer examination, none of these belief systems stands up when subjected to true scientific scrutiny because at least one or more of the essential elements that I have listed are missing.

In each of these belief systems, the hypotheses are compelling, emotionally engaging narratives that can never be falsified because they are assumed to be true. Evidence is often in the form of anecdotes. Statistical comparisons are based on self-selected data because all evidence contrary to the hypotheses are explained as some special case and ignored. Reproducibility of results by independent investigators is non-existent. People who raise questions are vilified as enemies of the good. In fact, false choice is a defining feature of these belief systems because the response to all criticism is framed in terms of "us versus them." You cannot choose to seek the truth; you can only choose sides.

In reality, the predictive capabilities of these belief systems, if they exist at all, are no better than chance, but data is manipulated and skewed to make it seem otherwise. Because the nature of randomness is such that anyone who makes enough predictions will be correct some of the time, compelling success stories will continually emerge to feed and sustain the faithful.

As a result, pseudoscience will never be stamped out, but it should be recognizable by thoughtful educated people. Unfortunately, scientific illiteracy is rampant in our culture, even socially acceptable. For example, a 2007

Republican Party presidential debate featured candidates who publicly stated that they did not believe in evolution [12]. In contrast, try to imagine any of the candidates publicly and proudly stating an inability to read and still being taken seriously upon such an admission. Scientific illiteracy ought to be equally shocking—indeed, none of our modern technology would work if science was as wrong as many people claim.

Take, for example, the modern smartphone I alluded to earlier and contemplate all of the technological components that must work for you to make a call or text, access the Internet or use it to navigate: the battery, the antenna, the GPS system that relies on satellites, the touch screen, the optical display, the wireless communication, the Internet connection, the integrated circuit chips, the computer CPU, the programming, and so on. All of these components were developed as a result of the scientific method and scientific understanding. Put simply, the smartphone would not work if the modern scientific understanding of the world was as completely wrong and misguided as many people claim. What also would not work? The modern practices of medicine, transportation, agriculture, construction… the list goes on.

Sadly, as we shall see, many of the "data-driven" evaluation procedures being applied to education are closer to pseudoscience than real science. What is especially disturbing is that this pseudoscience is enacted by smart, educated people who should know better than to engage in the kind of magical thinking that has become the trend in education reform.

References

1. Gregory Derry, *What Science Is and How It Works* (Princeton: Princeton University Press, 2002).
2. Carl Sagan, *Demon-Haunted World: Science as a Candle in the Dark* (New York: Ballantine Books reprint edition, 2011).
3. Robert L. Park, *Superstition: Belief in the Age of Science* (Princeton: Princeton University Press, 2008).
4. Karl Popper, *The Logic of Scientific Discovery*, Originally published in German (Vienna: Verlag von Julius Springer, 1935), English edition (London: Hutchinson & Co., 1959).
5. Joseph Ganem, *The Two Headed Quarter: How to See Through Deceptive Numbers and Save Money on Everything You Buy* (Baltimore: Chartley Publishing, 2007) p. 379.
6. B. S. Everitt & A. Skrondal, *The Cambridge Dictionary of Statistics*, 4th Edition (Cambridge, UK: Cambridge University Press, 2010) p. 314.

7. Benjamin Snyder, "If You're a Market Bull Then Root for These Teams in the Super Bowl," *Fortune*, January 2016, http://fortune.com/2016/01/20/super-bowl-predictor-2016/.

8. Alyssa Fetini & Frances Romero, "Election Prognosticators," *Time*, November 3, 2008, http://content.time.com/time/specials/packages/article/0,28804,1856094_1856096_1856102,00.html.

9. Ron Berler, "The Ex-Cub Factor: Theory will decide the World Series," *Boston Herald*, October 15, 1981. https://web.archive.org/web/20070405034627/www.all-baseball.com/ref/berler.html.

10. John R. Huizenga, *Cold Fusion: The Scientific Fiasco of the Century* (New York: Oxford University Press, 1994).

11. J. Robert Schrieffer (editor) and J. S. Brooks (associate editor), *Handbook of High-Temperature Superconductivity* (New York: Springer Science + Business Media LLC, 2007).

12. "The Republicans' First Presidential Candidates Debate," filmed at Ronald Reagan Library in Simi Valley, CA on May 3, 2007, Transcript available at: http://www.nytimes.com/2007/05/03/us/politics/04transcript.html, video, 00:26, accessed May 1, 2018, https://www.youtube.com/watch?v=t4Cc8t3Zd5E.th

2

Data-Driven Education Reform: A New Pseudoscience

"I write to express my displeasure, in the strongest terms possible, at Loyola College's decision to no longer require standardized testing for undergraduate prospects ("Loyola joins SAT-optional colleges," June 7). This decision threatens to directly undermine, financially depreciate and otherwise academically devalue the bachelor's degrees granted by Loyola."

— Richard M. Fogal, New York, N.Y.
The writer is a 2009 graduate of Loyola College.
Excerpt from a Letter to the Editor
Baltimore Sun
June 10, 2009

In June of 2009, the school where I teach, Loyola College in Maryland (since renamed Loyola University Maryland), announced that it would join a growing list of universities and colleges with "SAT-optional" admissions policies. This means that prospective students are no longer *required* to submit SAT scores when applying for admission. Students may choose to submit their scores, but students who do not can still be admitted based on other criteria in their applications, such as high school grades and activities.

Do SAT-optional admissions result in a positive or negative change for a college? Like most new policies, we can see both costs and benefits. The question of whether the benefits outweigh the costs is a complex one and somewhat outside the scope of this book. What I want to examine are the roots of the vitriolic response from some of Loyola's alumni who denounced the new policy as a direct threat to their livelihood and potential earnings in the greater job market. As the alumnus in the quote above indicated, some interpreted

J. Ganem, *The Robot Factory*, https://doi.org/10.1007/978-3-319-77860-0_2

the decision as threatening to "financially depreciate" the bachelor degrees granted by Loyola.

Most of us go through school believing that our performance on tests impact us as individuals. We are taught that if we work hard at academics and achieve good grades (presumably through tests), we will be rewarded with greater opportunities and better paying jobs. So the idea that someone else's performance on a particular test, or in this case not even taking the test, has an impact on my personal earning power fascinates me. What is the rationale for that belief? Why are tests so important?

Quantifying the value and effectiveness of educational outcomes and practices has become a multi-billion dollar industry in the United States, reflecting an American obsession with using numerical measures instead of human judgment to assess performance. Numbers are believed to be more "scientific" and less prone to bias than the judgment of professionals. Decisions should be, according to a recently constructed buzzword, "data-driven." Given that Americans rank rather low in scientific and quantitative literacy, I have always found this faith in numbers and data-driven policies puzzling. After all, a great deal of professional judgment goes into making up a test and quantifying its outcome. If you don't have the math and science skills necessary to understand the test creation, the data collection, and the analysis, how can the test score be meaningful?

In this chapter I examine the underlying logic and assumptions behind the testing and assessment craze that has swept through education, and I uncover the erroneous chain of reasoning based on tests and related metrics that leads to dangerous education policy decisions. As we shall see, many of the "data-driven" education policies and reforms resemble pseudoscience more than real science because they are missing one or more of the essential elements of science identified in Chapter 1.

The "Mathematical Intimidation" of Teachers

Because of the push to improve education, many school districts use student test scores to determine the retention, promotion, and compensation of teachers. The underlying assumptions: student achievement depends on the abilities of the teachers, such achievement is measurable with standardized tests, and, therefore, test scores can identify effective teachers. According to this logic, high test scores result from high-quality teaching that should be rewarded and emulated; low test scores indicate that the teachers are incompetent, and that schools with consistently low scores should replace their teachers or be closed.

The flaw in this reasoning is so glaring that I am amazed that these assumptions drive so much of national education policy. A simple thought experiment exposes the fault. Imagine two schools at opposite ends of the test-score spectrum. For example, in Baltimore where I live, private college-prep schools filled with students who score in the 95th percentile and above on standardized tests share the city with public schools filled with students who cannot read at grade level and with graduation rates less than 50%. Many of the public schools are labeled as failures because of their low test scores. Imagine the following experiment: move all the students from one of the private schools to one of the failed public schools, and all the students from the failed school to the private school. Do not change the teachers, administrators, or curricula. A year later, test all the students again. If the hypothesis that test scores depend on the teachers is true, the test scores at the two schools should not change.

Of course, our assumption would be proven false. We don't have to actually do this experiment to know its outcome. Test scores would follow the students, not the schools or the teachers. In fact, we could keep the students in place at their respective schools and switch the teachers. Under these circumstances school test scores would not change, but rather the "successful" teachers at the private school would now be labeled "failures," and the "failed" teachers at the public school would now be labeled "successful."

This is not to say that teachers have no effect on student test scores—they do. But there are multiple factors involved and given that test scores correlate with family income and education levels more than anything else, teachers are not the primary factor. But is it possible to use statistical methods to isolate the effect of the teachers on their students' test scores and judge teachers solely on those outcomes?

Over-Fitting Data: Value-Added Models for Teacher Effectiveness

In fact, some school districts are aware of these differences in student populations and have recognized that the background of each student plays an important role in test outcomes. To adjust to these differences in student populations, school administrators have adopted "value-added models" (VAMs) to evaluate teachers. The basic idea of a VAM (several are in use) is to isolate the impact of the teacher using statistical methods to control and correct for the many other influences on student test scores. It is assumed that test scores for all students will change over the course of a year of instruction. Students at the suburban schools with high test scores and students in the urban schools with low test scores should all have increases in their test scores over time. A VAM focuses on that change, not the actual test score. The goal of a VAM is to "predict" the change in student test scores. If the actual change is greater than the predicted change, the teacher has "added value."

The logic behind value-added modeling is seductive because it appeals to our sense of fairness. Why should teachers in urban school districts be labeled failures simply for having poorly prepared students from the start? However, in practice VAMs use complex statistical models that are impenetrable to even the most mathematically sophisticated person. Take, for example, the statistical formula for determining the "value added" by teachers in New York City schools, published in a 2011 article in the *New York Times* [1]. The formula involves a complex weighted summation over nine different variables with names such as: "true total school effect," "true total district effect," and "classroom participation indicator."

According to this statistical model, it is not enough that teachers in New York City schools demonstrate that their students learn the material. Instead the statisticians "predict" the "expected proficiency" of students using an even more complex formula involving 32 variables, the results of which serve as one of the factors used in the "value added" formula. A teacher with students that all become proficient might not have any measureable "added value" if the statistical model "predicted" the students would all become proficient. Teachers without measureable "added value" do not get tenure. At least that is my best guess after re-reading the *New York Times* article several times on how this statistical model is supposed to work. I am in good company—the journalist writing the article admitted that the model was too complex for him to fully understand.

The elegant statistics are impressive, but if you need 32 variables to explain the performance of a particular teacher, then you don't have an explanation. It is simply not possible to identify and quantify 32 attributes of any person's performance at any job and claim that each of these is more meaningful than the random "good days" and "bad days" that we all experience at work. The VAM used by New York City schools is a classic example of "over-fitting," which I described in Chapter 1 as having a model with many more variables than the available data can support. In this case, the data simply doesn't contain enough information to support all of the insights about a particular teacher's performance that model claims it can.

As I explained, a signature of over-fitted data is when a model fits data from the past perfectly but is unable to predict the future, which is true in the case of VAMs. As one study on the effectiveness of VAMs in evaluating teachers found:

> "VAM estimates have proven to be unstable across statistical models, years, and classes that teachers teach. One study found that across five large urban districts, among teachers who were ranked in the top 20% of effectiveness in the first

year, fewer than a third were in that top group the next year, and another third moved all the way down to the bottom 40%. Another found that teachers' effectiveness ratings in one year could only predict from 4% to 16% of the variation in such ratings in the following year. Thus, a teacher who appears to be very ineffective in one year might have a dramatically different result the following year. The same dramatic fluctuations were found for teachers ranked at the bottom in the first year of analysis. This runs counter to most people's notions that the true quality of a teacher is likely to change very little over time and raises questions about whether what is measured is largely a "teacher effect" or the effect of a wide variety of other factors." [2]

These models fail to predict because they rely primarily on student test scores and *do not relate these scores to a causal chain of events initiated by the teacher*. In fact, advocates of using student test scores to evaluate teacher performance even admit that no causal connections can be found. As one policy paper states:

"… legislating "good teachers" is extraordinarily difficult, if not impossible. The currently available data provide little reason to believe that enough is known about good teachers to set appropriate training and hiring standards. The idea behind most certification requirements is to guarantee that nobody gets a terrible teacher. In other words, the general idea is that a floor on quality can be set. But doing this requires knowledge of characteristics that systematically affect performance. The prior evidence does not indicate that this can be done with any certainty." [3]

Incredulously, this very same policy paper goes on to advise that principals and superintendents make decisions about teachers "…based on the evaluation of potential and actual effectiveness in raising student performance rather than a set of prior attributes." [3] As Richard Rothstein, a research associate at the Economic Policy Institute specializing in education, pointed out, this reasoning is completely circular:

"Neither Hanushek and Rivkin nor Sanders claims to identify the characteristics of such good teachers other than by a circular description—good teachers can raise student achievement, and teachers are defined as good if they raise student achievement." [4]

Edward Haertel, a professor of education at Stanford, also pointed out the statistical flaws in VAMs when this circular reasoning is employed.

"Measurement error will lead to unrealistically large teacher-effect estimates if the very same student test scores used to calculate teacher value-added are then used again to estimate the size of the teacher effect. This incorrect procedure amounts to a circular argument, whereby highly effective teachers are defined as those producing high student test score gains and those same student test score gains are then attributed to them having been assigned to highly effective teachers." [5]

In other words, VAMs essentially encode a tautology—that good teachers have good students.

This glaring logical contradiction has not stopped administrators, and the media, from using VAMs to bully teachers. In 2010 the *LA Times* obtained seven years of test score data from the Los Angeles Unified School District and subjected it to a value-added analysis [6]. Then it published a series of articles naming the teachers ranked at the bottom by the VAM. John Ewing, President of Math for America, published an article thoroughly debunking the *LA Times* exposé of teachers, an act he decried as "mathematical intimidation." [7] He concluded:

"Unlike many policy makers, mathematicians are not bamboozled by the theory behind VAM, and they need to speak out forcefully. Mathematical models have limitations. They do not by themselves convey authority for their conclusions. They are tools, not magic. And using the mathematics to intimidate—to pre-empt debate about the goals of education and measures of success—is harmful not only to education but to mathematics itself." [7]

Despite this warning, as of this writing, there is a database posted on the *LA Times'* website that ranks the teachers and schools in the Los Angeles Unified School District according to a VAM [8].

Moreover, education reformers use the results of VAMs to make some absurd projections. In the Hanushek and Rivkin paper, they use analysis of teacher performance to project that the average seventh-grade mathematics achievement gap between lower- and upper-income kids can be closed by having five years of good teachers in a row [3]. Good teachers are defined as those in the 85th quality percentile as measured by VAMs, which are of course based on student test scores.

Other policy analysts have produced similarly absurd projections. For example, in a 2006 paper "Identifying Effective Teachers Using Performance on the Job," Gordon, Kane, and Staiger state that: "the average difference between being assigned a top-quartile teacher or a bottom-quartile teacher is 10 percentage points." [9] Of course this statement is a description of their model, not of teaching quality, because a distribution of test scores must have top and bottom quartiles with a certain number of percentage points separating the two categories. But rather than make an attempt to identify what the top-quartile teachers do to achieve their results, the authors instead infer that:

> "...the black-white achievement gap nationally is roughly 34 percentile points. Therefore, if the effects were to accumulate, having a top-quartile teacher rather than a bottom-quartile teacher four years in a row would be enough to close the black-white test score gap." [9]

Notice that by this logic, no matter what their teachers actually did, under-performing black students who catch up and close the achievement gap had four years in a row of top-quartile teachers. Declaring "greatness" in teaching using this reasoning process becomes akin to saying that lottery winners know how to choose winning lottery numbers. The fact is that any quantitative measure of performance—tests scores, student achievement, VAMs for evaluating teaching—has a statistical distribution associated with it that must have a top, middle, and bottom. Pure chance dictates that some students will be in the top category several years in a row, but creating a "Lake Woebegon" where "all the children are above average" is not mathematically possible.

The "Effective Teacher" Tautology

The "great teacher" or "highly effective teacher" concept as articulated in these policy papers and by many education reformers is an example of a tautology. Defining a "great teacher" as a teacher with a class of students that do well on standardized tests conveys no information because there will always be students at the top of the distribution who were taught by someone. And according to this definition, obviously any student who closed the achievement gap had highly effective teachers. This "data" in fact tells us nothing about what those teachers did and, more importantly, if their results can be reproduced.

A great teacher must be doing something different in the classroom that is *causally* related to student learning. If those differences that make for a "great teacher" cannot be identified and articulated, it is not possible to train or hire "great teachers." Simply saying that a great teacher is one with students who achieve high test scores explains nothing.

All professions—teachers, doctors, lawyers, priests, builders, etc.—have members who are grossly incompetent, who are practitioners unable, unwilling, or unfit to perform their duties at even the most basic or minimal level. In some extreme cases these practitioners betray the professional trust placed in them in order to engage in criminal acts. Horror stories of professional incompetence and deceit are told and re-told, and we can all recount instances of outrageously bad behavior by a teacher, doctor, lawyer, priest, and so on. It does a disservice to all when colleagues cover up for people who are incompetent and deceitful. The answer is to remove such individuals from their positions and disciplines when appropriate. The answer is *not* to employ broad policies as responses to anecdotes about people who should not be in professional practice anyway.

Much has been made in the media of the difficulty of firing teachers because of tenure protection. But blaming education shortfalls on teacher tenure is misdirection. Tenure is intended to protect teachers from arbitrary dismissal by requiring due process. This benefits teachers and students because education often requires confronting difficult and sensitive issues in a politically charged atmosphere. Whether "due process" is fair or unnecessarily time-consuming and expensive is a legitimate issue. But the idea that you can "fire your way" to excellence in education is ludicrous. Removing grossly incompetent teachers is a completely different problem than developing excellence in the many inexperienced teachers who are starting out in the profession.

It is not that hard to list the essential attitudes and actions of a good teacher:

- Demonstrate interest and enthusiasm for the subject and show genuine respect and care for the students and a love and desire to teach them.
- Be an expert in the field taught and know the subject matter well.
- Be prepared and organized and show up to class regularly and on time.
- Know the literature on the best pedagogical practices and implement them.
- Work collaboratively with colleagues.
- Be a mentor for those less experienced, and seek guidance and mentorship when needed.
- Commit to continuing professional development and life-long improvement of knowledge and skills.

Note that this list is common to all professions; just substitute terminology appropriate for law, medicine, etc. in the sentences above. Assessment of teachers should focus on to what extent they have these attitudes and take these actions.

The real issue for effective teaching isn't gross incompetence—it is what to do about the wide variability in skills and experience found in the population of good faith practitioners. What distinguishes a profession from an ordinary job is a person's commitment to ongoing development. Teachers unwilling or no longer able to make this commitment should not be in the profession. However, this is only one side of the coin: the profession must employ practices that offer sustainable mentorship, guidance, and development to aspiring practitioners. Teaching skills can vary greatly depending on an individual's interests, background, and experience. Matching the right person to the right job is as critical in teaching as in any other profession—a reality that education reformers do not want to admit.

But instead of identifying the attributes and actions of effective teachers, education reformers bully teachers with over-fitted statistical models, correlations with no identification of underlying causes, and tautological definitions of success. These value-added models are classic examples of pseudoscience. In her book *Weapons of Math Destruction,* Cathy O'Neil documents how value-added models become drivers of educational inequalities—excellent public school teachers, who for whatever reasons fare poorly in a value-added model, end up being hired by elite private schools [10].

The Statistical Impossibility of Adequate Yearly Progress in Schools

The reauthorization in 2002 of the federally mandated Elementary and Secondary Education Act, known as the "No Child Left Behind" (NCLB) Act, extended the testing used to evaluate teachers to entire schools [11]. NCLB mandates testing in reading and math for all students in grades 3–8 and once in grades 10–12 and requires that all schools demonstrate adequate yearly progress (AYP) towards the goal of bringing *all* students up to grade-level proficiency in math and reading by 2014. The law further threatens that schools that do not make AYP for three or more years face escalating sanctions, culminating in a required restructuring after seven years of failing to make AYP. Not surprisingly, in the decade that followed NCLB vast numbers of schools did not satisfy the AYP requirements, which led to many states requesting waivers from the law's requirements from the federal government.

NCLB was designed to hold schools accountable for student education outcomes and to force the closure of "failing" schools, that is schools in which there were students not up to grade-level in reading and math. Again, we see aspirations towards a laudable goal—grade-level proficiency for all—seducing policymakers into acceptance of a bizarre line of reasoning. There is simply no state or country on Earth in which *all* students are at grade-level in math and reading. There never has been and there never will be because students vary in abilities and interests. People who believe that students will magically meet certain standards upon simple communication and understanding of expectations of them have never worked with special education students, or gifted and talented students. Any classroom—and certainly any school—will always have a spread of student abilities; children progress at their own rates, sometimes in confounding ways.

Indeed, schools can be assured of their failure to make AYP year after year even before beginning such an inane undertaking because of the natural variability in student ability combined with a mathematical effect known as "saturation." Because the number of proficient students can never exceed 100%, AYP gains must level off once the center of the student distribution is moved to grade-level proficiency. It becomes mathematically impossible to bring students in the tail of the distribution to grade-level without moving students in the center to well above grade-level. In this case, student proficiency has "saturated," and gains in yearly test scores must cease because the number of students who can improve fast approaches zero. In other words, if a school reached the goal of having every student attain grade-level proficiency, that school would be labeled a failure because it would be impossible to make further progress towards achieving that goal.

Failure to Address Causality: Not Asking Why Schools Are "Failing"

But the real failure of the NCLB testing regimen is that nobody makes an attempt to find out *why* some schools are "failing." If a particular school has test scores that consistently lag other schools in an area, there must be reasons for the discrepancy. If those reasons are not identified and remediated, then not only will the school continue to fail, but a re-structured school that doesn't address the reasons for the low test scores will also fail. Identifying a failing school is not the same thing as identifying the reasons for the failure. NCLB relies on the same tautology that is encountered in identifying effective teachers through VAMs—those who have students with high test scores are effective—applied to entire schools. And the reasoning is equally circular: effective schools have high test scores so therefore a school with high test scores is an effective school. What the test scores do not reveal are the differences between an effective and ineffective school.

For example, in the United States, schools with consistently low test scores, the ones that have been targeted for re-structuring, tend to cluster in impoverished urban areas. That pattern would suggest that the reasons for failure might be causally related to conditions associated with urbanization and poverty. We could construct and possibly investigate a large number of potential hypotheses to probe the underlying causes.

It might be that schools in these areas are either not attractive to highly effective teachers and administrators, or very attractive to ineffective ones. If that is the case the reasons should be identified and the incentives for working at these schools changed. It might be that the schools lack resources for facilities, books, or enrichment activities. In that case more resources should be invested in the schools, not less. It might be as simple as hungry students don't learn well. In that case school breakfast and lunch programs might have a bigger impact on test scores than any changes to the teachers or curriculum. More likely it is a synergistic mix of these reasons and others. Consequently, solving the low-test score problem will not be simple—the solution will depend on the unique circumstances of the community in which the school is located. Until an attempt is begun to understand the mix of reasons, any changes made will be a stab in the dark.

Again we see an example of magical thinking—the belief that failure results entirely from character flaws rather than from external factors. Without actually determining the reasons for a past failure, the assumption is that a new school will be better because the new people will be more motivated, or dedicated, or determined, or hardworking, or possessing of some character trait that their predecessors lacked. It is analogous to thinking that my inability to fly is the result of some character flaw within, rather than an external force called gravity. Not surprisingly, studies show that closing schools and beginning new ones, either private, charter, or public, doesn't result in dramatic change. On average, the new schools do no better or worse than what came before [12].

Data Manipulation: Teaching to the Test

But NCLB mandated testing is not simply an exercise in magical thinking. It has far more serious consequences, changing the entire nature of education in ways that undermine its long-term goals. The enormous pressure placed on administrators and teachers to raise test scores has changed both teaching methods and curricula in unintended ways. Teachers must adhere to rigid schedules and have little flexibility to accommodate natural variations in student interests and abilities. The tests no longer assess the effectiveness of curricula; instead curricula are determined by the tests.

The result is the phenomena of "teaching-to-the-test" that I observed in my daughter's third-grade math class. As a teacher, I have always found that expression strange. After all, I give tests, and I only test what I teach. To do otherwise would be unfair to the students. Few people argue against tests as a method to assess students' learning nor against test scores as a basis for assigning grades. Used appropriately, tests are a useful learning tool, for both teachers and students. Tests motivate students to study, and they inform teachers about the effectiveness of their instruction.

But, "teaching-to-the-test" is something different. It is an educational mindset in which test scores are not measures of learning outcomes; rather, the test scores are the outcomes. While that distinction might be subtle, it has real effects on how classes are taught, and on the messages we communicate to students about the goals of an education. Tests are measurement tools; they should not be the reasons that students come to class.

The aversion to "teaching-to-the-test" arises because, at its essence, it is a form of manipulation. Children are perceptive, and they can figure out when adults are manipulating them. Teachers are perceptive, and they will adjust their actions to the reward structure in place. The net result is a poisonous class atmosphere not conducive to learning.

Teachers and students are perceptive. What we need are leaders who are perceptive, and willing to use judgment instead of hiding behind meaningless numbers. A school is not a factory turning out robots with identical product specifications. But, too often, the characterization of educational outcomes solely in terms of test scores results in the mindset of a manufacturing company, rather than an educational institution. Our leaders need to look beyond the numbers and judge the context in which the numbers arose. Each child, each teacher, each school is unique. We should celebrate that uniqueness instead of trying to eliminate it.

On the surface it appears that the motivation for the education-testing craze has gone badly off track. Many high-stakes tests appear to no longer *have* a motivation; instead the test *is* the motivation. It is like saying that the purpose of an experiment is to use the equipment in a laboratory, or the purpose of doing a math problem is to use a calculator. However, I suspect that the real motivation for all of the testing that leads to no insight is misdirection. I believe that most of this testing is for political show and that the politicians do not actually want to know the reasons that schools fail to educate. If we uncovered the real reasons, the fixes would be costly and politically painful. No one really wants to know the truth, and the mindless collection of test data keeps everyone busy and not having to face this truth.

Data Manipulation: The Accountability Hoax

Accountability is touted as the justification for the extensive use of testing and other metrics in education. As the business model for education is promulgated throughout K-12 and higher education, so with it is the idea that each person in the organization must be "held accountable" for outcomes. However, the flaw in this reasoning causes serious problems even in businesses that adhere to it. People can only be held accountable for their *actions*—no one controls outcomes. The use of carrot and stick incentives to reward and punish outcomes can backfire because people can only change their actions. If the desired outcomes don't materialize as a consequence of changed actions, these kinds of reward systems become strong incentives to make it look otherwise.

The corporate world provides innumerable examples of employees and executives manipulating metrics to give false appearances when they were rewarded by incentive plans for doing so. The financial crisis of 2008–09 was precipitated by massive fraud in mortgages and mortgage-backed securities. The only thing unusual about that was its scale. Another recent example of a smaller, but still costly fraud was the collapse of Enron in 2001 and with it the long-time accounting firm Arthur Andersen that enabled Enron's financial deception. In the prior decades of the 1990s and 1980s, systemic fraud contributed to the Savings and Loan Crisis and collapse of many of those institutions.

The fact is that a business model of "accountability" through the use of metrics does not ensure desired outcomes, or even ensure that anyone will be held accountable. This applies also to education. When test-based metrics for accountability for education outcomes are put in place, so too are strong incentives to manipulate the numbers. An investigation using statistical analysis by the *Atlanta Journal Constitution* found roughly 200 school districts around the country with high concentrations of suspect test scores [13]. While the analysis didn't prove cheating per se, investigators in several large school districts with suspect scores did uncover allegations of teacher and/or administrator-assisted cheating. Scandals beset schools in St. Louis, Houston, Dallas, Detroit, Baltimore, and Atlanta, and in many of these cases evidence was strong enough to warrant firings and criminal prosecution.

Consider, for example, Beverly Hall. Hall was superintendent of Atlanta's public schools and was named national superintendent of the year in 2009 by the American Association of School Administrators because of "significant gains in student achievement over the past 10 years." She resigned the next year amid an investigation by the Georgia Bureau of Investigation that discovered that 44 out of 56 schools had cheated on state standardized tests. Hall was indicted in March 2013 by a grand jury for her role in the scandal, along with 34 other educators who worked in the school system under her. Hall never faced trial because of failing health that eventually resulted in her death from breast cancer in March 2015. Most of the other educators took plea deals, but some went to trial. In April 2015, 11 teachers were convicted of racketeering, a criminal charge usually reserved for mobsters [14]. However, the motivations were similar: to earn bonuses and career advancements.

Some might argue that these episodes provide further proof of sociologist Donald T. Campbell's observation made more than three decades ago. "Campbell's Law," as it is known, states that the more a quantitative measure is used for social decision-making, the more it will be subject to corruption pressures that distort the social process it is intended to monitor [15]. While I agree with that assessment, I would go further and argue that testing scandals are symptomatic of a more insidious societal problem: a refusal by its leaders to accept responsibility for the consequences of their decisions. Defining accountability in terms of a quantitative measure—a number—is actually an elaborate hoax perpetrated by the leadership to avoid being truly accountable to their communities.

Basing education policy decisions on standardized test scores (numbers) means that the educators in charge are relieved from using professional judgment. Consider all of the effort school leaders no longer need to exert and decisions they no longer have to defend. If students are judged based on test scores, there is no need to consider their natural abilities and inclinations. What becomes irrelevant is whether Bs on a math test result from overachieving C students who become inspired by a great teacher or from underachieving A students who are bored with the class. Similarly, if teachers are judged based on their students' test scores, gone is the need to go into the classroom and observe their methods and interactions with students. What becomes irrelevant is whether students are failing despite good teaching or succeeding by overcoming bad teaching.

If the schools are judged on test scores, there is no need to work at improving the schools. All that is necessary is to declare schools with low scores failures, fire the teachers and principals, and give the work of educating the students to others—even if there is no reason to believe that schools with different personnel would do any better.

In all of the above examples, the reliance on numbers indicates that decisions are automatic and require no professional judgment. As a result, none of the teachers or school administrators are accountable for the outcomes.

In fact, the standardized test scandals that came with high-stakes testing in many ways mirror the financial scandals that unfolded at the same time. The U.S. economy is still struggling to recover from the elaborate accountability hoax perpetrated by the mortgage industry in the mid-2000s. Home prices were appraised based on inflated "comparables," not on what the market could reasonably support over the long run. Credit scores were assigned based on past payment histories, not on the ability to make future payments. Securities were rated based on mathematical models with faulty assumptions, not on realistic assessments of risk. When the system came crashing down, no one was accountable because everyone's actions were in response to numbers, even though those numbers were meaningless.

Do we want the same kind of economic wreckage brought on by the banking industry for our education system? The obsession with test scores to the exclusion of other educational goals suggests that we are heading in that direction. The truth is that judging the quality of teachers and schools requires looking at more than just student test scores, that education has more dimensions than just reading and math, and that the single-minded goal of continually improving test scores is not realistic.

Professionals, whether they are in education, business, law, medicine, science, or engineering, are hired because their specialized training and extensive experience endows them with superior judgment. What is the point of hiring a professional if we do not want him or her to exercise that judgment? There will always be errors in judgment. But do we want a society in which to avoid blame, no one uses judgment? A society in which decisions are based solely on numbers instead of sound judgment is one in which no one is truly accountable.

The SAT: Promoting Equal Opportunity or Perpetuating a Hierarchy?

The Scholastic Aptitude Test (SAT) is a widely used instrument for college admission decisions. The SAT's original purpose was to provide a level playing field for admission to college by identifying the students most likely to succeed in college, without regard to social and economic background. In theory, a student from a poor inner city school district and a student from an expensive private prep school who have identical SAT scores should have equal abilities to succeed in college.

But the almost universal use of the SAT has also resulted in an industry that profits through the sale of expensive test preparation services to students. Private companies, such as Kaplan and Princeton Review, charge hundreds of dollars for SAT prep courses, and thousands of dollars for private tutoring. Both companies boast that the combined SAT scores of their students increase more than 100 points because of these services. As a result, we can never know if a raw SAT score represents innate ability or intensive—and expensive— prep work. A privileged background clearly provides an advantage on the SAT test, and this defeats its original purpose of assessing students regardless of background. Additionally, an SAT score is a single snapshot in time that tells how well a student did taking a test on a particular day, and some very smart students don't test well. In fact, students who take a deeper and more nuanced view of the questions can be at a disadvantage.

The SAT is also now linked to the belief that the test is necessary to preserve college standards and, moreover, that failure to test students prior to admission will result in lower standards. As mentioned at the beginning of this chapter, some alumni at the university where I teach, Loyola University Maryland, are concerned that dropping the SAT admission requirement will devalue their potential earnings on the job market. In their view, employers will no longer take students with a degree from Loyola seriously because students at the school are no longer tested for aptitude before admission to the university. If the SAT does determine future earnings, as these alumni believe, it is little wonder that millions of high school students spend so much money and time on prep courses in an attempt to game the system.

So how did the SAT go from being a tool of upward mobility intended to help disadvantaged students get into college, to being a means of preserving the existing socioeconomic structure by allowing students from wealthy families to game the system and to enhance their future earnings? To start, consider how colleges differ from public K-12 schools. The most striking difference is that colleges do not offer a one-size-fits-all standardized education. Unlike public K-12 education with its standardized testing and Common Core standards, colleges are decidedly not standard. In fact, higher education in the United States is successful because it lacks standardization and instead addresses individual needs.

Each college—and there are thousands in the United States—offers a unique educational experience. Students are looking for colleges with educational offerings that best match their needs and interests. Colleges are looking for students that are most likely to succeed in the educational programs being provided. On the surface it appears that there would be little incentive for students to game the system and gain admission to a college that is not a good fit for them.

Data Manipulation: The Murky Business of Quantifying Prestige

However, our obsession with prestige has resulted in extreme differentiation and a clear hierarchy among institutions of higher education. Colleges and universities are ranked not by student test scores, but by less transparent formulas such as the *U. S. News & World Report* annual ranking of colleges [16] and the Princeton Review's annual book on best colleges [17]. Students compete for acceptance into the most prestigious colleges and universities. In turn, colleges and universities, seeking to enhance their prestige, compete to attract the best students. Additionally, while the college ranking guides do not publish their exact formulas, colleges can deduce enough factors in order to game the ranking systems by manipulating the statistics that go into them. The net effect of the competition for prestige is to increase the cost of a college degree far beyond what is necessary. And students will pay the higher costs because the hierarchy perpetuates itself in the job market. Employers automatically assume students graduating from the more prestigious schools will be better employees and pay them more.

Thus, rather than leveling the playing field, the SAT is used as a sorting tool to perpetuate an existing hierarchy. The higher a student scores on the SAT, the more options to attend prestigious colleges become available and the higher prestige translates into a greater potential for future earnings—hence the incentive for students to game the system, and also the incentive for colleges to use the SAT in the admissions process.

SAT scores were meant to provide a level playing field for college admission by putting students from all backgrounds on equal footing. But, as it usually happens when a number is substituted for judgment, an inordinate amount of time, effort, and expense is allocated toward manipulating the number. This is not to say that SAT scores are meaningless. High school students with poor math scores will not do well in college majors that involve STEM majors—science, technology, engineering, or math. Those with poor verbal scores will struggle in just about all college majors.

The SAT is a crude measure of college readiness and loses its value even further when students game it. Studies have shown that, not surprisingly, high school GPAs are better indicators of college GPAs than SAT scores. As one report summarizes:

> "College and university cumulative GPAs closely track high school GPAs, despite wide variations in testing. Students with strong HS GPAs generally perform well in college, despite modest or low testing. In contrast, students with weak HS GPAs earn lower college Cum GPAs and graduate at lower rates, even with markedly stronger testing. A clear message: hard work and good grades in high school matter, and they matter a lot." [18]

Because of this evidence, many colleges have rethought the reliance on SAT scores for admission decisions. Success in college depends not only on scholastic aptitude, but also on many other intangibles, such as desire, focus, motivation, and maturity. Although these qualities defy quantification, competent admissions officers are able to make accurate judgments.

These qualities also translate into college success, which is more dependent on attitude than aptitude. Students will do well if they attend class, do the assigned work, and major in a subject that interests them. In other words, students should study subjects in which they are passionately interested and work hard to master them. That may sound simple and trite, but my experience is that students who fail in college haven't mastered those basic practices.

Colleges that decide to become SAT-optional need to examine their motivations. If the motivation is to provide opportunity to students who don't rise to the top on standardized tests, but give many other indications of succeeding in college and contributing to the campus community, that is admirable. That also means that the admissions officers need to do careful work examining all other facets of these applications. However, if the motivation is simply to accrue more students to fill out class sizes regardless of ability or prior preparation, that is not ethical. Incoming college students should not be set up to fail.

Additionally, employers and professional schools should learn to look beyond the reputation of the school that recent graduates come from. Put her on any campus in the country, and a student who consistently cuts class and misses assignments will receive the exact same education: none. And I would further argue that a C-average graduate of a highly ranked college may not be as good a worker as an A-average graduate of a lesser-known college; the A-average graduate probably works harder and learns more. The same can be said when comparing majors. Even for technically oriented jobs, I would recommend hiring an A-average philosophy major over a C- or D-average STEM major. To this point, employers should be careful about using keywords in screening resumes because they might be rejecting some outstanding potential hires. Graduates with high GPAs in any major are capable of learning on the job, while graduates with low GPAs in the specified major might not be able to learn the tasks the job requires.

Students should understand that the prestige of their degrees might help in landing them their first jobs, but that their value to employers in the long-run will be in the work that they do. College degrees have no "financial value" so it is not possible for them to "depreciate." A degree is a non-transferable status that cannot be bought or sold. I know this seems like a strange assertion given the wide disparity between the average lifetime earnings of college graduates compared to those without college degrees. But students are mistaken if they believe that degrees are the cause of the higher income typically earned by college graduates.

No employer pays a person because he or she has a college degree. Employees are paid for the performance of work; that is, if the performance has sufficient value, it then becomes in the financial best interest of the employer to pay accordingly. It happens that the knowledge, skills, and insights that are acquired through the process of obtaining a college degree often result in the ability to perform work that is of greater value to employers. But many people without degrees are highly paid because they perform valuable work. It is productive work that causes payment, not the abilities associated with the degree. Graduates who cannot establish themselves as productive workers will find that their degrees mean very little financially. For recent graduates entering the workforce, college reputation and courses of study are important because it is all employers have as a basis for judging competence and abilities. But within four to five years of graduation it will be performance on the job that counts.

Assessing Colleges: Self-Selected Data

So how is the quality of a college determined if the SAT scores of its students have little relevance? This too has become a murky business. In recent years colleges have come under increasing pressure to "assess" the effectiveness of their programs. "Assessment" is now a ubiquitous buzzword in education that had little usage a generation ago. Accrediting agencies and school administrators are now expected to provide evidence of effective and desirable outcomes from the resources—human or capital—allocated to their schools. The goal of assessment is to answer a reasonable set of questions in regards to educational programs:

• Are students learning?
• Are teachers effective?
• What teaching methods ("pedagogies" in educational jargon) should be used?
• Are resources effectively allocated?

Practitioners of assessment seek to provide answers based on data, not expert opinions, which they often distrust. By collecting and analyzing data, the process of assessment is intended to mimic the scientific method and provide objective, evidence-based answers to these questions.

This is a laudable goal, but what becomes disturbing about the current "assessment" frenzy is that the scientific method has been co-opted, corrupted, and distilled to only one thing: the accumulation and analysis of data. It is highly doubtful whether much of the collected data and convoluted analysis schemes will ever identify a chain of causation that can be used to produce better educational outcomes.

One might think that the institutions of higher education—our colleges and universities—might be immune to assessment practices that require the collection of reams of insignificant data. However, they serve as a perfect case in point. Take, for example, the agency charged with accrediting many of the nation's college and universities, the Middle States Commission on Higher Education. Its requirements on assessment, outlined in its handbook, *Student Learning Assessment: Options and Resources,* must be followed or schools will lose their accreditations.

The handbook, which purports to "clarify the principles and methods to assess student learning," leads faculty members through a multi-stage process for developing assessment practices for their courses [19]. One step in the process is to use a "Teaching Goals Inventory (TGI)" to "identify the priority of various learning goals in their courses and programs." This "self-scorable" inventory asks a faculty member to rate the relative importance in a particular course of 52 separate goals on a scale of 1 to 5, with 1 being "not-applicable" and 5 being "essential." The instructions are to "assess each goal in terms of what you deliberately aim to have your students accomplish rather than in terms of the goal's general worthiness…"

A sample of the 52 goals includes:

- Develop an ability to perform skillfully
- Develop a commitment to accurate work
- Improve self-esteem/self-confidence
- Develop a sense of responsibility for one's own behavior
- Develop a capacity to make wise decisions
- Develop aesthetic appreciations
- Learn to appreciate important contributions to this subject
- Develop an informed concern about contemporary social issues [19, pp. 23–26]

The list contains an additional 45 goals—all laudable, certainly, but also arguably vague and un-assessable.

Once the faculty member decides on the learning goals for a course, the next step is to collect evidence to document that the chosen learning goals have been met. Of course, teachers have always assessed student learning by using grades. But, according to the assessment handbook: "grades are not direct evidence of student learning" because a "grade alone does not express the content of what students have learned; it reflects only the degree to which the student is perceived to have learned in a specific context." Only if grades "are appropriately linked to learning goals" are they an indicator of student learning." If you are confused by what all this verbiage means, so am I.

What it means in practice is that accreditation teams want to see actual examples of the tests and assignments that grades are based on. It is no longer sufficient for a professor to read an English paper and assign it a grade such as a B. The accreditors want to see the actual paper, see how it was graded, and if the paper shows evidence that the student achieved any of the goals the professor chose from the Teaching Goals Inventory, such as developing aesthetic appreciation, commitment to accuracy, informed concern, capacity for wisdom, and so on.

My concern is not with the goals themselves, but rather with their misappropriation. Notice that the teaching goals in the inventory are byproducts of the *education process*, not the actual *content* goals that most professors typically teach in their courses. It can be argued that the byproducts are more important than the content, because the byproducts become lasting personal traits while content is often forgotten. It can be argued just as strongly, however, that it would be presumptuous for professors to explicitly teach character traits such as wisdom, concern, aesthetic appreciation, self-esteem, and self-confidence. The inculcation of these traits usually comes through immersion, struggle, and mastery of intellectually challenging course work. No one, for example, would obtain genuine self-confidence from a course designed to explicitly teach self-confidence.

Most importantly, there is no clear way that a professor can change her teaching methods in response to this kind of overly detailed data on vaguely stated learning goals. She could, however, discover ways of changing her teaching methods based on legitimate studies on effective teaching, which directly link *mastery of content* to the *methods used to teach the content*. For example, if she wants her students to come away from a lesson with a conceptual understanding Newton's first law of motion, there are teaching methods that have been identified through research as being more effective than others. She could use the "deductive explanation task (DET)" described in the paper "Deductive Reasoning to Teach Newton's Law of Motion" and published in a peer-reviewed journal on science and mathematics education [20]. The authors of this paper reported that using the DET they developed, students achieved a good conceptual understanding of force and motion.

But if the learning goal is "capacity for wisdom," will that ever be linked in a causal way to what the teacher is doing? The student might be acquiring a greater "capacity for wisdom" through normal development and maturation outside of anything in the course that the professor can control. List enough character traits as learning goals and I can guarantee that "evidence for success" will be found for some of them, regardless of the teaching method. The professors and the college administration will soon learn what traits are most often demonstrated and very soon those will be the ones assessed. After all, the professors are being asked to choose the learning goals. With enough data you can always demonstrate the success of something, but this is just another manifestation of over-fitting – it does not qualify as doing science.

Determining the best teaching methods and conditions for student mastery of content is a valid area of scientific study: specific research questions can be formulated and tested. It is possible to teach a specific topic with different teaching methods and test student recall and understanding to determine which method worked best. In fact, the vast literature on best teaching practices is often ignored by administrators and accreditors who both lack the disciplinary expertise to understand the studies, and who also do not want to commit the recommended resources to implement them.

The motivating questions that assessment practices are intended to answer are significant. Are student learning outcomes worth the enormous commitment of time and financial resources required to attend college? But assessment practices are unlikely to produce better outcomes if they conflate teaching methods with quality of life issues, which is often the case.

Determining the best teaching practices and classroom conditions for inculcating desirable character traits and improving the quality of life for students is a much more difficult scientific undertaking. When studying character traits it is difficult to isolate causes and effects, and quality of life criteria are difficult to define. However, a great deal of accumulated evidence shows that college graduates have a vastly improved quality of life in many dimensions. College graduates earn significantly more money, are much less likely to be unemployed [21], more likely to marry, less likely to divorce [22], are healthier, and even have longer life expectancies [23], than people without college degrees.

But how improved quality of life comes about is more likely to be found in the program of study rather than specific teaching methods. The questions that should be asked are: What kinds of long-term outcomes result from different college programs? Do some programs serve students better in the long run? How do long-term outcomes differ for students receiving liberal arts degrees, technology degrees, business degrees, Jesuit education, attending a conservatory, reading great books, having most of their courses dictated or choosing their own course of study? These are interesting questions that should be addressed separate from classroom strategies. Conflating programming with individual teaching methods when conducting assessment leads to little insight about either facet of the college experience.

It may also be that there is no "best" program for all students. Most likely an education that matches an individual student's strengths and passions will be the "best." A talented musician would be best off at a conservatory, an aspiring engineer best off at a technology institute, and so on. Figuring out how best to match students to programs of study, rather than trying to determine if specific programs are "better" than others might be much more useful.

In either case, understanding the causal reasons for the improved quality of life for college graduates would be useful knowledge to obtain. Perhaps, with that understanding, it would be possible for people to enjoy a better quality of life without the expense of college. But doing so will require formulating scientifically testable questions and conducting controlled studies. Collecting reams of self-selected data on vaguely stated learning outcomes will not provide us with that insight. Actually, I doubt the purveyors of assessment want that insight, because their real motive in collecting all this data is to justify the ever-escalating cost of a college education. I don't know of anyone using assessment to try to figure out how to deliver the desired learning outcomes for less money.

Facts Versus Stories

"Facts tell; Stories sell." I learned this mantra in a workshop on writing ad copy; it also sums up a great deal about the human condition. A powerful, emotionally engaging narrative moves people to act regardless of the facts. This is why pseudoscience continues to flourish in the modern era. Tell a good story and find just enough facts to make it plausible and anyone can have a following. In contrast, science works by aiming to gather all the available facts and piecing together a causal explanation consistent with them all—even if it's not an explanation people want to hear—and then probing further for contradictions. Unfortunately, an examination of "data-driven" educational policies uncovers more pseudoscience than real science—pseudoscience driven by powerful narratives that cover up inconvenient truths.

• **The teacher narrative, particularly in public K-12 schools, is that all educational failure is the result of bad teachers.** Bad teachers lurk around every corner in the educational system, waiting to inflict a lifetime of damage on unsuspecting children entering the system. Like zombies, these bad teachers cannot be killed off because they are protected by all powerful teachers unions obsessed with maintaining lifetime job security for members too incompetent to work anywhere else. Because no one knows for sure why certain teachers are bad, or even who the bad teachers are, heroic reformers armed with sophisticated statistical algorithms that can crunch reams of data are needed to ferret out the bad teachers hiding in their classrooms in plain sight of students and parents. With enough data and analysis, these bad teachers can be exposed and publicly shamed and humiliated into either changing their ways or leaving the profession.

The truth is that in any school I've ever been associated with, it has always been common knowledge among all the interested parties—students, teachers, administrators, parents—who the good teachers are, who the bad teachers are, and the reasons why a teacher falls into one category or the other. No sophisticated statistical analysis was ever necessary. I think everyone I've ever known could say the same thing about their schools. Teachers, being real human beings, are of course all different, and they interact every day with students who are also human and therefore all different. Those differences, and the richness of human interactions that result from them, should be celebrated. But, instead those differences have become an anathema to a standardization movement that seeks to have common curricula, common texts, and a testing regimen to enforce conformity to all these standards. Because humans are not robots with identical product specifications, the stated goals of the standardization movement are doomed to failure. However, that is not a concern. The real point is for politicians to say they are doing something about education, have the numbers to prove it, and someone to blame—the teachers—for any real or perceived failures.

• **The school narrative is that the United States is in a state of educational crisis—and has been for decades.** President Regan's National Commission on Excellence in Education's 1983 report, *A Nation at Risk: The Imperative for Educational Reform,* issued a dire warning of "a rising tide of mediocrity that threatens our very future as a nation and a people." [24] Almost four decades later in 2010, the message was still the same in the documentary *Waiting for "Superman,"* released with a companion book carrying the subtitle "How We Can Save America's Failing Public Schools": for the United States to be economically viable in the twenty-first century the entire failed school system must be reformed [25].

The truth is that most schools work. In fact, as Diane Ravitch documents, student test scores on the National Assessment of Education Progress (NAEP), which is administered by the U. S. Department of Education, are at all-time highs [26]. Most students are studying and learning more than they did four to five decades ago. However, schools in urban areas with high concentrations of poverty are not working well. There is nothing new or surprising about the failure of these schools, certainly nothing that requires widespread testing to uncover. These schools did not work five decades ago and despite all the "reform" since then these schools still do not serve their students well. Until the actual causes for the failure of these schools are addressed, no amount of testing and reform is going to change their educational outcomes. Of course, the elephant in the room is that the causes for the failure of schools in highly impoverished areas are mostly external to the schools. Addressing these causes will require politically painful choices that no one wants to face.

• **The SAT narrative is that being "smart" matters most and that the "smart" trait is quantifiable with an appropriate testing instrument.** This belief is instilled in students from an early age. In my daughter's third grade class, the teacher exhorted the students to do well on a standardized test in order to show "what smart students we have at our school." Implicit in this statement is the assumption that all good schools have "smart students." Also implicit is the assumption that colleges need the SAT to identify and admit smart students in order to maintain the prestige of the college. According to this narrative, failure to restrict entrance to only the smart students is a betrayal to all the students and alumni because it "financially depreciates" the value of their degrees. Higher education is a sorting process performed for the benefit of future employers that identifies the smartest individuals to be awarded the higher paying jobs.

The truth is that being "smart" neither is a fixed trait nor does it equate with success. In fact, studies have shown that those who believe in fixed intelligence will learn less; for example, one study demonstrated that praise for intelligence can actually undermine children's motivation and performance [27, 28]. Children praised simply for intelligence—for being smart—come to believe that intelligence is a "fixed" trait, one that the child is born with and cannot be improved. Consequently, children with perceptions of their intelligence as "fixed" come to view the purpose of school as documenting their innate abilities, as opposed to growing their intelligence and abilities. Such a belief causes students to avoid challenging tasks out of fear that failure will demonstrate a lack of intelligence and ability.

In contrast, children who are praised for effort instead of aptitude—for working hard instead of being "smart"—do not see failure as a blow to their self-worth and seek higher and higher levels of achievement. Instead of viewing their academic abilities as innate and fixed, they learn that hard work does result in higher levels of achievement. The third-graders being exhorted to show "how smart they are" are being misled and so are college students who believe a high SAT score is the pathway to future financial security. Yes, employers need people who are smart, but they need people who can actually solve problems, and most importantly, they need people who can continue to learn.

At the same time students can learn how to learn—or increase their overall aptitude for academics. Most skills of value involve what I call "deep expertise," that is skills that have no upper limit to the extent that they can be improved. Achievement in most academic subjects—reading, writing, mathematics, science, visual and performing arts—requires the development of skills with deep expertise. Practitioners can spend their entire lives improving and honing their skills. Academic achievement is just one aspect of the rich and complex process of human development. Ultimately this is a biological process that will continue for a lifetime. Learning a skill that involves deep expertise requires the formation of complex neural pathways in the brain, an active process that cannot be shortcut. A teacher cannot simply transfer knowledge to a passive unengaged student.

• **The assessment narrative in colleges and universities is that a college education should instill character traits and habits of mind that go beyond mastery of the subject matter.** Professors and administrators are asked to provide classroom data to demonstrate that students are achieving these learning outcomes. The ever-escalating costs demanded of students and their families are defended by such a narrative.

The truth is that graduates from legitimate colleges experience enhanced quality of life in many dimensions. Hard data from the U. S. Census Bureau and that the U. S. Department of Labor collected over decades support this claim, and that is the real reason students and parents keep paying so much for college. Self-selected assessment data from classrooms is not going to change this basic reality one way or the other. However, college costs rise much faster than inflation because colleges continue to move far beyond their core mission of teaching and scholarship. The obsession with prestige has spurred a race to create all manner of programming beyond what is necessary to achieve their core educational goals. The rise in cost this programming creates is fast approaching a level of unsustainability, and soon no one will be able to afford a college education. No amount of assessment data is going to change that basic financial math.

While all these narratives are powerful and emotionally compelling, they all fail to provide *causal* explanations for student learning. The underlying reasons for why some teachers are more effective than others, why some schools succeed while others fail, why some students succeed in college while others drop out, why some college programs achieve their learning outcomes while others do not, are left unexamined. Instead the narratives provide tautologies—successful programs, teachers, schools, and students have successful outcomes.

Nonetheless, these narratives thrive for the same reason that pseudoscience continues to thrive—choosing willful ignorance over harsh and inconvenient truths. Teachers must work with students with a wide variety of backgrounds and abilities, and not all students are ready and able to learn at grade-level. Schools reflect their communities, and failed communities will have failed schools. Success requires hard work; simply being smart and credentialed isn't enough. College doesn't need to be as expensive as it has become, and not everyone needs to go. Rather than deal with the complexities of these realities, it is easier to remain ignorant of them and instead tell a good story.

References

1. Michael Winerip, "Evaluating New York Teachers, Perhaps the Numbers Do Lie," *New York Times*, March 6, 2011, http://www.nytimes.com/2011/03/07/education/07winerip.html?pagewanted=all.
2. Eva L. Baker, et al., "Problems with the Use of Student Test Scores to Evaluate Teachers," *EPI Briefing Paper #278* (Washington, DC: Economic Policy Institute, 2010). http://s2.epi.org/files/page/-/pdf/bp278.pdf.
3. Eric A. Hanushek, and Steven G. Rivkin, "How to Improve the Supply of High Quality Teachers," *Brookings Papers on Education Policy*, (Washington, DC: Brookings Institution Press, 2004) 7–25. http://muse.jhu.edu/journals/pep/summary/v2004/2004.1hanushek.html.
4. Richard Rothstein, "Comments" *Brookings Papers on Education Policy*, (Washington, DC: Brookings Institution Press, 2004) 25–39. http://muse.jhu.edu/journals/brookings_papers_on_education_policy/v2004/2004.1rothstein.html.
5. Edward H. Haertel, "Reliability and Validity of Inferences About Teachers Based on Student Test Scores," 14th William H. Angoff Memorial Lecture on March 22, 2013 (Princeton: Educational Testing Service, 2013). https://www.ets.org/Media/Research/pdf/PICANG14.pdf.
6. Jason Felch, Jason Song, and Doug Smith, "Who's teaching L.A.'s kids?" LA *Times*, August 14, 2010, http://www.latimes.com/local/la-meteachers-value-20100815-story.html#page=1.
7. John Ewing, "Mathematical Intimidation: Driven by Data," *Notices of the AMS* 58, no. 5 (2010): 667–673.http://www.ams.org/notices/201105/rtx110500667p.pdf.
8. "Los Angeles Teacher Ratings," *LA Times*, accessed May 1, 2018, http://projects.latimes.com/value-added/faq/#what_is_value_added.
9. Robert Gordon, Thomas J. Kane, and Douglas O. Staiger, "Identifying Effective Teachers Using Performance on the Job," *The Hamilton Project* (Washington,

DC: Brookings Institution, 2006). Accessed May 1, 2018, https://www.brookings.edu/research/identifying-effectiveteachers-using-performance-on-the-job/.

10. Cathy O'Neil, *Weapons of Math Destruction: How Big Data Increases Inequality and Threatens Democracy* (New York: Crown Publishing, 2016).

11. Public Law 107 – 110, An Act "To close the achievement gap with accountability, flexibility, and choice, so that no child is left behind,"Enacted by the Senate and House of Representatives of the United States of America in Congress Assembled, January 8, 2002, https://www2.ed.gov/policy/elsec/leg/esea02/107-110.pdf.

12. Diane Ravitch, *The Death and Life of the Great American School System: How Testing and Choice Are Undermining Education* (New York: Basic Books, 2010).

13. Emily Merwin, John Perry, and M. B. Pell, "Suspect scores, substantiated cheating," *Atlanta Journal-Constitution*, September 22, 2012, http://www.ajc.com/news/cheating-our-children/district-bios/.

14. Erin Fuchs, "An epic cheating trial has come to an end, and teachers could go to jail for 20 years," *Business Insider*, April 1, 2015, http://www.businessinsider.com/atlanta-teachers-convicted-of-racketeering-2015-4.

15. Donald T. Campbell, "Assessing the Impact of Planned Social Change," *Occasional Paper Series* Paper #8, (Dartmouth College: The Public Affairs Center, 1976). http://portals.wi.wur.nl/files/docs/ppme/Assessing_impact_of_planned_social_change.pdf.

16. "Best Colleges: U. S. News and World Report Rankings," U. S. News & World Report, accessed May 1, 2018, http://colleges.usnews.rankingsandreviews.com/best-colleges.

17. Princeton Review, The Best 379 Colleges, 2015 Edition (New York: Random House, 2014).

18. William C. Hiss and Valerie W. Franks, "Defining Promise: Optional Standardized Testing Policies in American College and University Admissions" (Arlington, VA: National Association for College Admissions Counseling, 2014). http://www.nacacnet.org/research/researchdata/nacac-research/Documents/DefiningPromise.pdf.

19. Middle States Commission on Higher Education, *Student Learning Assessment: Options and Resources*, 2nd edition (Philadelphia: Middle States Commission on Higher Education, 2007). accessed August 6, 2014, http://www.msche.org/publications/SLA_Book_0808080728085320.pdf.

20. Han Su Lee and Jongwon Park, "Deductive Reasoning to Teach Newton's Law of Motion," *International Journal of Science Mathematics Education* 11, (2013): 1391–1414.

21. U. S. Bureau of Labor Statistics, "Earnings and Employment rates by educational attainment," (Washington, DC: U. S. Department of Labor, 2013): Fig. 1, accessed August 6, 2014, http://www.bls.gov/emp/ep_chart_001.htm.

22. U. S. Bureau of Labor Statistics, "Marriage and Divorce: Patterns by gender, race and educational attainment," *Monthly Labor Review*,(October 2013), http://www.bls.gov/opub/mlr/2013/article/pdf/marriage-and-divorce-patterns-by-gender-race-and-educational-attainment.pdf.

23. S. Jay Olshansky, et al. "Differences In Life Expectancy Due To Race And Educational Differences Are Widening, And Many May Not Catch Up" *Health Affairs* 31, no. 8 (August 2012): 1803–1813. http://content.healthaffairs.org/content/31/8/1803.abstract.

24. The National Commission on Excellence in Education, "A Nation at Risk: The Imperative for Educational Reform," A Report to the Nation and the Secretary of Education, (Washington, DC: United States Department of Education, 1983). https://www2.ed.gov/pubs/NatAtRisk/index.html.

25. Karl Weber, ed., *Waiting for Superman: How We Can Save America's Failing Public Schools*, Participant Media (New York: PublicAffairs, 2010).

26. Diane Ravitch, *Reign of Error: The Hoax of the Privatization Movement and the Danger to America's Public Schools* (New York: Alfred A. Knopf, 2013).

27. Claudia M. Mueller and Carol Dweck, "Praise for Intelligence Can Undermine Children's Motivation and Performance," *Journal of Personality and Social Psychology* 75 (1998): 33–52.

28. Carol Dweck, *Mindset: The New Psychology of Success* (New York: Random House, 2006).

3

The Complexity Myth: The Opposite of Science

"He uses statistics in the same way that a drunk uses lamp-posts—for support rather than illumination."

— Andrew Lang
19th century Scottish novelist and literary critic

In the battles over education, much has been made of the roles of teachers. Education reformers espouse a belief in the central role of the teacher; presumably under the tutelage of an effective, highly-qualified teacher, students will meet proficiency standards. The advocacy group StudentsFirst, founded in 2010 by former Washington DC schools' chancellor Michelle Rhee, asserts: "Teachers make all the difference." [1] and they claim that "Research shows that no other in-school factor has a greater effect on a child's future." [2] Specifically, the research they cite to support this claim is a paper by Rivkin, Hanushek, and Kain, which deploys an elaborate statistical analysis to reach the conclusion that teachers matter more than class size for student achievement [3]. But as this chapter will explain, despite the rhetoric in support of the teacher's role, administrators dictate more and more of the curriculum and instructional methods.

In the narrative given by reformers, the teachers matter more than anything else; moreover, the research cited is convenient for school boards resisting calls for reducing class sizes as a means for improving schools. Just find better teachers. However, the authors of the cited study also qualify their own research, stating: "little of the variation in teacher quality is explained by *observable characteristics* such as education or experience." The emphasis is

© Springer International Publishing AG, part of Springer Nature 2018
J. Ganem, *The Robot Factory*, https://doi.org/10.1007/978-3-319-77860-0_3

mine. In other words, the underlying implication is that there is no way to find better teachers because we can't identify high-quality teaching, other than through our finding that great teachers have high achieving students. In Chapter 2 I discuss this fallacious, circular tautology by these same two authors in an earlier 2004 paper [4]. In this chapter I turn from a focus on the students to a focus on teachers. Specifically, I demonstrate how complexity-for-complexity's sake is invoked in the assessment of teachers at the expense of an appreciation for the actual complexity of the student-teacher relationship. I then show how these impossible expectations result in shortages of qualified teachers rather than improved classroom instruction.

The Quest for the Perfect Teacher

Federal law requires that teachers be "highly qualified," meaning that they hold a minimum of a bachelor's degree in the subject that they teach, be fully certified, and pass rigorous state tests on core subject knowledge. In addition to meeting these requirements, teachers are expected to demonstrate "effectiveness," defined as their students making "adequate yearly progress" on standardized tests. Teachers are also expected to be "effective" with students from different backgrounds and with different instructional needs. In other words, in addition to subject mastery, teachers must be experts at managing a diverse range of relationships with their students.

Finding "great teachers" has been a long-time quest for Michelle Rhee and her like-minded reformers. Indeed, over a decade before beginning StudentsFirst, Rhee founded The New Teacher Project (TNTP), whose initial purpose was to recruit mid-career professionals in other fields to become teachers in underperforming schools. In their report titled, "The Irreplaceables," TNTP states their primary recommendation: "smart retention." [5] The report summarizes smart retention as rewarding top teachers with merit pay and letting low performing teachers go. And how does the report recommend improving the ability of existing teachers? It states: "Strengthen the teaching profession through *higher expectations*." Again, the emphasis is mine. This line of thinking—that expectations for teachers need to be raised—has become influential and pervasive in schools around the country.

In the example I gave in the introduction of this book, my daughter's third grade teacher cut off discussion with the confused students by invoking the old parental standby: "It's for your own good." Another common expression that parents use to silence children is: "I expect better _____ from you." (Fill in the blank with grades, behavior, work, etc.) Its usage is based on a wide-spread belief that "expectations" matter above all else, that children will magically fulfill the expectations set by their parents, and—therefore—expectations should always be kept "high." End of discussion. That attitude has been carried over into many workplaces—schools in particular—when managing subordinates and is discussed further in Chapter 8. But, in this context, notice that this expression is fundamentally meaningless. It provides no information to the person being admonished on what *actions* qualify as "better."

It bears repeating from Chapter 2: people can only control their actions. No one controls outcomes. The only way to influence outcomes is to take actions which are causally aligned with the desired outcomes. Even then, there is no guarantee that the outcome causally aligned with an action will occur. For example, smoking is one of the causes of lung cancer, but habitual smoking does not guarantee getting lung cancer.

Nonetheless, even though we cannot guarantee that an action will always cause its associated outcome, when we ignore causal mechanisms and look only for correlations, we risk interpreting random events as meaningful. This is the trap that practitioners of pseudoscience fall into. An astrologer, out of pure chance, will make some correct predictions. However, this does not indicate that *any* of the predictions are meaningful because there is no causal mechanism in operation for generating correct predictions.

For education reform, a legitimate use of the scientific method to improve teaching must focus on the *actions* of the teacher that are *causal* to student learning outcomes. When causal actions are identified and then repeated, successful learning outcomes can therefore be reproduced, and, finally, effective teachers can be identified, hired, and trained. As noted in Chapters 2 and 5, the rich literature on effective pedagogy and child development, especially in the STEM fields, documents scientifically validated teaching practices and serves as foundational best practices. A motivated teacher can acquire and apply this knowledge base to become a more effective teacher.

Reformers, unfortunately, have chosen to ignore much of the literature on effective pedagogy, and instead serve up another tautology: effective teachers do everything right. Effective teachers are, in the words of Mary Poppins, "practically perfect in every way." But perfection is not only impractical, it runs counter to what is perhaps most valuable about the educational experience. The teacher-student interaction is between two autonomous human beings and thus brings with it the complexity inherent in all human relationships. Students are not robots being assembled and programmed in a factory. Teachers are not idealized, perfect, fantasy people.

The Teacher-Student Relationship

By way of example, let's consider some of my memorable teachers in high school. Did my teachers possess the abilities that reformers seek in regard to teacher-student relationships? I went to a large (over 2000 students) homogeneous (all middle-class white) suburban high school. Of course, even for a student body lacking ethnic or economic diversity, there is always a diversity of interests and abilities.

Memorable teacher number 1: Dr. E. Senior year I took AP calculus with Dr. E. Credentialed with a Ph.D., Dr. E was the most highly qualified teacher in the math department. A soft-spoken middle-aged bearded man, he projected the aura of a stereotypical college professor. He had a deep understanding of calculus and relished teaching it to the select group of 20 students in my class. We were the top math students in the school and all of us aspired to pass the AP exam on the subject. He treated us more like colleagues than high school students. I enjoyed his class, and I would go on to pass the AP exam and earn college credit for calculus.

Of course, Dr. E taught other math classes. My sister, a high school junior, took his algebra class at the same time I took calculus. It could be said that Dr. E was a demanding algebra teacher who had high expectations of his students. The truth is that like many people with a Ph.D. in math, he regarded algebra as rather obvious. He responded indignantly to less than perfect homework, crumpling the offending paper, throwing it to the floor and stomping on it. In his mind, students who submitted incorrect answers to problems must not be taking him or his class seriously. He put my sister, for whom algebra was not obvious, in this category, often driving her to tears with frequent outbursts directed at her. Eventually algebra class became unbearable for her, and my mother decided to intervene.

My mother contacted the school to request a meeting with Dr. E so that she could mediate the conflict between him and my sister. Indeed, she was rather perplexed by the situation, as my sister and I told such conflicting stories about Dr. E. How could we possibly have the same teacher?

Dr. E. responded that he was busy and unsure of a time that he would be available to meet. Furious, my mother spoke to the principal and demanded that my sister be transferred to an algebra class with a different teacher. Her request was initially denied; school rules allowed dropping a course and foregoing any credit, but transferring to a different teacher was not permitted. My sister was presented with the option of either quitting algebra altogether or continuing with Dr. E. My mother would hear none of it, and the principal finally backed down and transferred my sister to a class with a different teacher.

Blindsided by the exception to what he thought was an unbreakable rule, Dr. E approached me to ask what happened. I didn't know what to say and just shrugged. He appeared hurt and confused by the events. He did not know how badly his relationship with my sister had deteriorated, and he had clearly underestimated my mother. My sister finished algebra that year with a different teacher.

Unfortunately, my sister's experience was not an anomaly. The eldest son of a neighbor also incurred the wrath of Dr. E. He had struggled in school, but math was a subject he felt good at. That is until he landed in Dr. E's algebra class. According to our neighbor, Dr. E constantly berated her son's performance in math and destroyed whatever little remained of his self-confidence. She further claimed that it was her son's experience with Dr. E that provoked her son to run away from home at age 16. She had not heard from her son since, and had no idea what had happened to him. As far as our neighbor was concerned, Dr. E should be fired.

After spending many years searching for her son, our neighbor finally got a lucky break, a tip that her son lived in a particular city in a different state. She found him alive and well. In fact, he was gainfully employed, owned a home, and was happily married. His reason for leaving and cutting off all contact with his family: to escape from an abusive and alcoholic father, who our neighbor eventually divorced.

The same year that I had Dr. E, a group of his students held a tribute for him. They performed skits that gently spoofed his erudite mannerisms and gave glowing personal testimonials about his impact on their lives. Dr. E was visibly moved as he arose at the end of the production to accept some gifts of appreciation. I watched the event, but not liking how Dr. E treated my sister, I did not participate. It struck me then, and it strikes me still, how students and parents had such different reactions to Dr. E. I had not seen students express this kind of heartfelt public thank you for any other teacher in the school. Clearly Dr. E had touched many young lives, changing them for the better. And yet he also had the opposite reputation among other students.

Memorable teacher #2 and #3: Dr. T and Mrs. S. Two additional examples from my education further demonstrate the importance of context in establishing teacher effectiveness. In my senior year, I took AP English with Dr. T and a college-accredited psychology course with Mrs. S. Both were highly qualified teachers. Dr. T held a Ph.D. in English literature, chaired the English department, and had taught for many years. A jovial, somewhat pompous man, Dr. T loved words, lots of words, big words, flowery words. He insisted that writing should have "flair." He found my writing stilted, dull, and lacking in the verbosity he relished. All my papers came back marked up in red ink with a cursory B for a grade.

Mrs. S asked for writing sample from each of us on the first day of class. Her psychology course required substantial amounts of writing and she wanted to see our writing abilities. She specifically instructed the class that anyone taking AP English from Dr. T should ignore his writing instruction. I had never heard a teacher criticize another teacher in that manner. I soon learned that Mrs. S didn't mince words when she bluntly told me that she loved my writing sample. She found my writing crisp, direct, and focused. Throughout her course I received little red ink on my papers and all A's for grades.

So, who had the greater impact on my life: Dr. E, Dr. T, or Mrs. S?

The answer may surprise you: Dr. T, but for reasons having nothing to do with his AP English course. I knew Dr. T long before I arrived in his class because his son and I were friends. I looked up to his son, one year older than me—an excellent student and an outstanding chess player. I aspired to play chess as well as his son, who graciously taught me about the game. But more importantly he and his father introduced me to the world of competitive chess tournaments. Dr. T drove his son and me to chess tournaments on weekends and coached us on the rigors of playing serious high-level chess.

My relationship with Dr. T had reverberating consequences on my life, particularly in my transition to college. When I arrived at college I found instant acceptance by the group of chess players on campus. These upper classmen had previously taken many of the courses I found myself in and provided mentoring and support, as well as camaraderie and friendship.

I learned from my experiences with high school teachers that relationships do not exist in a vacuum between two and only two people; rather, all relationships matter and are part of a complex web. I also learned that the web of relationships often has more consequences than simply acquiring knowledge in the actual content of the courses.

All examples of highly-qualified, effective teachers, it would be impossible to characterize Dr. E, Dr. T, and Mrs. S with a list of attributes off a job description of the ideal teacher. Like most of us, they had complex personalities that meshed with some people and conflicted with others. Moreover, all of this relationship drama occurred in a homogenous educational environment—the school student body was all white, middle-class and suburban. And yet two students from the same family, my sister and I, had vastly different educational experiences with the same teacher, Dr. E. It is not possible to have students with less diversity than those coming from the same family. Yet Dr. E, for all his brilliance at math and his desire to teach, was not able to adjust his methods to our different inclinations and personalities. A trait that is all too human.

Teaching in Diverse Urban Schools

But what happens in a school with true diversity? What is expected of teachers in these environments? By the standards of today, teachers must do just about everything and anything completely right at all times and with all students.

In his memoir, *Confessions of a Bad Teacher*, John Owens recounts a year he spent teaching at a public school in New York City's South Bronx [6]. He describes an environment in which teachers are both tightly scripted, and yet responsible for everything that happens—both the learning outcomes and student behavior. For Owens, the scripting began with a retreat and orientation before classes started. Owens describes a weekend filled with PowerPoint presentations on "New York State standards, curriculum maps, lesson plans, syllabi, baseline data, acuity tests, Regents exams, S.M.A.R.T. goals, and the Blackboard Configuration." In addition to the delivered PowerPoints, teachers were given "notebook-filling rules, rubrics, standards, demands, and musts." A few samples from the "must" list: "We must provide children with rich purposeful lessons. We must support the social, emotional, and academic needs of all students. We must help students who fail nonetheless recover credit for their failed courses. We must provide our students with at least two community service projects a year." [6, p. 32]

The school principal, whom he identifies as Ms. P, dictated all of these guidelines in elaborate detail using legalistic language that governed all aspects of school life—from how the students dressed, to how the students behaved, to how the teachers conducted class, and even to how hallway bulletin boards were to be decorated. For example, a teacher could receive an unsatisfactory performance rating for not adhering to a five-column set of standards on bulletin boards. The student work had to be presented on the bulletin board alongside a display of the New York State learning standards that the student work addresses. Owens notes that the state standards went on for pages and pages with headings and subheadings.

Take, for example, the eighth grade writing standards heading 1: "Write arguments to support claims with clear reasons and relevant evidence." Subheadings included such dictates as 1c: "Use words, phrases, and clauses to create cohesion and clarify the relationships among claims(s), counter-claims, reasons, and evidence" and 1d: "Establish and maintain a formal style." As Owens notes: "Not the sort of language that immediately connects with any eighth graders I have ever met." [6, p. 140]

Ms. P's obsession with order and precision meant that useful pedagogies were turned into tight scripts that teachers had better adhere to or else. One such tried-and-true pedagogy is the "workshop model," a popular format because it promotes co-operative learning and allows teachers to provide differentiated instruction by grouping children at similar levels. For the New York City school system, the workshop model became a standard format for organizing class time, with a lesson taught during a typical 50-minute class period divided into the following segments: Do Now (5–10 minutes), Mini-Lesson (10–15 minutes), Group Work (15 minutes), Share (10 minutes), Summary (5 minutes), and Learning Log or Exit Slip (3 minutes). Under the direction of Ms. P, the workshop model morphed into a tight script that required choreographing classroom activities to the precise minute. If she walked into a class 18 minutes into the period and the children were not doing group work the teacher's professional evaluation would suffer.

Owens' memoir recounts a web of teacher-student and student-student relationships unimaginably more complex than my high school experiences. Expectedly for an urban school, Owens first class was ethnically, racially, and socio-economically diverse, with a number of children who were not native English speakers. When observed by his lead teacher and assistant principal, Owens' evaluation suffered for not adhering precisely to the script and for additional offenses:

- "Start-of-class rowdiness."
- "Do Now takes too long."
- "Students off task."
- "Pacing" too slow ("free time = misbehaving!")
- "Assignments lack "clarity" ("clear instructions: verbal & written").
- "All lessons should be data based. What data do you have to justify the teaching of the lesson aside from the fact that it is in your curriculum map?"
- "Since your students' notebooks are either disorganized or nonexistent, I was not able to find much archival evidence showing that you assess students' learning on a regular basis."
- "Yelling at the eighth graders." [6, p. 154]

Chapter 2 discussed the practice of "over-fitting" data on evaluations of teachers using statistical methods, and as explained in Chapter 1, over-fitting occurs when so many variables are present in the statistical model that even random noise can be "explained." Observational evaluations like those made of Owens are another example of the practice of over-fitting. An equally disturbing example of over-fitting: how Owens was told to assess the students. Owens had to put more than 2000 entries per week into the online grading system for his students. Scores were required for homework, classwork, notebook, and core values (academic excellence, community citizenship, unity of being, reflective living, self-determination, compassion, and integrity), along with attendance. He realized the following:

> "In all, the evaluation system for the kids was a lot like Ms. P's sixty-six-point teacher evaluation system—there were so many elements and so many variables and so many subjective grades that anything good or bad could be "proven." And it could be "proven" with the weight of online reporting systems, spreadsheets, and other "data." The trouble was, some of the kids had no positive data at all. No work, no quizzes, not much of anything except maybe showing up." [6, p. 194–195]

In addition to the pseudoscientific practice of over-fitting data, and the tautology of asserting that an effective teacher does everything absolutely right at all times, another logical fallacy arises in this scenario: holding teachers completely accountable for everything that happens in a classroom that is almost completely scripted by someone other than the teacher. Obviously a person whose every action is dictated cannot be responsible for anything.

John Owens left a lucrative job as an executive in the publishing industry to become an English teacher at a public school. A middle-aged professional who loved literature, he thought he could give back to society by teaching writing to underprivileged children. Owens thus fit the profile of a mid-career professional that TNTP purported to recruit. He taught for less than one year. After being told that his work as a teacher was unsatisfactory, he resigned and returned to the publishing industry.

Teachers Are Real Human Beings (Not Idealized Fantasy People)

As I explained in Chapter 2, the school reform movement uses pseudoscientific methods that rely on reams of regulations, data, spreadsheets, and dense statistical analysis to mislead the public; moreover, they also rely on the public's widespread misunderstanding of the purpose of science. Many people mistakenly believe that science is about complexity. It is easy to see why people think this way: not only are a great many of the cutting-edge experiments in science complex, but also the results of science have been used to create an artificial environment for ourselves that is radically complex compared to the environment in which we evolved. A human hunter-gatherer from the dawn of modern *Homo sapiens* more than 50,000 years ago would be bewildered by the 21st century information age we live in.

Although complex in practice, the truth is that science seeks to simplify. Scientists search for consistent patterns that provide clues to the underlying laws of nature that are, in fact, remarkably ordered compared to the apparent chaos of events in nature. As explained further in Chapter 5, Einstein observed (1) that the laws of nature must be profound and subtle, and (2) the remarkable fact that science is even possible. Science is possible because nature at its core is predictable and orderly. In fact, imposing the kind of control that we have over our environment would not be possible if nature wasn't predictable and orderly. I often remark that if the underlying laws of nature were as complex as people imagine, scientists would have no hope of understanding anything. Science is about finding order within the apparent chaos.

The school reform movement seeks to invoke the authority of science while turning the process of science on its head. The process of science if rightly applied to education reform would be an investigation for underlying patterns in the data that could lead to simpler explanations for learning outcomes and a possible reduction in the workload needed to accomplish these goals. Instead, more and more data is collected as a means of creating more and more complex explanations, and this complexity necessitates an increased workload. Massive data collection to impress the public becomes the goal and the resulting incoherent complexity is elevated as a mark of success. Lost in all this mindless busywork is any real insight as to what teachers do to affect and inspire learning. Instead chaos is created from order, which is the reverse of the scientific process.

Standardized Teaching Evaluation Systems

Owens' experience in New York is not an anomaly; we can also see complexity erroneously invoked in a nationally used observational teacher evaluation system: *Charlotte Danielson: The Framework for Teaching Evaluation Instrument 2013 edition* [7]. This scoring system ("rubric" in educational jargon) for evaluating teaching performance is broken into four broad "Domains": (1) Planning and Preparation (2) The Classroom Environment (3) Instruction (4) Professional Responsibilities. This is a good start for thinking about the overall activities that comprise the job of teaching, a job that is much more than just standing up in front of a classroom and explaining the lesson of the day.

Each Domain is then broken down into "Components"—a total of 22 Components are listed. For example there are five Components for Domain 2: (a) Creating an environment of respect and rapport (b) Establishing a culture for learning (c) Managing classroom procedures (d) Managing student behavior (e) Organizing physical space. This is not a bad way to think about running a classroom, and a teacher should think about establishing procedures and policies based on a consistent teaching philosophy for classroom management. The teacher, for example, should have predictable patterns of behavior towards students so that they are not surprised by the teacher's expectations and reactions.

But rather than providing a guide for aligning actions and policies with a consistent philosophy of teaching, the Charlotte Danielson rubric devolves into a scoring system of mind-numbing complexity. Each of the 22 Components is further broken down into "Elements"—a total of 76 Elements are listed—and teachers are rated on a scale of 1 to 4 for each Element. The 4-point rating scale corresponds to (1) Unsatisfactory, (2) Basic, (3) Proficient, and (4) Distinguished. In each of these four performance categories, for each of the 76 components, are about three to five examples of actions that would trigger a particular rating. The example actions are the "indicators" associated with the "critical attributes" of each Component.

Consider, for example, the six indicators in Domain 2, Component 2a:

- Respectful talk, active listening, and turn-taking
- Acknowledgment of students' backgrounds and lives outside the classroom
- Body language indicative of warmth and caring shown by teacher and students
- Physical proximity
- Politeness and encouragement
- Fairness

The two Elements for Component 2a are (1) Teacher interactions with students including both words and actions (2) Student interactions with other students, including both words and actions. To be rated "unsatisfactory" for Element 1 of Component 2a, the teacher would have to show patterns of disrespect, or unfamiliarity with the students, such as not calling students by their names. At the "basic" level, the patterns of interaction between teachers and students in class would be generally appropriate but uneven. For example, the students might listen passively to the teacher, but not to each other.

To move up to the "proficient" level, teacher-student and student-student interactions would be "uniformly" respectful. The teacher "greets students by name when they enter the class and during the lesson." Students would "attend fully to what the teacher is saying and wait for classmates to finish speaking before beginning to talk." At the "distinguished" level all interactions would be highly respectful. The teacher would demonstrate knowledge and caring about individual students beyond the classroom, such as "inquiring about a student's soccer game last weekend." There would be no disrespectful behavior among students because, for example: "Students say 'Shhh' to classmates who are talking while the teacher or another student is speaking."

Keep in mind that I have just discussed the indicators and examples for just two of the 76 Elements in total that make up Charlotte Danielson teacher evaluation rubric. Fully charting all 76 Elements with their "critical attributes" and examples of "indicators" goes on for a hundred pages. This extreme attention to detail is marketed as an advantage for administrators using this evaluation system; it touts in its list of updates to the 2013 edition, "Even clearer rubric language and descriptions of each performance level within each component to help observers make tighter distinctions between performance levels."

It further claims that the examples given are not meant to be "all-encompassing" but are used to "illustrate the meaning of the rubric language," addressing the needs for "Higher stakes, higher expectations require increased accuracy with increasingly limited resources."

It seems to me that an accurate scoring of the 76 distinct Elements in the rubric would require many hours of observation to discern patterns in teacher and student performances. Undoubtedly, this would only further strain limited resources. Moreover, once an administrator has completed rating on the scale of 1 to 4 for all 76 Elements of a teacher's performance, and described the observations to justify each rating, what would be the next step? Obviously there would need to be another rubric in place for the material consequences of the Charlotte Danielson rubric—cutoff levels for the performance ratings to determine raises, remediation, termination, and so on. Would there be equal weighting across Domains, Components, or Elements in setting the cutoff levels? More importantly, what would a performance evaluation with this level of detail and complexity mean to the person receiving it?

Consider for example an evaluation of Dr. E for the aspect of the rubric I just detailed: Domain 2, Component 2a, Element 1, an evaluation of performance on teacher interactions with students. Would Dr. E's behavior be unsatisfactory, basic, proficient, or distinguished? I think any given observer on any given day, in any given class could have given Dr. E any one of these four ratings.

However, there were patterns in Dr. E's behavior that I'm sure readers already discerned from my brief description of him. These patterns are common in many teachers and it is not necessary to use an elaborate scoring system to uncover them. Dr. E had a difficult time remembering what it was like to not be an expert on his subject and had difficulty empathizing with students who struggled. I think all teachers have this difficulty to some degree. I certainly do. It can be difficult to remember what it was like to be baffled by something that is now second nature.

In addition, Dr. E, while he reveled in working with the top math students, lost patience with average students. This is also a common fault for some teachers that the principal could have worked to remediate. The principal could have insisted that Dr. E meet with my mother, mediated the breakdown in the relationship with my sister, and coached Dr. E on more appropriate methods for dealing with students with average math ability. Instead the principal chose a non-confrontational approach for dispensing with the issue—avoid it altogether by separating the combatants—which is a common technique used by many administrators that resolves immediate problems but leads to no long-term improvement.

Should the principal have handled the situation the way he did, or coached Dr. E on more appropriate behavior for dealing with average students? I don't know the long-term context that the principal operated in—that is dealing with Dr. E year after year. My suspicion is that the principal was well aware of Dr. E's shortcomings as well as his strengths. Remember the glowing tribute his students gave him. I suspect that the principal long ago decided that Dr. E's contributions outweighed his liabilities and decided it wasn't worth intervening in this particular dispute. These kinds of compromises are made routinely in all work relationships. If all of us used a Charlotte Danielson-type system to score our relationships with our bosses, subordinates, and colleagues, soon none of us would have a job. Nobody says and does the exact right thing at all times and in all places. Instead we learn the patterns of behavior for those we work with and decide if, on balance, the job is worth it or not.

Observational evaluation systems, like the Charlotte Daniel Framework that provide an elaborate scoring system for teachers' actions, are the exact opposite of science. A scientific-based system would elucidate which actions the teacher takes that result in successful outcomes. But the pseudoscience based systems in place—as evidenced by both the New York educational system and the Charlotte Daniel Framework—obscures the causes of student learning by drowning whatever effective actions the teacher is taking in an ocean of meaningless numbers. Such meaningless complexity also allows the evaluator to construct any narrative on the effectiveness or ineffectiveness of the teacher. Such narratives are then impossible to falsify because of the reams of supportive "data" provided.

Teacher evaluation systems like these certainly have their uses, but I would argue that the uses are nefarious. A great deal of power is shifted to administrators, power that can then be wielded over teachers. Simultaneously, the elaborate complexity, reams of data, and veneer of scientific authority are used to impress the public while contributing nothing to the long-term improvement of educational outcomes.

Impossible Expectations = Teacher Shortages

The net result of this approach to managing and evaluating teachers is a cognitive dissonance that strains all rational attempts at comprehension—and has negative material consequences on the lives of teachers. At the same time performance expectations for teachers are rising, more and more of the curriculum is dictated by administrators from outside the classroom. Teachers are being given less freedom to use their own judgment on what is best for their students. The same administrators who clamor for better teachers work hard to make teachers irrelevant.

John Owens' experience of having all his lessons scripted by the administrators has become the norm in this era of high-stakes standardized testing. Consider some of the email I've received from actual teachers in response to some of my previous education commentaries. Here are three quotes from three different teachers:

(1) "Our state standards have become so high and numerous and the stakes of the statewide testing so enormous that most personal judgment of what is best for kids is not considered valid. I long for the days when I could decide how much time to spend on a topic, work on the 'why' and not just rush through the 'how . . .' I have seen more change in teaching in the last few years than in all the previous ones. As the state is making teachers feel more and more inadequate, pulling money and resources from us while still requiring more, and wanting to base everything on the test scores."

(2) "I'm told not to modify; just teach the program. It's ridiculous. Administrators in my school are adamant about this point, though. They do not trust teachers to make decisions about teaching in their own classrooms."

(3) "Recently, I retired from teaching grade 6 science at a prominent middle school in Baltimore County. I regret having felt compelled to spend time on the curriculum rather than pursue students' questions/interests. Because of the pressure placed on teachers to ensure that their students perform at the expected levels on the Baltimore County benchmarks, class time is spent on the county prescribed curriculum! These anxiety producing tests for both teachers & stu-

dents are given at the end of each unit. If a teacher's students' performance is unsatisfactory, that teacher's credibility can be questioned! I would also like to add that county benchmark test questions were on occasion unclear & deviated from the curriculum. Also, at times, the provided answers were grossly incorrect!"

It is impossible to distinguish between good teaching and bad teaching if we strip away the freedom of professional judgment. Teachers cannot be essential and irrelevant at the same time. You cannot demand excellence from a group of people that you vilify.

An increasing challenge is finding people willing and able to teach under these conditions, especially in impoverished urban areas. Take, for example, the state of Arizona. In the fall of 2014, there were severe shortages of school-teachers across Arizona, leading the *Arizona Republic* to report that "Low pay and tough new expectations for teachers have led to a shortage of qualified people willing to take jobs in Arizona's classrooms." [8]

According to the Arizona Department of Education, of the 95,000 teachers certified to teach in Arizona, only 52,000 were teaching at the beginning of the 2014 school year. A survey of the Arizona Association of School Administrators found that 2100 teachers across 64 school districts had quit. One reason for the loss was that teachers could find higher paying jobs with less stress than teaching. The average starting salary for an Arizona School teacher was $31,874 in 2012, the last year that salary data was available. This is consistent with the data contained in the Georgetown University jobs report, cited in Chapter 5, which found that jobs in education *paid the least* of any professional-level job requiring a bachelor degree.

Additionally, Arizona's loss of teachers was also attributed to the increased demands to collect student performance data and drill students for standardized tests. The executive director of the Arizona Association of School Administrators, Deb Duvall, explained, "Many people go into teaching because they want to interact with students, but there is less time for that." [8]

Well into the 2014 school year, Arizona news media reported teacher vacancies at "crisis levels." [9] If the available qualified people are no longer willing to do the work, a rational response might be to remedy the low pay and high-performance expectations that drive teachers away. Does making expectations impossibly high and the work onerous improve the quality of classroom teaching? Probably not, if it results in large numbers of experienced teachers leaving the profession. Since the reasons for the shortages of qualified teachers are known, it might be expected that the school districts would work to ameliorate them. That was not the course of action chosen.

Rather than remediate the actual reasons teachers were leaving the profession, the school administrators decided to greatly enlarge the available pool of applicants for the vacancies. The method for getting more applicants: recruit teachers from abroad. The school superintendents hired Filipino teachers to come to teach in Arizona schools.

Hiring Foreign Teachers to Cope with Shortages

A read of articles in the Arizona press in the fall of 2014 on using Filipino teachers to fill school vacancies might leave the impressions that (1) a teacher shortage is a recent problem and (2) overseas recruitment is a novel solution. Neither impression would be correct. It is a little known fact that for years there have been chronic shortages of teachers, especially in urban school districts, and for over a decade school administrators have been covering this up by hiring teachers from overseas to fill the vacancies. The Philippines is a particularly popular country for recruiting teachers for urban U.S. school districts.

For example, in 2005, Baltimore city public schools hired 108 Filipino teachers to help meet shortages. Some were placed in schools labeled by the state as "persistently dangerous." [10] By 2009 more than 600 Filipino teachers worked in Baltimore and accounted for about 10% of the work force in the city school district [11]. Baltimore was not alone in its quest for foreign teachers. By 2007 an estimated 19,000 teachers were working in the United States on temporary visas, a trend that prompted the American Federation of Teachers to issue a report titled: *Importing Educators: Causes and Consequences of International Teacher Recruitment* [11]. It stated: "Unwilling or unable to address the root causes of a growing teacher shortage, public school systems around the country have begun importing teachers to meet their staffing needs." [11, p. 7]

A further inducement to the practice of hiring Filipino teachers: recruitment efforts cost the school districts nothing. In other words, schools were able to meet their staffing needs with foreign teachers with practically zero effort and at zero cost. Profit-driven companies facilitated the process of hiring and bringing teachers from overseas to the United States. So how did these companies make money? They charged the teachers. Each of the Filipino teachers in Baltimore paid between $5000 and $8000 to the recruitment agency that placed them.

These recruitment practices require a large upfront payment from the job applicant with the expectation that the U.S. job will pay enough to justify the initial outlay. Obviously, this leaves many foreign teachers vulnerable to abusive labor practices—and I would argue—sounds dangerously close to the definition of human trafficking. Some examples:

- In 2004, the U. S. Department of Justice indicted the owners and operators of the teacher recruitment company Omni Consortium on charges of alien smuggling and visa fraud, mail fraud, and money laundering [12]. A total of 273 Filipino teachers each paid the company fees as high as $10,000 with the expectation of receiving jobs in Texas school districts. Less than 100 of the teachers were actually hired. In 2008, two of the indicted recruiters pleaded guilty in federal court to conspiracy to defraud the U.S. government in exchange for dropping the other charges [13].
- In 2010, more than 350 Filipino teachers filed a class action lawsuit against the East Baton Rouge Parrish school district in Louisiana and the firm Universal Placement International of Los Angeles. Advocates for the Filipino teachers claimed that the district's recruitment scheme mirrored human trafficking. In particular, the teachers had to pay about $5000 in non-refundable recruitment fees to obtain their teaching jobs. Only after paying this initial fee were the teachers told about additional fees and expenses required for placement. In total the firm collected about $16,000 in fees from each teacher. Those who could not pay were referred to private lenders who charged usurious interest rates of between 3 and 5% per month, and these teachers had their visas and passports confiscated until they did pay. In a 2012 trial, a jury found that this scheme did not constitute human trafficking; however, the court did award the teachers $4.5 million after finding that the recruitment firm violated the law by not adequately informing them of all of the required fees [14, 15].
- In 2011, the U. S. Department of Labor fined the Prince Georges County, Maryland school district $1.7 million for violating federal laws for its hiring practices of Filipino teachers. It also ordered the county to pay the teachers $4.2 million in back wages [16].

The practice of hiring foreign teachers by school districts in the U. S. is widespread. While in most cases, laws technically are not violated; however, the practice nonetheless raises ethical and humanitarian issues. Is it ethical to charge foreign teachers their recruitment costs? Are foreign teachers and their U.S. students best served by these practices? What is the impact of teacher loss on the educational systems of their home countries?

In *Teachers Without Borders? The Hidden Consequences of International Teachers in U. S. Schools*, Alyssa Hadley Dunn examines these issues using case studies of four Indian teachers working in the United States [17]. She found a common belief justifying the practice of recruiting foreign teachers, as well as mid-career professionals like John Owens: mastery of the subject matters above all else. Teachers must meet the federal requirement, stated earlier, that they be "highly qualified," meaning that they have a degree in their subject. It is assumed that if a teacher knows and thoroughly understands the subject, that knowledge and understanding can be imparted to the students. But as Alyssa Hadley Dunn argues, culture and context matter. The foreign teachers possess deep knowledge of their subject matter, but often little knowledge of American culture, and African-American culture in particular. This obviously limits their effectiveness in the urban schools in which they are most often placed.

Aftermaths

Recruiting foreign teachers turned out not to be a panacea for Baltimore. In 2012, visas were not renewed for many of the teachers. The school district could not make the case to the U. S. Department of Labor that the foreign workers were doing jobs Americans could not, a legal requirement for obtaining a visa. Many of the Filipino teachers and their families felt bitter and abandoned when the school district admitted it had no longer-term plan in place for their continued employment in Baltimore [18].

Hiring foreign teachers also runs counter to a central tenet of the narrative pushed by school reformers—that tenure and unions are the primary impediments to staffing schools with "great teachers." For example, when she was Washington, D.C. schools chancellor, Michelle Rhee sought to eliminate tenure and link teachers' pay to their students test scores, a move opposed by the teachers union [19]. In Rhee's view, tenure and unions protect "bad" teachers and both should be eliminated. Isn't this another fallacious argument? If teaching jobs are so easy and secure that the incompetent aspire to seek and hold them, why would school districts need to resort to ethically and legally questionable tactics in order to fill these jobs with foreign workers? Apparently, teaching is a job that anyone can do and yet, at the same time, no one is capable.

Rather than being a quick fix for teacher shortages in low performing schools, the practice of staffing U.S. schools with foreign teachers illustrates the complexities of learning. Teachers and students are active participants in the educational process, and culture and context matter in regards to the quality of their relationships, which are essential for effective education.

Whether U. S. schools are staffed by American teachers, or teachers from abroad, as long as the pursuit of "data" is elevated above the establishment of high-quality interpersonal relationships between teachers, students, and administrators, none of the problems plaguing urban schools will be solved. Instead the result is what John Owens describes as a "cheater's paradise." With so much data being collected, and so much at stake in the data, everyone—students, teachers, and administrators—has the means, motive, and opportunity to manipulate the data, and everyone does. Owens states: "Those who insist they are not lying are liars." The education career of the antagonist in Owens' memoir, the all-powerful principal Ms. P, ended a few months after Owens resigned. Department of Education officials escorted her and her assistant principal from the school after finding falsified records of student progress. [6, p. 240]

Across Time and Space: The Complex Web of Human Relatedness

"When I was a child, I talked like a child, I thought like a child, I reasoned like a child. When I became a man, I put the ways of childhood behind me."
  I Corinthians 13:11

When I was a child, I lived in a world populated by perfect people. My parents and my grandparents, my aunts and uncles, my parents' friends and neighbors, and above all, my teachers were all models of perfection that I, one day upon achieving adulthood, would obtain. As I aged, one by one, the people around me dropped off my perfect list. Each year the list shortened until, as an adult, I discovered there were no perfect people in my world, and I would never be perfect either. Everyone I knew struggled and fell short to live up to expectations. Everyone was limited in some way by deep-seated fears and various kinds of insecurities. Everyone experienced the painful losses of unattained aspirations, of failed relationships, of loved ones through death. I learned that maturity didn't mean attaining perfection, but rather an understanding that joy and sorrow are both part of the human condition. I learned that to be successful, not only must you risk failure, you will at times fail.

When I embarked on my career in science, I was fortunate to have mentors who were amazingly good at what they did and patient enough to teach me. Their deep understanding of physics, skills in the laboratory, and facility with all aspects of the process of doing science seemed unattainable to me. But as I advanced in my career, I realized that my mentors were not born with the deep insights they possessed, but rather struggled to obtain them in the same way that I struggled. Their accomplishments were not foreordained, but rather the outcomes of years of hard work that included failures and dead ends.

My mentors did not have magical powers. In fact, they had mentors who they looked up to and guided them. Relationships matter for everyone.

As of this writing, I have a wife, three children, two grandchildren, two parents, three siblings, and a large extended family. I teach students, interact with colleagues, supervise people, and am supervised myself. I am an active participant in social and community organizations. Through the normal course of a month, I relate to dozens of people in many different ways. Each of these relationships is unique, and in total they define my life. I know that I don't live up to everyone's expectations of me all of the time, but I contribute what I am able, and I hope that my interactions make positive differences in people's lives. Of course my situation is not unique. All adults live within a complex web of relationships and face the same challenges.

Therefore, it is willful ignorance to assert that teachers should be perfect the moment they begin teaching, relating to each student in the exact way that each student needs at all times. There must be patience for the years of development a craft as complex as teaching requires for mastery. The expectation of instant perfection is an example of the kind of magical thinking characteristic of children. How ironic that many adults engage in childish thinking on how teachers should educate children, especially given that the goal is to transition children into thinking like adults.

Magical thinking has destructive consequences. Expectations and tests are not pedagogies. Learning happens for a reason, not because of a test. And the belief that collecting reams of data on teacher and student performances causes learning is akin to believing that measuring the temperature everyday will somehow change the weather.

References

1. "The Reform Solution," StudentsFirst, accessed July 7, 2015, https://www.studentsfirst.org/TheReformSolution.
2. Same as reference 1, further down on page.
3. Steven G. Rivkin, Eric A. Hanushek, and John F. Kain, "Teachers, Schools, and Academic Achievement," *Econometrica* 17, no. 2 (2005):417–458.
4. Eric A. Hanushek, and Steven G. Rivkin, "How to Improve the Supply of High Quality Teachers," *Brookings Papers on Education Policy* 2004 (2004): 7–25. http://muse.jhu.edu/journals/pep/summary/v2004/2004.1hanushek.html.
5. The New Teacher Project, *The Irreplaceables, Understanding the Real Retention Crisis in America's Urban Schools* (New York: TNTP, 2012). http://tntp.org/assets/documents/TNTP_Irreplaceables_2012.pdf.
6. John Owens, *Confessions of a Bad Teacher: The Shocking Truth from the Front Lines of American Public Education* (New York: Sourcebooks, 2013).

7. Charlotte Danielson, *The Framework for Teaching Evaluation Instrument*, 2013 Edition (Princeton: Danielson Group, 2013). http://danielsongroup.org/framework/.

8. Cathryn Creno, "Arizona teacher shortage forces schools to go international," *Arizona Republic*, October 1, 2014, http://www.azcentral.com/story/news/local/arizona/2014/10/01/arizona-teacher-shortage-international-candidates/16519807/.

9. Joe Dana, "Arizona Schools: 527 job vacancies at 'crisis' levels," *USA Today*, September 22, 2014, https://www.usatoday.com/story/joedanareports/2014/09/21/12news-education-teacher-legislature/16030749/.

10. Sara Neufeld, "Filipino teachers learn life lessons in Baltimore," *Baltimore Sun*, August 28, 2005, http://articles.baltimoresun.com/2005-08-28/news/0508280105_1_teachers-mercado-baltimore.

11. American Federation of Teachers, *Importing Educators: Causes and Consequences of International Teacher Recruitment* (Washington, DC: American Federation of Teachers, 2009). http://www.aft.org/sites/default/files/wysiwyg/importingeducators0609.pdf.

12. Liz Austin, "Federal authorities crack teacher smuggling ring," Associated Press, *Plainview Daily Herald*, October 22, 2004, accessed May 1, 2018, https://www.myplainview.com/news/article/Authorities-say-ring-was-smuggling-teachers-into-8893442.php.

13. Louie Gilot, "2 accused in teacher smuggling ring plead guilty," *El Paso Times*, January 5, 2008, https://www.alipac.us/f12/tx-2-accusedteacher-smuggling-plead-guilty-90980/.

14. Southern Poverty Law Center, "Mairi Nunag-Tanedo et al. v. East Baton Rouge Parish School Board et al., accessed May 1, 2018, http://www.splcenter.org/get-informed/case-docket/mairi-nunag-tanedo-et-al-v-east-baton-rouge-parish-school-board-et-al.

15. Diana Samuels, "Filipino teachers win $4.5 million jury verdict, claim they were forced into 'exploitative contracts'," *Times-Picayune*, December 18, 2012, http://www.nola.com/news/baton-rouge/index.ssf/2012/12/filipino_teachers_win_45_milli.html.

16. Robert Samuels, "Prince George's owes foreign teachers millions, federal investigation finds," *Washington Post*, April 4, 2011, http://www.washingtonpost.com/local/education/federal-investigation-pr-georges-owes-foreign-teachersmillions/2011/04/04/AFucbodC_story.html.

17. Alyssa Hadley Dunn, *Teachers Without Borders? The Hidden consequences of International Teachers in U. S. Schools* (New York: Teachers College Press, 2013).

18. Erica L. Green, "For children of Filipino teachers, an uncertain future," *Baltimore Sun*, May 7, 2012, http://articles.baltimoresun.com/2012-05-07/news/bs-md-ci-filipino-teacher-students-20120430_1_filipino-teachers-immigrant-teachers-work-visas.

19. Michelle Rhee, *Radical: Fighting to Put Students First* (New York: Harper, 2013).

Part II

Misunderstanding Math and Science Education

4

Why Our Kids Don't Get Math

As a physicist, I hear a lot of complaints about math. Conversations with people meeting me for the first time and learning my occupation often have responses along these lines:

"Physics interests me, but I could never do the math."
"Math didn't like me in high school. I can't imagine doing physics."
"I have no talent for math. I flunked algebra in high school."
"I really disliked math in school. It's too confusing."

Math is one of the least favorite subjects for students in school and one of the most difficult to relate to students' lives. After all, most adults cannot get through their workday without being able to read and write, and many people read and write for pleasure. The importance of learning reading and writing skills is self-evident. But relatively few people use algebra, trigonometry, and geometry in their work, and almost no one does math for pleasure. Some understanding of basic arithmetic is needed to shop, bank, and manage budgets at home and at work, but the actual arithmetic operations can be offloaded to a calculator. In practice, for the vast majority of people, most of the math that frustrates and vexes them in school will not be used later in their adult lives. The one exception: when their own children go to school and need help with learning math.

For all the seemingly pointless frustration that surrounds math, it is hard to understate the importance of modern mathematics. Simply put, the modern economy, with its production of all the goods and services that we consider essential to our well-being, would not exist without it. Math is employed all around us in modern technology, communication, transportation, medicine,

J. Ganem, *The Robot Factory*, https://doi.org/10.1007/978-3-319-77860-0_4

public health, finance, manufacturing, marketing, and the list goes on. It is one of humanity's greatest intellectual achievements, and is as essential as reading and writing in maintaining the vast interconnected networks of people and resources that provide the complex products and services that no one person, or even a small group of people, could ever provide by themselves.

Everyone benefits from math even though relatively few people use high-level math in their daily work. But even people who do not routinely use high-level math can benefit from learning to think mathematically and from applying mathematical thinking to their daily lives. Math is part of the school curriculum for the same reason that physical education is (or at least should be) part of the curriculum. While even fewer people become professional athletes than professional scientists and mathematicians, the physical skills and overall level of fitness that school athletics confers on students provides them with lifetime health and wellness benefits.

Jordan Ellenberg makes this point in *How Not To Be Wrong: The Power of Mathematical Thinking*, likening practicing computations in math class to the weight training and calisthenics drills practiced by athletes [1]. The drills are boring, repetitive, and tedious and apparently of no use because the players will not be lifting weights or doing stretches during play of a game. But, the "players will be using the strength, speed, insight, and flexibility they built up by doing those drills, week after tedious week."

Most adults do not participate in competitive sports and yet still practice the boring weight training and calisthenics routines used by athletes because the same advantages in strength, speed, insight, and flexibility are useful in their daily lives. In a similar way, mathematical practice and training also confer advantages. As Ellenberg writes: "Math is woven into the way we reason. And math makes you better at things. Knowing mathematics is like wearing a pair of X-ray specs that reveal hidden structures underneath the messy and chaotic surface of the world."

Students going on to college who want to major in any of the mathematics, sciences, engineering, or social science disciplines will be required to take college-level math courses. Most likely, the majority of math computations they learn will not be used later in their careers, but the insights they gain from doing those computations will be essential for understanding the disciplines of their chosen majors. Not being able to do college-level math severely limits a student's choice of major. A major in the humanities should be a choice, not a default because of inability to do math. Even students in majors that don't require math would still benefit from college-level math courses. The usefulness of mathematics arises in many contexts.

My advice to high school students—study as much math as you can.

However, despite the importance of math, and the many attempts at reforming curricula and pedagogy, there continues to be systemic failure in the math education of students. Our kids still do not get math. There is a widening gap between what is taught in high school math and what is expected in college. There is a troubling disconnect between how math is taught in school and how professional scientists, engineers, and mathematicians use math. There is confusion in teaching why math is relevant by using clumsy examples that require much more facility with reading comprehension than with mathematical reasoning.

The Widening Gap Between High School and College Math

There are dire consequences to this disconnect between how math is taught and how math is practiced by professionals. As more states strive to improve math curricula and raise standardized test scores, more students show up to college unprepared for college-level math. We are thus in the midst of a paradox that begs the question: what math should be taught in high schools?

Statistics compiled in 2010 by the U. S. Department of Education report that for the 2003–04 academic year 34.7% of freshmen entering college needed at least one remedial course. In many instances an individual student needed more than one remedial course. That number inched up by the 2007–08 academic year, with 36.2% of freshmen entering college needing at least one remedial course [2]. This data challenges the efficacy of the implementation in 2002 of the Elementary and Secondary Education Act (No Child Left Behind), a law that mandated testing for proficiency in reading and math. Clearly, the readiness of graduating high school students for college-level studies did not improve as a result of NCLB.

The Department of Education reports were backed up by the National Mathematics Advisory Council, that reported in 2008 that proficiency in mathematics declined during high school. For students in 8th grade, 32% were proficient in math, but by 12th grade, the fraction of proficient students declined to 23%. The final report of the Advisory Council stated: "Consistent with these findings is the vast and growing demand for remedial mathematics education among arriving students in four-year colleges and community colleges across the nation." [3]

We have no evidence that the math proficiency of high school graduates has improved since 2010. In fact, education reporters for local newspapers just about anywhere in the United States can fill column space by writing about the need for remedial math. Here are just a few samples.

- A *Cleveland Plain Dealer* January 2014 article reported that 40% of high school graduates enrolled in a public college in Ohio in 2012 needed either remedial math (34%) or English (20%), or both (14%). According to the Ohio Board of Regents "nearly every Ohio high school sent students who were not prepared to take college-level math or English to a public two or four-year college." [4]
- An *Oklahoman* September 2014 article reported that 4 out of 10 high school graduates in Oklahoma were required to take at least one remedial class when they entered college, and for 90% of those students a remedial math class was needed [5].
- A *Milwaukee Journal Sentinel* August 2014 article reported that 1 out of 5 freshmen entering the University of Wisconsin system needed remedial math to prepare them for the high-level math classes required for their degrees [6].
- A Southern California Public Radio February 19, 2014 broadcast reported:

"A look at each freshman class each year at the California State University system in the last decade reveals a paradox in academic achievement: all the students have met CSU's class and grade requirements to gain acceptance yet every year a significant portion test unable to do college level math and English work." [7]

In my state, Maryland, which has one of the country's better education systems, a 2009 study [8] found similar results upon examining the alignment between the state's high school assessment tests and the Accuplacer college placement tests [9] that many colleges use to determine the need for remedial math. The study reported substantial disconnect between Maryland's high school curriculum and the expectations for the Accuplacer test.

With national averages for the need for college remedial math on the rise, statistics, studies, and articles like these routinely appear in the media in just about every state. In short, students are becoming less and less versed in math in high school, and need more and more remedial math courses upon entering college. What is also disturbing about these statistics is their singular focus on the elite subset of high school graduates that enroll in college. What about those students who don't go to college? There is no accounting for how many non-college bound students are also math deficient.

These statistics, studies and articles do not shock me. As I first wrote in 2009, I've witnessed first hand with my three children the disconnect between the high school and college math curricula [10]. As a parent of three children who all graduated from Maryland high schools, I tutored them in middle school and high school math and I know how little understanding is conveyed in those math classes. Nothing has improved since then, and—ironically— much of the problem arises from a blind focus on raising math standards.

Bizarre Math Expectations

For example, the math problems assigned to my children became progressively more difficult through the years to the point of being bizarre. When my daughter was in eighth-grade, she asked me one evening to help her perform matrix inversions. I teach matrix inversion in my sophomore-level mathematical methods course for physics majors. It is difficult for me to do matrix inversions off the top of my head. Needing to refresh my memory, I had to pull Boas' book: *Mathematical Methods in the Physical Sciences* off my shelf [11]. Not exactly eighth grade reading material.

On another night that same year, my daughter brought home a word problem that read: "If John can complete the same work in 2 hours and that it takes Mary 5 hours to complete, how much time will it take to complete the work if John and Mary work together?" That's an easy problem if you know about rate equations. Add the reciprocals of 2 and 5 and reciprocate back to get the total time. However, it took me a lot of thought to arrive at an explanation of my method comprehensible to an eighth-grader.

My other daughter struggled through a high-school trigonometry course filled with problems that I might assign to my upper-class physics majors. I wouldn't even assign problems at such a high level to college freshmen. I kept asking her how she was taught to do the problems. I wondered if the teacher knew special techniques unknown to me that made solving them much easier. Alas no such techniques ever materialized. The problems were as difficult as I judged.

For example, one problem involved proving a complicated trigonometric identity. My daughter brought it to me saying she had tried but couldn't find a solution. I saw immediately that the textbook had an error that rendered the problem meaningless. One side of the problem had a combination of trigonometric functions with odd symmetry and for the other side the symmetry was clearly even. I told her it was therefore not an identity and that fact could be proven with a simple numerical substitution on each side. If it is an identity, then the equality condition must hold for all values of the angle. A single numerical counter example proves that it is not an identity. It only took one try to find a counter example.

The next day she reported to me that the teacher couldn't solve the problem.

> "Did you tell him that it is impossible?" I asked.
> "I told him it was not an identity and if he put numbers in he would find that out. He didn't believe me. He just said: 'We'll see'."

The teacher never talked about that problem again. Although he had taught the class about the symmetry properties of trigonometric functions, evidently, he didn't understand the usefulness of that knowledge.

What's more is that such difficult math does not serve students well as they transition to college. I often work the summer orientation sessions at Loyola University registering incoming first-year students for classes. Time and again students cannot pass the placement exam for college calculus; many students also cannot pass the exam for pre-calculus, saddling them with a non-credit remedial math course. Without the ability to take college-level math, students' choices for majors are severely limited. No college-level math course means not majoring in any of the sciences, engineering, computer, business, or social science programs.

For all practical purposes readiness for calculus as an entering first-year student determines choice of major and career. My colleagues in the engineering department similarly complain that many students who want to major in engineering cannot place into calculus. The engineering program is structured such that no calculus means no physics freshman year and no physics means no engineering courses until it's too late to complete the program in four years. The math placement test given to incoming freshmen at orientation has much higher stakes than any test given in high school. With no course grade or teacher evaluation associated with it, no one but the student has any responsibility for or stake in its outcome.

Through the years I've found it discouraging as a faculty member to see so many high aspirations dashed at orientation before classes even begin. I tell students with poor math placement scores to go home, review high school math over the summer, and take the test again. But, few take my advice. Most students with poor placement scores switch to majors that do not have significant math requirements.

Three Problems with K-12 Math Curricula

If eighth graders are taught math at the level of a college sophomore, why are graduating seniors struggling? How can students who have studied college-level math for years need remedial math when they finally arrive at college? This is not a reflection on a lack of ability for an entire generation. Rather, it is a reflection of a flawed curriculum. From my knowledge of both high school and college curricula I see three problems.

1. Confusing Difficulty with Rigor. It appears to me that the creators of K-12 math curricula believe that "rigor" means pushing students to do ever more difficult problems at a younger age. It's like teaching difficult concerti to novice musicians before they master the basics of their instruments. Rigor—defined by the dictionary in the context of mathematics as a "scrupulous or inflexible accuracy"—is best obtained by learning age-appropriate concepts and techniques. Attempting difficult problems without the proper foundation is actually an impediment to developing rigor.

Rigor is critical to math and science because it allows practitioners to navigate novel problems and still arrive at a correct answer. Students need to be challenged, but in such a way that they learn independent thinking. If the problems are so difficult that a higher authority must always be consulted, rigorous thinking will never develop. The student will see mathematical reasoning as a mysterious process that only experts with advanced degrees consulting books filled with incomprehensible hieroglyphics can fathom. Pushing problems that are always beyond students' abilities to comprehend teaches *dependence*, not independence—the opposite of what is needed to develop rigor.

2. Mistaking Process for Understanding. Just because a student can perform a technique that solves a difficult problem doesn't mean that he or she understands the problem. There is a delightful story recounted by Richard Feynman in *"Surely You're Joking, Mr. Feynman!": Adventures of a Curious Character* that recounts an arithmetic competition between him and an abacus salesman in the 1950s, before the invention of calculators [12].

The salesman came into a bar and wanted to demonstrate the superiority of his abacus to the proprietors through a timed competition on various kinds of arithmetic problems. Feynman was asked to do the pencil and paper arithmetic so that the salesman could demonstrate that his method using the abacus was much faster. Feynman lost when the problems were simple addition, but he won easily at the apparently impossible task of finding a cubed root. The salesman was totally bewildered by the outcome: how could Feynman have a comparative advantage at hard problems when he lagged far behind on the easy ones?

Months later the abacus salesman met Feynman at a different bar and asked him how he could do the cubed root so quickly. When Feynman tried to explain his reasoning he discovered the salesman had no understanding of basic arithmetic. All he did was move beads on an abacus. It was not possible for Feynman to teach the salesman additional mathematics because, despite appearances, the salesman understood absolutely nothing.

This is the problem with teaching eighth-graders techniques such as matrix inversion. The arithmetic steps can be memorized, but it will be a long time, if ever, before the concept and motivation for the process is understood. This raises the question of what exactly is being accomplished with such a curriculum? Learning techniques without understanding them does no good in preparing students for college, where the emphasis is on understanding, not memorization and computational prowess.

3. Teaching Concepts that Are Developmentally Inappropriate. Teaching advanced algebra in middle school pushes concepts on students that are not developmentally appropriate for their age. Walking is not taught to six-month olds and reading is not taught to two-year olds because children are not developmentally ready at those ages for those skills. Math involves knowledge and understanding of symbolic representations for abstract concepts, development skills that are particularly difficult to speed up. Of course all math teachers dream of arriving at a crystal clear explanation of a concept that will cause an immediate "aha" moment for the student. But those flashes of insight cannot happen until the student is developmentally ready.

To quote my daughter, when I tutored her in seventh grade algebra, she "found it creepy" that I knew how to do every single problem in her rather large textbook. When I related the remark to a fellow physicist he nonchalantly remarked: "But it's algebra. There are only three or four things you have to know." He is correct; however, it took me years of development before I understood there were only a few things you had to know to do algebra. I can't tell my seventh grader or anyone else without the proper developmental background those few algebraic concepts and send them off to do every problem in the book.

All three of these problems—confusing difficulty with rigor, mistaking process for understanding, and teaching concepts that are developmentally inappropriate—are the result of the adult obsession with testing and the need to show year-to-year improvement in test scores. Age-appropriate development and understanding of mathematical concepts does not advance at a rate fast enough to please test-obsessed lawmakers. But adults using test scores to reward or punish other adults are doing a disservice to the children they claim to be helping.

It does not matter the exact age that you learned to walk. What matters is that you learned to walk at a developmentally appropriate time. To do my job as a physicist I need to know matrix inversion. It didn't hurt my career that I learned that technique in college rather than in eighth grade. What mattered was that I understood enough about math when I got to college that I could understand calculus.

Students Learn Mimicry Instead of Math

Memorizing a long list of advanced techniques to appease test scorers does not constitute understanding. Conflating the ability to do something with an understanding of what is being done is perhaps the greatest flaw with using testing metrics for educational accountability—a topic that is expanded upon in Chapter 9. Students are fully capable of learning and following procedures without understanding them. I observe this frequently when interacting with students, especially with calculus. A typical calculus textbook teaches various operational procedures that most students can reproduce by mimicking their instructor and examples in the textbook; however, they do not necessarily understand the meaning of the operations.

I observed a memorable example of this when I was in college. A friend told me that she was struggling in calculus and could not obtain any of the correct answers to problems in the textbook. I asked her to work on some problems in my presence so that I could observe at which points in the procedures she went off track. She began a procedure by correctly manipulating the mathematical form of an equation, but only on the left side. She then proceeded to the next step. I stopped her.

"What about the right side of the equation?" I asked.
"What are you talking about?"
"It's an equation. Whatever procedure you perform on one side of the equation, you have to perform the same procedure on the other side. Otherwise you destroy the equality and the expression no longer makes any sense."
"Is that why I can't get any of these problems right?"

Here was a very smart woman who had graduated high school, did well at an elite college, and made it into college-level calculus, but she had never grasped the meaning of the most fundamental mathematical concept of all: the equal sign. For her math was an exercise in mimicry, not an understanding of the deeper meaning expressed by the equations.

The Disconnect Between the Math Curriculum and Professional Practitioners

"The astronomer may speak to you of his understanding of space,
but he cannot give you his understanding.
The musician may sing to you of the rhythm which is in all space,
but he cannot give you the ear which arrests the rhythm nor the voice that echoes it.
And he who is versed in the science of numbers can tell of the
regions of weight and measure,
but he cannot conduct you thither.
For the vision of one man lends not its wings to another man."

----Kahlil Gibran
"On Teaching"
The Prophet [13]

Imagine a football coach who does not spend practices drilling his team and running plays. Instead players watch videos of football games, analyze and diagram the actions, discuss the reasons that some plays work and others don't, and plan strategies for upcoming games. His reason for this approach is that drill work is tedious, repetitive, and exhausting. Players will enjoy practice much more if they can study the underlying strategies and concepts of football, have engaging discussions, and learn to think like a professional football player.

We would call such a coach delusional, not because of what he is doing, but because of what he is not doing. Obviously everything he is doing needs to be done, but his team will not stand a chance on an actual football field without putting in hours of tedious, repetitive, and exhausting drill work.

For an activity like football that has a kinesthetic component, it is immediately obvious that learning will only be possible through repetitive drill work [14]. No one would entertain the notion that they could learn to play tennis by watching the Wimbledon tournament on television, learn to play piano by attending a concert at Carnegie Hall, or learn to dance by going to a performance of the New York City Ballet. Although math lacks a kinesthetic component, this line of reasoning also applies.

Consider the debates on math education that have run on for decades. Should students be taught standard algorithms for operations such as multiplication and division and focus on getting correct answers, or should students be taught conceptual thinking and focus on discovering mathematical knowledge on their own? Educators have argued both sides of this issue; in reality, it is a false choice.

Without a conceptual understanding of math, the subject is of little use. Applying math to real-world problems and knowing if the results of a mathematical analysis make sense requires an understanding of the concepts. That said, it is not possible to have a conceptual understanding without the extensive practice, memorization, and drill work needed to achieve computational fluency.

I tell my students that expertise in any subject, math or otherwise, has three components: facts, skills, and understanding. Each of these components is learned in a different way. Facts are static and must be memorized. Skills are actions that must be practiced in order to become proficient. Understanding evolves and comes only through experience and reflection.

This explanation of mathematical learning is different from Bloom's Taxonomy, a widely influential educational theory that many teachers can probably recite [15]. Bloom saw learning as a hierarchical process, with separate learning domains—cognitive, affective, and psychomotor—each with its own hierarchy. I rather see the learning process as iterative, not hierarchical, with the learning process much the same in each of the different learning domains.

In Bloom's taxonomy, first published in 1956, the hierarchy in the cognitive domain from the bottom up is: knowledge, comprehension, application, analysis, synthesis, and evaluation. In this model of learning, comprehension (or "understanding" in updated terminology) is necessary before students can actually do something with their new knowledge. Hence many educational reform movements in the decades following the taxonomy have emphasized "conceptual" learning over practice. However, because I believe understanding to be an ongoing process, I disagree with the idea that a conceptual understanding is necessary before higher order activities, such as application, analysis, and synthesis can take place,

Chess as Example

For example, consider learning chess. It is an activity without a kinesthetic component; hence, it would fall under Bloom's cognitive domain of learning. But no one would believe that the game could be mastered without practice, or that novice players could discover the principles of strong play on their own.

To learn chess, an aspiring player must memorize the names and movements of the pieces, and the object and rules of the game. These are what I refer to as facts. But the acquisition of skill in playing the game requires a program of study and practice. In order to improve, players must read texts on chess tactics and strategies and attempt to implement those ideas by playing actual games. There is no substitute for practice, but at the same time players must learn additional facts and acquire more knowledge about the game.

Moreover, an understanding of chess evolves in time. A novice, a skilled player, and a grandmaster can all look at the same chess position. The novice will see individual pieces. The skilled player will see groups of pieces. The grandmaster will see the entire position.

But if the grandmaster articulated his understanding of the entire position to the novice, the narrative would be of limited use. The novice would not have the knowledge base and the skills necessary to make sense of most of what a grandmaster would say about a given chess position. But that does not mean that the novice is incapable of applying, analyzing and synthesizing chess ideas. Those ideas might be relatively crude, and obvious to the grandmaster, but the process is necessary to reach a high level of understanding.

Expertise

As in the case of the chess grandmaster, experts are experts because they think about their subject of expertise differently than novices. Those thought processes cannot be transferred directly to a student; rather, they must develop through study and deliberate practice [16]. There is no shortcut to that development. This should be especially obvious in a subject such as math. Apparently it is not.

Many years ago, before calculators and optical scanners had been invented, I made a purchase at a bakery counter tended to by a young woman who had to pencil in prices on the bags of pastries being sold. I asked for 5 donuts priced at 26 cents each. She placed them in a paper bag and on the outside of the bag she computed 26 × 5 using the standard algorithm for multiplication that I, and countless other students, had learned in elementary school. She of course was very proficient at multiplication problems using this method, because throughout the day, everyday, a steady stream of customers patronized the bakery counter.

Before she could write out the problem, I said to her: "It's $1.30."

She completed the problem, writing all the steps on the bag, and the result was $1.30. Startled by my seeming clairvoyance, she looked at me for an explanation. She knew of no other way to multiply but the standard algorithm, and that process required time and writing. How could I multiply the numbers instantly in my head and arrive at the correct answer?

> I said to her: "If the donuts were 20 cents each how much would 5 cost?"
> She replied: "A dollar."
> I said: "And what is 5 times 6?"

She understood immediately what I had done, but only because she was already proficient at multiplication. If I tried to teach my methods for doing mental math to people not already proficient in the use of standard algorithms, my explanations would lead to confusion rather than enlightenment.

Real learning is iterative, not hierarchical, and it doesn't matter whether the subject is—to use Bloom's terminology—in the cognitive, affective, or psychomotor learning domains. When learning is systematized, it often leads to rigid ideologies riddled with false choices. The argument over whether math instruction should focus on concepts or computation is in many ways analogous to the argument on whether reading instruction should focus on phonics or whole language. Fluent readers use and understand both approaches.

Likewise, learning math is an iterative process that cycles between concepts and computation. Experts in math are proficient in both because it is impossible to master one without the other. Ultimately math is about recognizing patterns. It is impossible to achieve fluency in pattern recognition without lots of practice.

Making Math Relevant: Assessing Reading Comprehension or Math?

I began this chapter with the assertion that while math is one of the most difficult subjects for students to relate to their daily lives, it is also at the same time absolutely essential to our modern economy. Understandably, designers of K-12 math curricula want to teach students that math is relevant and that they can benefit from applying mathematical reasoning to real-life situations. Unfortunately, this is often done in clumsy ways with poorly worded questions that test reading comprehension more than math fluency.

Consider, for example, some sample math questions from the new PARCC assessment tests. The PARCC acronym stands for "Partnership for Assessment of Readiness for College and Careers" and is comprised of a consortium of states working together to develop assessments aligned with the new "Common Core Standards" [17]. As many states adopt the Common Core, the PARCC standardized tests will replace the previous state tests used to assess student

and school performance. The PARCC assessments also differ from prior standardized tests in that they are implemented on computers; instead of filling in
bubbles with a number two pencil, students type answers into online forms
and click on menu commands.

I decided to test my math knowledge beginning with a sample question for
third graders [18].

Vans for a Field Trip

For a school field trip, 72 students will be traveling in 9 vans. Each van will
hold an equal number of students. The equation shows a way to determine
the number of students that will be in each van.

$$72 \div 9 = ?$$

The given equation can be rewritten using a different operation.
Use the drop-down menus to select the operation and numbers to complete
the equation.

9	+	9	=	72
72	−	72		
?	x	?		
	÷			

*Note: The shaded areas above highlight the choices available in three vertical
drop-down menus, while the boxes with "=" and "72" are fixed on the page.*

The vocabulary—rewritten, determine, operation—in this question strikes
me as advanced for third grade. Can we assume all third graders have this level
of fluency with technology, such as knowing how to use "drop-down menus"?
While it might appear that all children have access to computers at home and
walk around fixated on their smartphones, that is just not the case. Many
students from low-income families lack consistent access to technology.

I, however, do at least know the vocabulary and am adept at using technology. Nonetheless, similar to my experience visiting my daughter's third grade
math class a few years ago, I'm stumped for an answer. I just don't know. I discern that the "field trip" framework is irrelevant and has nothing to do with the
answer because the number 8, which is the number of students to load into each
van, is nowhere to be found. That means that knowing multiplication tables,

which is what I spent my third grade memorizing, isn't going to help me. Instead this question assesses whether third-graders understand the much more abstract concepts—that multiplication and division are inverse operations, that the "?" symbol represents the 8 students in each bus, and that an equation can be rewritten with different arithmetical operations and convey the same meaning.

These are algebraic concepts that are developmentally inappropriate for third-graders struggling to learn arithmetic. Furthermore, this one test question is packed with at least three mathematical concepts; if a significant number of students answer the question wrong, it will be impossible to know which of these three concepts the students failed to grasp. This is an example of an assessment that cannot be used to improve pedagogy because there is no direct causal link between a wrong answer and the reason(s) the answer is wrong.

Apparently, the "answer" is an "equation" that looks like $9 \times ? = 72$. Or is that the answer? Unlike the operation of division, the operation of multiplication is commutative, meaning that the order of operations doesn't matter. The expression $? \times 9 = 72$, which can also be constructed from these drop-down menus would mean the same thing as $9 \times ? = 72$. Would the testers ask a question with two correct answers, or is there a clue in the wording that would deem only one of the orders correct? I re-read the question several times and cannot find a clue. I don't know which expression to use. It appears that once again I am failing third-grade math. I turn the page to find the scoring instructions. Both answers are deemed correct. This is a multiple-choice question with two equally valid correct answers, another abstract concept.

I move on to a fourth-grade assessment test [19]. I do better on this one.

Three Friends' Beads

Ms. Morales has a bag of beads.

- She gives Elena 5 beads.
- She gives Damian 8 more beads than Elena.
- She gives Trish 4 times as many beads as Damian.

Ms. Morales then has 10 beads left in the bag.

Part A

How many beads did Damian and Trish each receive? Show or explain how you arrived at each answer.

Part B

How many beads were in Ms. Morales' bag before any beads were given to students?

I can do this problem. Damian received 5 + 8 = 13 beads. Trish received 4 × 13 = 52 beads. Since 10 beads are left, Ms. Morales must have had 5 + 13 + 52 + 10 = 80 beads to start. I check the scoring rubric to find that my answer of 80 is correct, but by itself it earns only 1 point on a scale of 0–3. The other 2 points are earned for "fully describing the steps necessary to find the number of beads that Damian and Trish each received." I'm not sure if I've done that. I realize that this question assesses my reading and writing ability far more than my understanding of multiplication and addition.

I decide to skip ahead to sixth-grade questions. I find one that requires data analysis, so it should play to my strengths [20].

Proportion of Instruments

Mr. Ruiz is starting a marching band at his school. He first does research and finds the following data about other local marching bands.

	Band 1	Band 2	Band 3
Number of brass instrument players	123	42	150
Number of percussion instrument players	41	14	50

Part A

Type your answer in the box. Backspace to erase.

Mr. Ruiz realizes that there are _____ brass instrument player(s) per percussion player.

Part B

Mr. Ruiz has 210 students who are interested in joining the marching band. He decides to have 80% of the band be made up of percussion and brass instruments. Use the unit rate you found in Part A to determine how many students should play brass instruments.

Once again, I am stumped. Does the ratio asked for in Part A refer to one particular band or the average of all three? I re-read the question several times, but it offers no clue. Then I look more closely at the data and realize that it is highly contrived. The ratio of brass to percussion players is exactly 3 for all three bands. That means it doesn't matter whether I (a) compute a ratio by randomly picking one band, or (b) compute an average ratio for all three bands; the answer will be 3 in either case.

I think I can now do Part B, although I've never seen the expression "unit rate." I think "unit rate" refers to the ratio I just computed, and the question is asking me to compute how many brass players Mr. Ruiz needs if the ratio of brass to percussion players for the 80% of students playing these instruments is kept at 3. The computation is (¾) × 0.8 × 210 = 126 brass players. (Note that a 3 to 1 apportionment requires division into ¾ and ¼ sections, not 2/3 and 1/3, which many people might guess upon first glance.)

I check the scoring rubric to see how I've done. On a scale of 0–4, my correct answers of 3 and 126 are good for 2 points. Earning the other 2 points depends on how well I've explained my reasoning in Part B. Curiously, the reasoning employed for Part A is not required or scored. It appears that the test scorers don't want to confront the ambiguity in this question when evaluating student reasoning.

I examined many other sample problems at the PARCC website, and I invite readers to do so too. It quickly became clear to me that performing well on PARCC math assessments requires sophisticated reading and writing skills in English. It also requires the ability to interact with computers by operating menus and typing. This causes me to suspect that male students, students who have a first language different than English, low-income students, and students who are truly gifted at math may be particularly challenged by these math assessments.

Boys are simply less verbal than girls at young ages, and no matter how much reading and writing skills are pushed back to younger and younger ages, that basic fact of biology and brain development isn't going to change. When it comes to explaining their reasoning strategies, boys will be less expressive than girls. Students for whom English is not their first or primary language will have difficulty decoding the sophisticated vocabulary these questions require to comprehend. Low-income students won't have the same fluency with the computer technology used to provide the answers because their families cannot afford to have as many electronic devices in the home.

It might seem surprising that I include students gifted in math as a category of students who would do poorly on these math assessment tests. It is because true math expertise is often a visual, rather than a computational or linear way of thinking. Ask someone who is extremely good at math to solve a math problem and frequently he or she will "see" the answer and then have to reverse engineer an explanation for why that answer is correct. Usually there are multiple explanations and some might be very visual and not easy to translate into words.

In fact, what makes math beautiful, and appeals to the aesthetic senses of those gifted in math, is its ineffability. It is a way of thinking that transcends language. Turning math assessments into frustrating exercises in reading comprehension and written explanation will drive away the students who may not be particularly adept at expressing themselves in English, but have the potential to excel at math.

The Need for Quantitative Literacy

The emphasis on reading in these problems is an attempt to make math relevant. But, relevancy should be authentic, not contrived. I am a strong advocate for making math relevant and have argued for this in prior papers I've published. In a 2009 paper—"Quantitative Reasoning Applied to Modern Advertising,"—I argued that consumers can make better financial decisions if they can use quantitative reasoning methods to "re-frame" sales pitches [21]. "Framing" is a concept from behavioral economics that posits that consumers often perceive financially equivalent propositions as different depending on how the choices are presented [22]. Anytime a financial cost can be re-framed as a financial gain, consumers are more likely to buy. The ubiquitous use of "sale pricing" is an obvious example of this phenomena.

In a 2011 paper—"Integrating Quantitative and Financial Literacy"—I argued that financial literacy should be integrated into the current math curriculum rather than taught separately because it is an ideal subject for teaching quantitative reasoning [23]. The personal finance examples I gave were what I termed "obvious benefit/hidden cost" financial propositions. All were examples of using quantitative reasoning skills to reframe sales pitches. I also showed how an understanding of algebra arises naturally from applying quantitative reasoning to these kinds of problems.

Applying quantitative reasoning to personal finance is just one example of Ellenberg's "X-ray specs"—referred to in the quote from earlier in this chapter. There are many other kinds of decisions in which the "X-ray specs" can be useful if we have them. But the foundation must be quantitative reasoning. Asking children to allocate students to vans for a field trip by using algebraic reasoning, before they have learned their multiplication tables, is a prescription for confusion, not a way to teach the relevancy of math. By jumping to algebra before quantitative skills are mastered, students never understand the motivation for algebra and why it is so important. It is like teaching children to read before teaching them how to recognize the letters in the alphabet.

The "Chinese Room"

In 1980 the American philosopher, John Searle published a paper in which he presented a thought experiment that has come to be known as the "Chinese room" argument [24]. Imagine that you are alone in a room. Outside of the room are native Chinese speakers who write questions on pieces of paper using Chinese characters and slip them under the door. You have no understanding of written (or spoken) Chinese, but you do have access to instructions written in English that you can follow to respond to the questions. No translation or understanding of the characters is necessary. You simply look up the string of characters given to you in your instruction set, and a string of characters with a logical response in Chinese is given next to it. Then you write those Chinese characters on a piece of paper and slip it back under the door to your interrogators. This back and forth goes on for a while and eventually the Chinese speakers on the outside become convinced that you know and understand Chinese.

Searle's thought experiment is one of the most famous in the philosophical literature because of its obvious implications for the fields of computer programming and artificial intelligence (AI). It is meant to be an argument against AI, and much ink has been spilled over it. Google "Chinese room argument," and you can spend days reading all the explanations, responses and counter responses that will appear in the search results. But, leaving philosophical considerations aside, imagine this being a real situation rather than a thought experiment. You are in a room sending and receiving Chinese characters, the back and forth going on for years; one day the door will be opened and your lack of understanding of Chinese will become obvious.

When it comes to math education, we have turned our schools into real-life versions of Searle's Chinese room. Children are provided the instructions needed to solve highly sophisticated math problems. Standardized assessments are like the Chinese questioners. As long as the questions are answered correctly, the evidence shows that the children understand the math concepts. That evidence is all that is needed to convince educators that the math taught is "rigorous," and that "standards are being raised."

But one day the door to the school will be opened and the children will leave. They will discover, that like the abacus salesman in Feynman's story, following instructions and providing correct answers to the questions posed does not constitute an understanding of math. In fact they may never have had a chance to understand math because many abstract concepts were taught at a developmentally inappropriate age. Biology cannot be sped up. A third-grader's brain is not yet wired to process the abstractions needed for algebra.

Fundamentally, all mathematics, no matter how advanced, technical, or sophisticated, is built from numbers and the basic arithmetic operations for their manipulation. Algebra is a generalization of arithmetic, in which an unknown number is represented symbolically. Calculus generalizes algebra by allowing static algebraic formulas to become dynamic, as the unknown quantity takes on a range of possible values that change over time and/or space. Without an understanding of arithmetic, none of this higher order math makes any sense.

Offloading arithmetic to calculators and substituting what amounts to algebra instruction in its place makes no sense pedagogically, developmentally, or in achieving the overarching goal of raising math standards. Children need a solid foundation in quantitative literacy. They need to have a sense of numbers and quantity. Learning how to do arithmetic without a calculator, manipulate fractions, decimals, and exponentials and connect quantitative literacy to some fundamental ideas in geometry must be mastered first. An understanding of algebra will follow naturally after a solid sense about numbers is instilled.

Instead, I see a steady arrival of students in college who have no sense about numbers, but they are expected to learn calculus in order to complete their degree requirements. They are completely befuddled. It is akin to placing a student in an advanced literature course for a foreign language before they have taken the first introductory course in that language. Setting students up to fail at any level—K-12 or college—is unethical and a waste of time and resources. Yet this has become standard practice in education, a furtherance of the willful ignorance documented in the first chapter, all in the name of "raising standards and rigor" to arbitrarily defined levels that benefit no one but the policymakers, who can claim that they are doing something to "improve education."

References

1. Jordan Ellenberg, *How not to be Wrong: The Power of Mathematical Thinking* (New York: Penguin Press, 2014).
2. National Center for Education Statistics, "2003–04 and 2007–08 National Postsecondary Student Aid Study," (Washington, DC: U.S. Department of Education, 2010), NPSAS:04 and NPSAS:08. http://nces.ed.gov/programs/digest/d10/tables/dt10_241.asp.
3. National Mathematics Advisory Panel, *Foundations for Success: The Final Report of the National Mathematics Advisory Panel* (Washington, DC: U.S. Department of

Education, 2008). https://www2.ed.gov/about/bdscomm/list/mathpanel/report/final-report.pdf.

4. Karen Farkas, "Forty percent of high school graduates who enrolled in a public college in 2012 required remedial math or English," *Cleveland Plain Dealer*, January 17, 2014, http://www.cleveland.com/metro/index.ssf/2014/01/forty_percent_of_high_school_g.html.

5. Adam Kemp, "Many Oklahoma students start college taking remedial classes," *The Oklahoman*, September 2, 2014, http://newsok.com/manyoklahoma-students-start-college-taking-remedial-classes/article/5337902.

6. Karen Herzog, "UW spotlights 'tragedy' of students needing remedial help," *Milwaukee Journal Sentinel*, August 22, 2014, http://archive.jsonline.com/news/education/uw-spotlights-tragedy-of-students-needing-remedial-help-b99336149z1-272339141.html/?ipad=y.

7. Adolfo Guzman-Lopez, "More than a third of Cal State freshmen ill-prepared for college-level math, English," *Southern California Public Radio education blogs*, February 19, 2014, http://www.scpr.org/blogs/education/2014/02/19/15882/more-than-a-third-of-cal-state-freshman-illprepar/.

8. G. Martino and W. S. Wilson, "Doing the Math: Are Maryland's high school math standards adding up to college success?" (Baltimore: Abell Foundation, 2009). http://www.abell.org/sites/default/files/publications/ed_DoingMath_0409.pdf.

9. "Accuplacer Tests," College Board, accessed May 1, 2018, https://accuplacer.collegeboard.org/students.

10. Joseph Ganem, "A Math Paradox: The Widening Gap Between College and High School Math," *APS News* 18, no. 9 (October 2009): 8. http://www.aps.org/publications/apsnews/200910/backpage.cfm.

11. Mary L. Boas, *Mathematical Methods in the Physical Sciences*, 2nd Edition (New York: John Wiley & Sons, 1983).

12. Richard P. Feynman, *"Surely You're Joking, Mr. Feynman!": Adventures of a Curious Character*, Ralph Leighton (contributor), Edward Hutching ed., (New York: W. W. Norton, 1985).

13. Kahlil Gibran, "On Teaching," *The Prophet* (New York: Alfred A. Knopf, 1923).

14. Howard Gardner, *Frames of Mind: The Theory of Multiple Intelligences* (New York: Basic Books, 1983).

15. Lorin W. Anderson, et al., *A Taxonomy for Learning, Teaching, and Assessing: A Revision of Bloom's Taxonomy of Educational Objectives* (New York: Pearson, 2000).

16. K. Anders Ericsson, Neil Charness, and Paul J. Feltovich, eds., *Cambridge Handbook of Expertise and Expert Performance* (New York: Cambridge University Press, 2006).

17. "About PARCC," Partnership for Assessment of Readiness for College and Careers, accessed June 15, 2015, http://www.parcconline.org/about-parcc.

18. "Sample Mathematics Item Grade 3: Vans for a field trip," Partnership for Assessment of Readiness for College and Careers, accessed January 15, 2015, http://www.parcconline.org/sites/parcc/files/PARCC_SampleItems_Mathematics_G3Vansforfieldtrip_081513_Final.pdf.

19. "Sample Mathematics Item Grade 4: Three Friends' Beads," Partnership for Assessment of Readiness for College and Careers, accessed January 15, 2015, http://www.parcconline.org/sites/parcc/files/Grade4-ThreeFriends%27Beads.pdf.

20. "Sample Mathematics Item Grade 6: Proportion of Instruments," Partnership for Assessment of Readiness for College and Careers, accessed January 15, 2015, http://www.parcconline.org/sites/parcc/files/Grade6-ProportionsofInstruments.pdf.

21. Joseph Ganem, "Quantitative reasoning applied to modern advertising," *International Journal of Science and Society* 1 (2009): 87–96.

22. Amos Tversky and Daniel Kahneman, "The framing of decisions and the psychology of choice," *Science* 211 (1981): 453–458.

23. Joseph Ganem, "Integrating Quantitative and Financial Literacy," *JSM Proceedings*, (Alexandria, VA: American Statistical Association, 2011), 1562–1574.

24. John R. Searle, "Minds, Brains and Programs," *Behavioral and Brain Sciences* 3 (1980): 417–457.

5

Misunderstanding Science Education

According to stories promulgated through the media, if we want to solve all of our financial problems, we should all become scientists and engineers. Perennially, starting salaries for college graduates with STEM degrees are higher than those for graduates with degrees in the arts and humanities. This fact appears in a 2015 report, *What's It Worth? The Economic Value of College Majors,* published by the Georgetown University Center on Education and the Workforce that generated a slew of articles in influential financial publications [1]. A random sampling of headlines and advice includes:

"Choosing a College Major? Read This First"
"Studying petroleum engineering will net you $3.4 million more, over time, than a degree in early-childhood education." ---- *Fortune*, May 7, 2015 [2]

"College Majors Figure Big in Earnings"
"Study finds some study areas pay more than others, with engineering earnings triple those for education." ---- *Wall Street Journal*, May 7, 2015 [3]

"College Majors that Make the Most Money"
"Then there are the jobs people do more for love than cash: Early childhood education majors pulled in the least, making an average of $39,097 a year. While that's still a significant bump over high school graduates, who typically pull in $22,000 a year, it's a drastic cut of what STEM and business majors reported making a couple years out of college." ----- *Bloomberg Business*, May 7, 2015 [4]

© Springer International Publishing AG, part of Springer Nature 2018
J. Ganem, *The Robot Factory*, https://doi.org/10.1007/978-3-319-77860-0_5

And this information wasn't actually new. A prior 2011 report released by the Georgetown group was similarly held up by post-financial meltdown, business reporters as evidence that all students should chose STEM majors. Examples:

"Students Pick Dumb Majors Despite Pay Gap"
"Students are ditching head-scratching majors in science and engineering in favor of more manageable fields, even though anyone who's read a jobs study recently knows that lab geeks earn more."---- *Business Insider*, November 9, 2011 [5]

"College Students Need to Look at These Charts Before Deciding on a Major"
"May we suggest you look into engineering." ---- *Business Insider*, November 21, 2011 [6]

The reasoning behind this advice is straightforward. Supporting a post-college student debt load, and justifying the high financial investment needed to attend college, requires a high-paying job after graduation. It would appear that the solution for all student debt and financial problems would be for them all to obtain degrees in a STEM field. The federal government is even moving in this direction. A proposal by the Obama administration to rate colleges using complex metrics that would factor in the post-graduation earnings of their students might cause college administrators to start pushing as many students as they can toward STEM degrees [7].

In fact, it has become fashionable for politicians to malign degrees granted in the arts and humanities. Former President Obama himself said:

"I promise you, folks can make a lot more, potentially, with skilled manufacturing or the trades than they might with an art history degree."
--- President Barack Obama, Waukesha, Wisconsin, January 30, 2014 [8]

And not to be outdone by Obama, some high profile Republicans have weighed in.

"If you want to take gender studies that's fine, go to a private school and take it. But I don't want to subsidize that if that's not going to get someone a job."
---- North Carolina Governor Patrick McCrory, Radio Interview with Bill Bennett, January 29, 2013 [9]

"If I'm going to take money from a citizen to put into education then I'm going to take that money to create jobs. So I want that money to go to degrees where people can get jobs in this state. Is it a vital interest of the state to have more anthropologists? I don't think so."

---- Florida Governor Rick Scott, Radio Interview with Marc Bernier, October 10, 2011 [10]

Bashing certain degrees might make for good sound bites, but there are multiple flaws with this line of reasoning—too many to address in this chapter alone, and I'll raise some of these flaws later in the book. But first, note the obvious economic problem of supply and demand. If everyone received a degree in a STEM field, the glut of graduates would depress starting salaries and drive up salaries for students with other degrees that would now be in short supply. Starting salaries are high for graduates with STEM degrees because there are fewer of them in relation to the demand. In a similar manner, starting salaries for pro-football players are much higher than for those who have STEM degrees, because in relation to the demand, there are even fewer college graduates with the skills needed to play in the NFL. And yet I don't read articles advising all students that college football is a path to future high-paying jobs and everyone should focus on sports rather than academics. In this context, it is easy to see how this is flawed logic and certainly bad advice.

It is also ironic to note that according to all of these studies on career choices, perennially the lowest paying jobs are in early childhood education. In a world that followed the advice of the media and politicians, in which students only choose majors leading to jobs with high salaries, there would be no pre-school or kindergarten teachers at all. The same political leaders urging all students to major in STEM fields so that they can get high paying engineering jobs, also carp incessantly about the need to recruit more "high quality" teachers into low-paying education jobs.

However, while the politicians and their media lackeys have at least a naive grasp of economics, for the most part they have no understanding at all of science and science education. In Chapter 1, I discussed what science is and what it is not. In this chapter, I will elaborate further on science and science education. I will explain that those pushing for more math and science education in schools often don't understand what that means. Those who think that the STEM subjects and the liberal arts are on opposite ends of an educational spectrum have serious deficits in their understanding of all these subjects and of education in general.

Technology and engineering, the T and E in STEM, are based on science and math, the S and M in STEM. In other words, S and M are foundational to T and E. In Chapter 4 I discuss M (math) and in this chapter I will discuss S (science). At the K-12 level of education, all aspiring STEM students need a firm foundation in math and science. However, everyone can benefit from scientific literacy regardless of whatever major and career is chosen. This is especially true in a world in which science is increasingly under attack for political reasons and in which pseudoscience continues to flourish. Additionally, more and more occupations require fluency with "STEM skills"—that is the ability to use mathematical reasoning and interact with complex hardware and software systems. Even if you don't get a degree in a STEM field, you should become scientifically literate and acquire some basic STEM skills.

There is no question that college-level math and science courses are difficult and are plagued by high dropout and failure rates for entering students. Science is hard for reasons inherent in the discipline that cannot be changed, but also for reasons associated with its traditional pedagogy that *can* be changed. In this chapter, I examine these reasons by exploring the question of what science is and how it differs from other approaches to acquiring knowledge. Science is often misunderstood and misrepresented in educational settings, which undermines efforts to foster more interest in science.

In explaining in further detail what science is, I further expand on the benefits of scientific literacy, specifically how scientific literacy provides inoculation against the increased politicization and misuse of science. I also discuss the limits of science and the kinds of questions that it cannot answer. Throughout this discussion I continue to visit my now familiar themes of data manipulation, willful ignorance, and tautologies.

Why Science Is Hard

A February 2012 report to the President of the United States issued by the President's Council of Advisors on Science and Technology (PCAST) advocated for an additional one million college graduates with degrees in STEM fields over the next decade. The report noted: "Fewer than 40% of students who enter college intending to major in a STEM field complete a STEM degree." [11] The problem with retention of STEM majors had already been reported in nationwide media outlets a few months prior to release of the report. That *New York Times* article, "Why Science Majors Change Their Minds (It's Just So Darn Hard)" reported that over half the students who enter college with the intention of getting a STEM degree end up switching to a non-STEM major or failing to get a degree [12]. The article sounded a prophetic alarm. Politicians and business leaders soon echoed the PCAST report and called on colleges to graduate more students with STEM degrees, claiming this to be the only way for the United States to remain competitive economically. But as the *New York Times* article made clear, while earning a college degree is difficult, obtaining a degree in a STEM field is even harder.

The statistic on the low rate of retention for STEM majors did not surprise me because I observe firsthand the attrition in the introductory science and math courses at my university. STEM careers are interesting, prestigious and rewarding, and as result attract many young people. But, the difficulty of the actual work that needs to be accomplished ends many aspiring STEM careers before they begin.

Science has a reputation for being difficult, but is it necessary that science courses be the most difficult at the university? Why is science so hard? The most concise answer to that question is Einstein's famous, albeit cryptic observation:

"Raffiniert ist der Herr Gott, aber boshaft ist er nicht."

This translates from German as: "Subtle is the Lord, but malicious he is not." Einstein elaborated on this thought by saying: "Nature hides her secrets because of her essential loftiness, but not by means of ruse."

In other words, while science is possible, it is difficult out of necessity. If nature was set up to trick us, something many people actually believe, science would be a meaningless activity. People who deny evolution and believe that the Earth came into being just a few thousand years ago also have to believe that nature is an elaborate ruse set up to fool generations of scientists with false evidence to the contrary. In such a sham universe, science would be pointless.

Moreover, an honest universe with simple, easy to understand scientific principles would most likely be sterile. Think for a moment about all the elaborate physical, chemical, and biological processes that are taking place in your body for you to be able to read this. Think about the eons of stellar evolution, planetary evolution, and biological evolution that took place prior to your existence. All of those complex evolutionary processes were necessary for you to come into being. A universe in which a phenomenon as extraordinary as you exists must, of necessity, have scientific laws that are deeply profound and subtle. Simplistic laws wouldn't do it.

In fact, instead of asking why science is so difficult, a more appropriate question is: Why is science so easy? By easy, I mean: Why is science even possible at all? Einstein also thought about this question and found no good answer. He stated: "The most incomprehensible thing about the world is that it is comprehensible."

But, while an education in a STEM field must by necessity be a difficult and challenging undertaking, does that mean that a high attrition rate for aspiring STEM students is also necessary? Are we squandering future scientific talent as some of the educators quoted in the *New York Times* article allege?

Traditionally scientists are selected in much the same way that athletes are selected—through a process of weeding and sorting. This fact might surprise many people who think of jocks and nerds as polar opposites. But in traditional science preparation, like in athletic preparation, advancement is competitive. To survive the process aspirants must demonstrate that they are better than the others.

In introductory science classes this competitive weeding process is accomplished by grading on a "curve." Professors lecture to large groups of students, and then give difficult open-ended exams that typically yield average scores around 50%, with a distribution of scores resembling a bell curve. Students on the high end of the distribution curve receive the As and Bs, those in the middle the Cs, and those on the low end receive Ds and Fs—and typically withdraw from the course. Obviously attrition is a natural part of such a grading system.

Like an athletic program, the competitive grading system is designed to select for specific abilities. However, the abilities being selected for are not the ones many incoming freshmen think are important. Frequently there is a disconnect between the expectations of the students and the expectations of the professors, which leads many students to feel that they are being treated unfairly.

Students transitioning from high school expect tests for which they can prepare by memorizing material. However science professors, who emphasize the processes of discovering and reasoning, give test questions designed to thwart memorized rote responses and force students to think through unfamiliar scenarios. The system selects those with the ability to successfully navigate the unfamiliar by applying known concepts and reasoning to solve novel problems. This skill is critical to the actual work of science. As a result, studying methods that worked in high school fail in college, and many students give up rather than make the adjustment.

The traditional method for training scientists, with its high attrition rate, persists because like many teachers, university science professors mimic their teachers. However, the method does have many drawbacks and can be improved. Here are my observations and recommendations:

• **Competitive grading systems discourage recreational interest.** This is true in school athletic programs and it is also true for science classes. Just as students who get picked last for sports teams conclude athletics is not for them, students who fail to make the cut in science classes conclude that they lack the "science gene," and should not even try to understand the subject. But we all understand that physical fitness is important for everyone, regardless of athletic ability; similarly, scientific literacy is important for everyone, regardless of college major or career aspirations.

We must all function in a complex, high-technology economy that is dependent on science. That dependence will continue to grow. The most challenging and difficult problems facing humanity in the future—such as developing new energy sources, managing the environment, and adjusting to climate change—will have solutions that come through science. The choice to be scientifically illiterate is a choice to be a bystander rather than an active participant in the economy of the future.

• **The competitive model for science education, and for education in general, is both ineffective and poor training for how work is actually accomplished.** [13] Corporations compete, athletes compete, politicians compete, but the vast majority of working people have to cooperate if they want to get anything done. The stereotypical researcher working alone for years in a laboratory to achieve a breakthrough was an anomaly in the past and is even harder to find today. In modern times, the most pressing scientific questions are exceedingly complex, and progress only results from scientists pooling expertise and resources.

Consequently, most scientists today work in groups, and have shared authorship on the publications that result from their coordinated research activities. Many of these groups are dispersed geographically, and even span the globe by including members from multiple countries. Some experimental research groups, such as the one building and operating the Large Hadron Collider (LHC) on the Franco-Swiss border near Geneva, Switzerland, involve thousands of scientists from around the world. Research papers that result from LHC experiments have hundreds and sometimes even thousands of co-authors [14]. In this modern day of science research, competition is a team effort; various research groups must compete for recognition and funding, just as corporations must compete for market share. Most importantly, the daily work of most individual scientists requires working cooperatively with others.

• **The traditional lecture format is not the best method for teaching science.** Again to draw an analogy with physical education, lectures are of limited use when the subject being taught is an activity. Science is a means and method for thinking about and interacting with nature. Scientists pose questions to nature in the form of experiments, and nature provides cryptic answers that must be analyzed and interpreted. In this back and forth dialog with the natural world, students will only learn to follow the conversation if they participate.

I referenced in Chapter 2 the vast literature on best pedagogical practices that administrators often ignore in favor of mindless data collection on ill-defined learning outcomes. The literature on effective pedagogy is especially rich in the STEM disciplines, and its recommendations are not ones that most school administrators want to hear. An extensive report on best pedagogical practices in STEM fields summarizes:

> "Studies clearly show that student-centered instructional strategies are more effective in improving students' conceptual understanding, knowledge retention, and attitudes about learning in a discipline than traditional lecture-based methods that do not include student participation." [15]

The term "student-centered" is defined in the same report as:

> "... instructional approaches, in which learners build their understanding by applying the methods and principles of a discipline and interacting with each other under the guidance of the instructor." [15]

Notice that this approach is incompatible with standards-based curricula, such as the recent Common Core curriculum being adopted by most states that rely heavily on traditional lecture-based pedagogy and standardized testing to assess effectiveness.

I am not taking the view, held by some, that lectures have no use in science education. Lectures came into use because they are an efficient method for transmitting information, and the sheer bulk of information needed to be absorbed in order to participate in modern science makes total reliance on activity-based based learning methods impractical. Science education must balance lecture-based and activity-based pedagogies so that students acquire both the know-what and the know-how. In striking this balance, it is essential that science education, particularly at the K-12 level be student-centered as opposed to test-centered.

• **Traditional classroom education does not select for some character traits that are critical for success in science.** Patience and above all persistence are necessary personal traits for a successful career in science. Scientific research is not an undertaking for those who need instant gratification, or even frequent positive feedback. I often marvel at how years of scientific work might be summarized with a single figure in a research paper. Real progress is painstaking and slow.

Students need to be made aware that the day-to-day work of being a scientist is not that much different than most other jobs. They will have a boss, be expected to show up for work on time, put in a required number of hours, follow directions, and be trustworthy and responsible. When parents of prospective students who visit Loyola University Maryland ask me how students can qualify for summer research opportunities in my lab I tell them that when choosing research assistants, I am not necessarily looking for the best student in the classroom, I am looking for the best employee. A student who tests well but has poor class attendance is not someone I want to hire.

None of these proposed changes for science education will change the fact that science is hard, or that just having the ability to do science makes it a suitable career choice. To be a scientist you need to have the interest and the ability, as well as *enjoy the work*. Aspiring science students may have the interest and ability, but that does not automatically mean that they will find the work enjoyable. The same can be said of any profession. Any professional career is a difficult undertaking and only students passionate about the profession should make the commitment.

A number of years ago I was asked to speak on "Career Day" to my son's middle school class about being a scientist. I told the students my life story, and the steps that were needed to become a scientist. I talked about taking lots of math and science classes in high school, going to college to study physics, becoming a graduate student, and working for several years on a doctoral thesis. I talked about the day-to-day work of being a scientist, how I needed to perform a variety of tasks, from operating equipment in a laboratory, to performing mathematical calculations, to writing research papers and proposals.

During the questions and answers afterwards, the inevitable question arose from one of the students: "Is it hard?"

"Yes it is hard," I replied. "That is why I do it. I have no interest in a career that is easy. I like being a scientist because it is difficult and constantly challenges me."

As I left that day, the teacher, in private, thanked me for that answer.

Science as a Noun

Science

Noun

1. a branch of knowledge or study dealing with a body of facts or truths systematically arranged and showing the operation of general laws: the *mathematical sciences.*
2. systematic knowledge of the physical or material world gained through observation and experimentation.
3. any of the branches of natural or physical science.

4. systematized knowledge in general.
5. knowledge, as of facts or principles; knowledge gained by systematic study.
6. a particular branch of knowledge.
7. skill, especially reflecting a precise application of acts or principles; proficiency.

----- Definition from *Dictionary.com.*

For an area of human activity and study that has become so important to the modern world, it is surprising that there is no universally agreed upon definition of science. The dictionary definition above reflects everyday usage of the word "science" in the English language; it is certainly not a summary of the epistemological arguments on the meaning of science, arguments that still preoccupy philosophers. The site from which this definition was taken – Dictionary.com – also rates the difficulty index of the word "science" as very low, meaning that "all English speakers likely know this word." Yet the word itself is relatively new to the English language, entering the lexicon in the nineteenth century when practitioners of what today is called science began to distinguish themselves from philosophers [16]. A seventeenth century scientist, such as Isaac Newton, would have called himself a "natural philosopher" because at that time what we today call "science" was the branch of philosophy that concerned the natural world. In fact the full title of Newton's landmark work containing his laws of motion is *Philosophiæ Naturalis Principia Mathematica,* which translates from Latin as "Mathematical Principles of Natural Philosophy."

The recurring themes in all seven uses of the word science listed in the dictionary definition above are "knowledge" and "systematic." One or both of these words appear in five of the definitions and are implied in the other two. This reflects a contemporary practice of labeling all systematic approaches to acquiring knowledge as science, even if the subjects of study are not part of the natural world. As a result, at academic institutions mathematics has become "mathematical sciences," computing has become "computer science," politics has become "political science," and even home economics has been rebranded as "family and consumer sciences." [17]

The Kansas State Board of Education's Redefinition of Science

However the practice of labeling all systematic approaches to knowledge acquisition as "science" can lead to problems. Consider, for example, the Kansas State Board of Education's 2005 revision to the definition of science in the state teaching standards.

Original: "Science n. – The human activity of seeking natural explanations for what we observe in the world around us."

New: "Science n. – A systematic method of continuing investigation that uses observation, hypothesis testing, measurement, experimentation, logical argument and theory building to lead to more adequate explanations of natural phenomena."

On the surface, the new definition appears to be a benign change that clarifies the learning goals by expanding on the processes and elements of the scientific method; the change is also better aligned with the actual usage of the word "science" as reflected in its dictionary definition. In reality, however, the change was highly controversial, garnered national attention in the press, drew strong criticism from teachers and the scientific community, and was reversed just two years later [18].

Understanding the controversy requires a bit of background on the motivation for the change. Just six years earlier, in 1999, the Kansas State Board of Education decided to remove the topic of evolution from state standardized tests, making teaching the theory of evolution allowed but not required. In 2005 the board drafted science standards that mandated equal time for the theories of evolution and of "intelligent design" (ID). Notably, ID does not fit the original definition of science in the state teaching standards, but it does fit with the new definition the board proposed. The difference is subtle but important.

The phrase "seeking natural explanations" is inconsistent with ID because it excludes supernatural explanations—an intelligent designer—from being causal in biological systems and speciation. But the phrase "more adequate explanations of natural phenomena" does not exclude ID because it allows for supernatural explanations as long as they can be deemed "more adequate," even if the explanation is like ID, an untestable hypothesis rather than a comprehensive theory. In fact, having a supernatural explanation that can never be tested is very "adequate" since it removes the need for further scientific inquiry and exploration. Invoking ID resolves the question over the origination of biological systems once and for all—no further research needed. We are back to a tautology.

The Difference Between a Hypothesis and a Theory

Advocates of ID are able to sow confusion on the definition of science in education curricula because many people use the words "hypothesis" and "theory" interchangeably. Scientists, on the other hand, have different and very specific meanings for these two words. A "hypothesis" is a question that can be answered by experiment. For example: Does the use of antibiotics result in the emergence of drug-resistant bacteria? This hypothesis can be tested by controlled experiments with bacterial cultures and antibiotics. For this hypothesis, the answer to the question, or in other words the experimental result, is yes—antibiotic exposure does result in the emergence of drug-resistant bacteria. If the experiment is consistently reproducible by many independent scientists around the world, the result becomes accepted as an immutable fact of nature. This is the case for the experimental result that exposure of bacterial cultures to antibiotics leads to the emergence of drug-resistant bacteria.

In contrast, a "theory" is a conceptual framework that explains a wide body of experimental results and allows scientists to correctly predict the outcomes of experiments that haven't yet been attempted. In contrast to experimental facts, theories do change over time as more experimental results accumulate and scientific understanding of phenomena deepens. A theory must offer a coherent explanation of a wide variety of experimental results and most importantly, have *predictive* powers for future experiments. A theory would have little use or meaning without predictive powers.

Evolution is a theory because it meets these criteria; in fact, the theory of evolution predicts the emergence of drug-resistant bacteria. In contrast, it is a hypothesis to ask the question: "Does an intelligent being redesign bacteria to make them resistant to antibiotics?" The existence and workings of that intelligent being must be experimentally verified first, before a theory of the nature of that intelligence can be constructed. Presumably once a theory is understood that outlines the reasons the intelligence has for re-designing bacteria to evade antibiotic usage, it might be possible to develop antibiotics that would not lead to the emergence of drug-resistant bacteria.

However, since the intelligent being controls nature, it must exist outside of nature, and as a supernatural being, it is not available for experimental testing. Since the hypothesis is untestable, no meaningful theory of "intelligent design" can ever be constructed, which is why ID is not science, but instead has all the characteristics of a pseudoscience.

The lesson from the ID controversy in Kansas is that automatically labeling all systemized approaches to acquiring knowledge as "science" can be treacherous if in doing so explanations become disconnected from the natural world and are no longer testable by experiments on the natural world. As a mentor of mine bluntly put it: "Any academic department with the word science in its name is not." Fundamentally, science is about gaining knowledge and understanding of the workings of nature. As I mentioned in Chapter 1, reproducibility of results is a defining characteristic of science, and only experiments focused on natural explanations for natural phenomena can be reproduced. This simple fact is frequently overlooked when using the word "science" to describe investigations not directly connected to nature.

Nature is Eternal and Unchanging

The reason for the importance of natural explanations is that nature is eternal and unchanging; nature can never give wrong answers. Nature cannot err or deceive. These assertions about nature might at first appear counterintuitive, but they are the foundation of all scientific inquiry. You might argue that change is all around. Evolution of physical systems—such as stars—and biological systems—such as ecosystems—is always ongoing. If nature appears to have one defining characteristic it is an aversion to stasis.

However, and this is an important if not paradoxical point, all change observed in nature must unfold in accordance with rigid and unchanging laws. All evolutionary processes must conform to the laws of physics and chemistry. All biological evolution observed on Earth involves rearrangements of the same genetic codes, and to date, Earth-based biology is all that we have observed. An extraterrestrial biology could conceivably use different genetic codes, but it would still rely on the same chemical elements and conform to the same laws of physics that govern terrestrial biology.

The fact that nature is eternal allows us to reproduce experiments. Given the same apparatus and the same initial conditions, the same results must ensue. If this were not the case, science would be futile. If every "discovery" were a one-time event there would be no point in publishing results. There would also be no application of science to technology because inventions would cease to function if the underlying natural laws on which they were based changed. Science would also be an exercise in futility if an "intelligent designer" or other supernatural being arbitrarily altered the laws of nature at times and places of the being's choice. Again, under those circumstances reproducibility of experimental results would not be possible. Moreover, there would be no assurance, for example, that technology that works today would work tomorrow.

Reproducibility is a constant challenge to scientists because experiments are often complex and creating conditions that are truly the same each time can be difficult. In addition, while nature does not change, our understanding of nature certainly does. This is of course what science is about—gaining a progressively deeper and more nuanced understanding of nature. As our understanding deepens, what might have seemed impossible in the past—air travel, radio transmission, video, etc.—becomes possible. But, and this is another oft misunderstood point, progress in science does not negate the past. An experiment performed a thousand years ago still gives the same results if reproduced today, even if our explanation and understanding of those results are radically different. Francis Bacon's dictum from the sixteenth century will always be true: "Nature, to be commanded, must be obeyed." Four hundred years later those words still ring true. For all the apparent wonders of modern science and progress made since Bacon's time, science has no power to change nature. Nature will always be obeyed.

Science as a Question

"To punish me for my contempt for authority, fate made me an authority myself."

-- Albert Einstein

Since natural laws are never violated, science must begin with learning how nature actually works. This requires an open and questioning mindset, the exact opposite of the "do as you're told and follow directions" mindset that schools desire and reinforce. Remember the emphasis on the "number sentence" format in the third grade math class I visited? The point of the lesson was to follow instructions, not to arrive at a correct understanding.

A scientific investigation should begin with a question. However, ironically, science is most often used in educational settings to invoke authority rather than to question it. Consider a typical example of the kind of authoritative approach to teaching science that is widespread in K-12 instruction. I received a phone call one day from a teacher preparing a lesson about solar energy by following a set of instructions for building solar cookers. Her question for me: If she substituted glass covers instead of the plexi-glass covers the plans called for, would that make a difference in the operation of the cookers? She was doing what many K-12 science instructors do: following the lesson plan to the letter and consulting with a scientific authority (me) before making any deviations.

For me, a physical understanding of her solar cooker project was straightforward. The idea was to cover the device with a material transparent to visible light, which allowed heating. But the same material would hopefully be opaque to infrared radiation, which would block cooling. It is essentially a very small-scale version of a greenhouse. So from my expert point-of-view her question comes down to: How does the visible/infrared optical transmission spectrum of glass compare to that for plexi-glass?

Off the top of my head, I didn't know, and if I were to look it up, I would need to know the exact composition of the materials she was using—glass comes in different grades—which is information I'm sure she wouldn't have.

My response: "Build three solar cookers identical in everyway but their covers. Cover one with glass, one with plexi-glass, and leave the remaining one uncovered. Put all three outside in the same place for the same length of time, with the same kinds of thermometers. See which one, if any, heats up more."

She replied: "That's a wonderful idea. We could do that ourselves."

As she thanked me, she sounded very excited about actually doing an experiment. Maybe her students will learn that science is much more fun and interesting when they answer questions with experiments of their own, rather than follow instructions and consult scientific authorities.

Indeed, my observation is that young children are born scientists, with innate curiosity to question, explore, and experiment. However, because K-12 schools do not nurture this natural curiosity, few students graduate from high school with an interest in science. Instead schools instill character traits that are the exact opposite—conforming to authority, averting risks, and following directions. Once, when I was doing outreach at a local elementary school for their "STEM-day," the principal, with great puzzlement, told me that compared to all the other students in the school, the kindergartners had done the best on all the "challenge activities." I told her that I wasn't surprised. Kindergartners are still willing to experiment. For most children, their natural inclination to experiment and explore will decrease the longer they stay in school.

That anyone graduates from high school with an interest in science is the real puzzle. Exploring on one's own and trying new things are not activities that schools usually encourage. The reason schools are so averse is that most experiments, even those conducted by professional scientists, result in failure. To be a scientist you must acquire a very high tolerance for frustration and failure. It takes a long time and much trial and error to get something right in a laboratory. A school with the track record of a typical scientist would certainly not be making adequate yearly progress (AYP)!

Science as a Conversation

A scientific investigation begins with a question, but it quickly becomes a dialog. Fundamentally science is a conversation with nature, a back and forth that begins with an initial question posed in the form of an experiment but then leads to more questions and more experiments. Nature is being interrogated, and while nature's answers are never wrong or deceptive, they can often be surprising, subtle, and difficult to interpret. Therefore the answers must be received with an open mind. Children possess this open mind and, what's more, the process of questioning nature—hypothesizing, testing, evaluating the results, and refining theories—is also understandable to young children.

For example, the youngest group whom I've spoken to about science were four-year-old preschoolers. I brought a flashlight and a set of color filters and invited the children to predict the color of the light that results after various filters and filter combinations were placed in front of the flashlight. Even at four years of age, children already have a good mental model of what will happen in these experiments. A red filter results in red light, a green filter in green light, a red-green combination results in yellow light. The children already know from their coloring and painting experience about color mixing and they can correctly predict the colors that result from various filter combinations.

It is remarkable that by four years of age children have already developed and internalized a theory of color that makes predictions that are both accurate and useful for their artistic activities. But, while their theory is correct in the context of drawing and painting that is familiar to them, it also has limitations. I demonstrated the breakdown of their theory by substituting a laser for the flashlight and inviting predictions on the colors that would result after placing various filters in the path of a red-colored laser beam. Using their theory, they predicted that the red laser through a yellow filter would produce orange, through a green filter it would produce yellow, and through a blue filter it would produce magenta.

We then did the experiment. The results: A red laser beam going through a yellow filter comes out red, through a green filter it also comes out red, and a red laser beam does not go through a blue filter. Much surprise and bewilderment followed. I explained that is the reason why experimentation is so important in science. Nature does not always behave the way we expect it to. Oftentimes it does, but sometimes the results of experiments are new and surprising and we have to re-think our expectations. That was the lesson I wanted to convey that day to the four-year-olds. I made no attempt to teach any part of my much more sophisticated understanding of light—an understanding that allows me to correctly predict the outcomes of both the flashlight and the laser experiments, and also an understanding that is developmentally inappropriate for four-year-olds. They will get there someday; that day, I just wanted them to learn why experimentation is so important.

These experiments on light with the four-year olds also show that science is not the rigid linear process portrayed in grade-school science textbooks. Being able to confirm our initial hypotheses on color using the flashlight did not ensure a rock-solid correct understanding of light, as demonstrated by our disproving of our follow-up hypotheses using the laser. However, our initial hypotheses were not wrong either, and had we not conducted the laser experiments we would have continued to believe that our understanding of light was correct. What we learned is that it is possible to have an understanding of light that is adequate for many purposes—like painting—and yet at the same time incomplete because it is inadequate for other purposes—like laser-light shows. In fact, our scientific understanding is always incomplete, which is a status that keeps people like myself employed. That incompleteness is a necessary and exciting part of science. It certainly does not mean that the understandings we do have are therefore incorrect, a conclusion that anti-science and pseudoscience advocates like to draw.

Science is an Iterative Process

On the website *UnderstandingScience.org*, the scientific method is portrayed with an interactive flowchart that, unlike most flowcharts, does not have a beginning and an end. Illustrated instead is a circuitous process with lots of loops and feedback mechanisms. In the center of the chart is "testing ideas," which is the activity that occupies much of a scientist's time, and that center feeds, and is fed by, the activities of "exploration and discovery," "community analysis and feedback," and "benefits and outcomes." The peripheral activities also feed each other. The point is that the real process of science is iterative.

> "Science circles back on itself so that useful ideas are built upon and used to learn even more about the natural world. This often means that successive investigations of a topic lead back to the same question, but at deeper and deeper levels." [19]

The website does not attempt to define science, admitting that a precise definition is difficult. But, it does provide a checklist of attributes that a scientific investigation should conform to. Included in the list are "focused on the natural world," "attempts to explain the natural world," and "uses testable ideas." [20]

Moreover, *UnderstandingScience.org* provides narrative summaries of some groundbreaking scientific discoveries to make the point that doing science isn't formulaic. In fact, many major advances in science have resulted from serendipity or even outright mistakes. In his book *Brilliant Blunders: From Darwin to Einstein Colossal Mistakes by Great Scientists That Changed Our Understanding of Life and the Universe*, Mario Livio examines the major mistakes of five of history's greatest scientists and shows how errors in their thinking resulted in major conceptual breakthroughs [21]. Similarly, in *Serendipity: Accidental Discoveries in Science*, Royston Roberts recounts how many things we take for granted today—x-rays, penicillin, photography, sugar substitutes, to name a few—were accidental rather than planned discoveries [22].

Actually, since science is an investigation of the unknown, by definition major discoveries cannot be anticipated or planned. A scientist must remain ever curious and alert to new possibilities. A failed experiment is almost always a failure, except in rare cases when the "failure" is so unanticipated that it leads to a major breakthrough. This is the paradox of science. Everyone expects scientists to have plans for tackling problems of the utmost urgency. But you can only plan based on what you know, and the whole point of science is to find out what you don't know.

Science as a Guide

Of course many people will claim that my plea for open-minded inquiry and exploration is somewhat hypocritical. Scientists are routinely accused of being close-minded on many controversial issues. I am no exception. If you have read this far, you probably sense that I am dismissive of ideas such as creationism, intelligent design, and climate change denial. I am so dismissive that I am not even addressing the arguments put forth in support of these ideas. In one sense, it is hard to imagine someone being more close-minded in regards to these ideas than scientists like myself.

But the reason that I will not even engage in a debate on these issues is that these are not scientific theories. In fact, creationism, intelligent design, and climate change denial have all the attributes of pseudoscience outlined in Chapter 1. Advocates of these ideas present emotionally engaging narratives that cannot be falsified. Ask a denier of climate change what evidence he or she would require to be convinced that climate change is real, and you will not receive an answer. Ask a denier of Darwinian evolution what evidence he or she would require to be convinced that evolution is real, and again you will find that there is none. This is true close-mindedness. I, on the other hand, could be convinced that the Earth is not warming, or that evolution has not occurred. It is just that no one has presented any compelling evidence to me that these statements are true. Cherry-picking facts, which is common among practitioners of pseudoscience, is not what I regard as compelling evidence.

The ability to discern science from pseudoscience, to recognize when evidence is compelling as opposed to cherry-picked, should be an important part of science education. I would argue that learning to recognize pseudoscience should have a high priority for educational outcomes. Because most children do not grow up to be practicing scientists, it is even more important that the science curriculum include instruction on how to recognize and reject pseudoscience.

Debunking Pseudoscience

Too often science classes expose students to as many scientific facts and theories as possible, but omit one of the most important uses of science—unmasking falsehoods. While the scientific method is useful for revealing novel truths about nature, it can also be used to debunk pseudoscientific claims. The ability to discern fact from fiction is often more important than just knowing facts. But too often science educators are reluctant to teach this skill. I believe it's out of fear of appearing offensive when challenging other people's cherished, albeit irrational beliefs. But clinging to falsehoods can have tragic consequences.

For example, one of my most memorable lessons from eighth-grade science, in fact one of the few lessons I remember from eighth grade, was being assigned to watch a two-hour television special titled *In Search of Ancient Astronauts* [23]. The year was 1973 and NBC aired this documentary, narrated by Rod Sterling of *Twilight Zone* fame that popularized the theories of the writer Erich von Däniken [24]. His claim was that extraterrestrial beings visited the Earth early in human history and profoundly influenced human culture.

The slick production with Sterling's mesmerizing voice made for compelling television. As a thirteen-year-old, it was hard not to be convinced that the world's major religions originated from contact with extraterrestrial beings. It was even suggested that humans themselves might be the genetically engineered creations of intelligent beings that landed on the Earth thousands of years ago. The television show made all this sound plausible.

The next day in science class our teacher discussed the documentary. He proceeded to systemically demolish every claim the show made. In fact, all the evidence cited in the documentary to support the ancient astronaut hypothesis had simple mundane explanations. No compelling evidence exists that the Earth has ever been visited by extraterrestrials. Despite the popularity of Erich von Däniken's writings—tens of millions of books sold worldwide—his ideas are a classic example of a pseudoscience.

The lesson my eighth-grade science teacher succeeded in teaching me is that scientific thinking has valuable uses outside of science. In science class we learn to interrogate nature, but the interrogation methods can be used to scrutinize many other ideas and beliefs.

While many pseudoscientific beliefs are harmless, some that have found widespread popularity are dangerous. People who sincerely believe that our

Paleolithic ancestors were genetically modified by extraterrestrials that landed on Earth in flying saucers are not doing anyone harm. But, to give one recent example of a dangerous belief, people who refuse to vaccinate their children because they believe vaccines cause autism are endangering entire communities.

The belief that vaccines cause autism originated from a 1998 medical study that has long since been discredited. There are now reasons to believe that the study might have been a deliberate fraud. However, the weight of scientific evidence has not been able to counter widespread publicity of the flawed finding and the celebrity endorsements it garnered.

Actress Jenny McCarthy, through her writings and appearances on *Oprah*, is able to promote unsubstantiated claims about vaccines that have more influence on parental actions than the public health professionals at the Centers for Disease Control. Seth Mnookin in his book *The Panic Virus* shows that even the educated and affluent have succumbed to irrational fears of vaccines. In his words, the "result has been as tragic as it is predictable." [25] Children have died from easily preventable diseases.

Of course the media likes to generate controversy by giving at least two sides to every story. But science does not work that way. The autism-vaccine link, like the long-running creation-evolution debate, does not have another side in scientific circles. When the weight of evidence on one side of an issue becomes overwhelming, scientists tend to move on. Unfortunately, the general public, ignorant of how scientific issues are decided, often doesn't.

Deliberately Distorting Science

Even more dangerous than the media-enabled spread of pseudoscientific ideas is the deliberate distortion of legitimate scientific investigations for political and/or financial reasons. Consider the aftermath of the disastrous Gulf of Mexico oil spill in April 2010 that resulted from a blowout on a drill platform chartered by British Petroleum (BP).

An investigation by the Mobile, Alabama *Press-Register* revealed that BP offered lucrative contracts to scientists engaged in research on the Gulf of Mexico oil spill. According to one source, BP attempted to hire the entire marine sciences department at an Alabama university. The *Press-Register* reported that the contract "prohibits the scientists from publishing their research, sharing it with other scientists or speaking about the data that they collect for at least the next three years." [26]

I find this tactic particularly disturbing because it would allow BP to pretend that it is doing science when it is not. Employing scientists for private purposes is not a new practice. Nor is the act of keeping data and results proprietary. Many scientists work for private companies and must uphold the terms of the contract agreed to by both parties. Open sharing of information is often not desirable because companies that invest in research should be the first to benefit from the results.

However, conclusions drawn from proprietary data are not necessarily scientifically valid. BP's contract is a deliberate attempt to control the publication of data on the effects of the Gulf oil spill, while at the same time invoking scientific authority for the conclusions obtained from the research. This is not how the scientific method works, and to pretend otherwise is dangerous.

The act of employing scientists to take data, publish results, and interpret findings, does not necessarily mean that valid scientific conclusions will result. Scientists are fallible human beings, prone to error and motivated, in part, by their own beliefs, prejudices, self-interests, and parochialisms. In other words, the work of science is hampered by the same human foibles that plague all human endeavors.

But in the past few centuries science has advanced at a remarkable rate because its method has a self-correcting mechanism built in. Scientists throughout the world usually work independently and openly share ideas and results. Independence and openness are two features of the scientific method that are little appreciated, but essential to scientific advancement. By reviewing and checking each other's work, scientists uncover errors and biases. Over time evidence accumulates to support valid results and interpretations. Ideas that are wrong get culled and eventually become relegated to the history books.

Independence and openness are qualities not typically valued by businesses, or for that matter governments and churches. In fact, these institutions tend to regard open sharing of information and independent questioning of established precepts as existential threats. How ironic, then, that these same institutions will often invoke scientific authority to buttress their own self-serving claims.

You cannot have it both ways. Scientific "authority" derives from a method that self-corrects because of a tradition of independent researchers openly sharing information. You cannot take away this part of the method and still claim that you are doing science.

To date, science has been a remarkably successful human endeavor; however, we should not take for granted the continued advancement of science, especially while the benefactors of science attack it. The recent phenomenon of people choosing scientific beliefs that are consistent with their choice of church, or career, or political party is deeply troubling. Obviously, nature has no affiliation with any churches, corporations, or governments.

More and more, we see organizations of various types cherry-picking data to advance their own agendas. BP will be very careful in regards to the proprietary data it releases, in the same way that pharmaceutical companies are very careful about the results of drug studies that they release. Creationist/intelligent design advocates are quick to point out any problems with evolution theory, while ignoring reams of supporting evidence. In the United States, belief in global warming now falls along party lines, a situation that could not possibly occur if people were independently evaluating the evidence.

In fact, it would be remarkably coincidental if natural phenomena just happened to perfectly align with the economic self-interests of a particular group or person. Such a coincidence is highly unlikely. In the aftermath of the space shuttle Challenger disaster, the Nobel prize-winning physicist Richard Feynman, who served on the investigative commission, noted that political pressures contributed to the disastrous decision to launch that day. He warned: "reality must take precedence over public relations, for nature cannot be fooled." It is a warning we should all keep in mind no matter what topic is being investigated.

As I pointed out in Chapter 1, if science were as wrong as many people believe, none of the technology that we have come to rely on would work. That is a fact that science teachers should have their students reflect on. When I observe the media presenting unsubstantiated claims as being equally plausible as settled scientific fact it reminds me of the late Senator Moynihan's statement: "Everyone is entitled to their own opinions, but not their own facts."

Nature is not a democracy in which everyone gets to vote on its laws. There are right and wrong answers to the questions that we pose to nature. In addition, willful ignorance does not change the laws of nature, nor does it render them irrelevant. The judgment nature imposes is swift and final. No appeal is allowed. The answers we seek might be subtle and difficult to find. We won't find the answers to all the questions, and some might be forever unanswerable. But that doesn't mean that all opinions are equally valid and all possible explanations are equally plausible. Learning these essential truths about nature is more important than learning the multitude of facts that are crammed into every science class.

Science as a Verb

"Physics is like sex: sure, it may give some practical results, but that's not why we do it."

--- Richard Feynman

Science is a systemized body of knowledge, a way of questioning, conversing and thinking about nature, but most importantly to a practicing scientist, it is an activity. Science is something to do and *knowing* about an activity is not the same as *doing* the activity. Authentic science education should be about engaging students in the activity of science. Just as scientific thinking has valuable applications outside of science, the skills acquired from doing science are valuable in many other contexts. The PCAST report, cited earlier, recommended training more STEM professionals and more "STEM capable" workers [11]. The report documented the growing need for more people with "STEM skills" in occupations not traditionally thought of as STEM. In other words, the skills scientists develop in the act of doing science have an economic value in their own right.

However, our education system, with its heavy emphasis on memorizing facts and following instructions, fails at teaching children actual hands-on skills. There is a difference between knowing how something works and actually making it work. I see this problem all the time when I teach lab classes. In setting up an experiment, students will follow instructions to the letter and assume everything is correctly assembled. At the end they will have a beautifully assembled experimental apparatus that doesn't work. It is then brought to me to figure out why and the students will often watch in dismay as I dismantle it piece by piece to search for the problem. Sometimes it is a mistake or misunderstanding on the first step, and that forces the students to begin all over again. The first lesson learned about making things work is that time-consuming testing after each step in the process actually saves time.

It's not only students that struggle with this lesson. A friend once asked me for help wiring an external keyboard he purchased for a handheld device. He had followed the instructions, but after making all the connections it didn't work. Frustrated and confused he didn't know what to do next. He took it apart, put it back in the box, and called me.

He came to my office where I spread the parts out on my desk and followed the enclosed wiring instructions. But, after making each connection, I tested it with an electrical meter while twisting and pulling to make sure it was secure. I did this for every connection, because I made no assumptions about reliability based on how it looked or the high probability that almost all the connections I make are secure. When I finished, I turned the device on and it worked.

My friend said: "But, I wired it the same way you did. Why didn't it work?"

"You didn't do it the same way I did. You didn't test each connection when you made it. When it didn't work, you had no good way of finding a single bad connection, which is all that is needed for it to fail. I made sure each connection worked before I continued to the next one."

Testing, debugging, and assembling often feel like time-wasting activities, which is why they are frequently left out of school curricula. However, they are essential skills for doing science, as well as useful life skills. I often quip to the parents of prospective Loyola students touring our introductory labs that "at the very least physics will prepare your children for the future joys of homeownership." They all nod in understanding.

Addressing the Growing Gender Gap in Education

In his book *Boys Adrift: The Five Factors Driving the Growing Epidemic of Unmotivated Boys and Underachieving Young Men*, Leonard Sax discusses the fact that there are two kinds of "knowing." [27] Knowing about something, which is the kind of knowledge obtained from a book, is different than experiential knowing, which is the know-how kind of knowledge obtained through action. In contrast to other European languages, English does not have separate words for the two kinds of knowledge. Therefore Sax borrows the German words *Wissenschaft* (for book knowledge) and *Kenntnis* (for experiential knowledge). Sax argues that education should provide a balance of *Wissenschaft* and *Kenntnis*. European pedagogy does this well. However, American pedagogy is heavily biased towards *Wissenschaft* because it is easier to impart and test.

The consequences of this bias towards *Wissenschaft* are profound. Boys, who are more engaged by experiential learning than book learning, have become increasingly alienated from education in the United States. The ratio of females to males entering college is currently about 1.4 to 1 and climbing [28]. This large and growing gender gap in educational attainment is documented and analyzed by Diprete and Buchmann in *The Rise of Women: The growing gender gap in education and what it means for American schools* [29]. However, as documented in Chapter 2, college graduates have a vastly improved quality of life in many dimensions—earnings, health, longevity, and relationships. Women have responded to the incentives of higher earnings and better quality of life. That men have not responded to these incentives is in the words of the authors "puzzling" and "demands examination." They find that one exception is that women still lag far behind men in obtaining degrees in engineering and physical sciences. They recommend a strong high school science curriculum as a way of reducing gender stereotypes and allowing both men and women to succeed.

It should be noted that in the previous paragraphs I cited two books to support my argument, but these authors are in sharp disagreement with each other. Sax's book argues that differences in educational outcomes for boys and girls arise primarily from biological differences combined with a school environment that is not conducive to boys' learning styles. He advocates single-sex education in which boys attend more "boy-friendly" schools as a means of compensating for these differences. Diprete and Buchmann explicitly disagree with this recommendation. They argue that boys' underperformance in school has more to do with societal norms about masculinity than with biological differences. They argue that the educational system needs to do a better job of showing boys and girls the clear link between educational attainment and future work-place rewards.

I am arguing that authentic science education that engages students in actually *doing* science allows both boys and girls to transcend gender stereotypes and benefits all. Both genders are equally capable of excelling in science. My own view on the gender gap that has developed in education is closer to Richard Whitmire's, who sums up the problem in his book *Why Boys Fail: Saving Our Sons from an Educational System That's Leaving Them Behind* as: "The world has become more verbal and boys have not." [30] I do not see single-sex education as the solution to this problem, but attributing all gender differences to cultural norms is to deny the obvious. Boys and girls are different for biological reasons, but those differences have more to do with verbal development and the consequences of demanding more language skills at younger ages, than it does with science and math ability.

Authentic science education should include both *Wissenschaft* and *Kenntnis;* to be a scientist you need to know facts and how to make things work. It should engage boys and girls in hands-on experiential learning, which is also necessary in learning the thought processes of a scientist. It is one skill to learn how to ask scientific questions, and it is another skill to learn to ask the kinds of questions that can be posed to nature in the form of an experiment. Science is about more than just knowledge; it is also about knowing how that knowledge is obtained.

It is also worth noting that the reason that "STEM skills" are in high demand is that employers typically pay workers for doing something. Relatively few people have jobs that only require them to recall facts. Authentic science education has benefits for all that extend beyond science. Students learn that nothing happens by magic. Everything in their environment works for a reason, and it requires vast networks of interconnected people with varied expertise to bring forth and sustain our modern technological world.

The Limits of Science

A scientific approach to acquiring knowledge is powerful, but it is not without its limits. Science can reveal the inner workings of nature, but it cannot answer questions as to what nature means, or for that matter what our own lives mean. The humanities, which include religion, philosophy, history, art, and literature, are the branches of knowledge that deal with questions of meaning. Consider that when religions intrude into science by trying to answer scientific questions with religious texts, they frequently become ensnared in logical traps like tautologies. But, the tautological trap can work both ways. Scientists attempting to use science to answer questions of meaning can also fall into tautologies.

Take, for example, renowned physicist Stephen Hawking's co-authored book *The Grand Design* [31]. He and collaborator Leonard Mlodinow set out to answer three central questions: Why is there something rather than nothing? Why do we exist? Why this particular set of physical laws and not some other? Notice that once questions are phrased using "why" the issue of meaning becomes unavoidable.

Answering these questions is an ambitious agenda for a single volume, but the newsworthiness of the book was its assertion that no creator was necessary for the universe. Hawking and Mlodinow wrote that "the universe can and will create itself from nothing," and declared "philosophy is dead."

The publicity these assertions generated reminded me of a famous quote from the nineteenth century French mathematician Pierre-Simon Laplace who also wrote a book on the laws of the universe. He presented the book to the emperor Napoleon who said to him: "M. Laplace, they tell me you have written this large book on the system of the universe, and have never even mentioned its Creator."

Laplace answered: "I had no need of that hypothesis."

When Napoleon told Joseph-Louis Lagrange, another renowned mathematician of the time, what Laplace said, Lagrange replied: "Ah, it is a fine hypothesis; it explains many things."

After reading *The Grand Design*, I couldn't help but think that nothing has changed in the two centuries since this back-and-forth between Napoleon and the mathematicians. Explaining the universe without God is about as futile as explaining the universe with God. To assert that the universe creates itself from nothing, Hawking and Mlodinow appear to lapse into the same kind of tautology that creationists use to defend their beliefs.

The Creationist and Anthropic Tautologies

As I explained in Chapter 1, the Christian understanding of God, in the words of the Nicene Creed, is that God is the "creator of all that there is." This statement alone provides no insight on the mechanisms or motivations for creation. Scientists have sought to understand the mechanisms for creation, and in doing so have amassed enormous amounts of evidence that the Earth and its inhabitants did not simply come into being over a one-week time span 6000 years ago as creationists believe based on a literal interpretation of the book of *Genesis* [32]. But, a creationist will argue that none of this evidence matters because God, as the omnipotent creator of all that there is, could just as well have created the "appearance" of an older Earth and evolutionary processes. This is a tautology because the creationist position is unassailable. All evidence that does not support the creationist's views can be dismissed as part of God's creation.

In Ken Miller's book, *Finding Darwin's God: A Scientist's Search for Common Ground Between God and Evolution*, he likens the belief that the universe was created with "the appearance of age," to a belief in God as a charlatan [33]. Miller is a committed Christian who believes in God, not in spite of evolution, but because of evolution. In Miller's view, the process of evolution is awe-inspiring. In response to creationists, Miller writes that a God that has negated science by "rigging the universe with fiction and deception" is not a plausible divine being. To Miller, embracing the God of creationists is to "reject science and worship deception itself."

However, the model of a universe devoid of God presented in *The Grand Design* falls into a tautological trap akin to creationism. The "M-theory" Hawking and Mlodinow advocate allows for the existence of innumerable universes, each with different laws of physics. To explain why our universe is so remarkable, they resort to a decades-old idea known as the "anthropic principle." The essential idea is that of the multitude of universes that can exist, only a tiny fraction of them have physical laws that allow us to evolve.

Therefore, our existence as observers means that our particular universe must appear to us as special in extraordinary ways.

Whether the alternative universes exist in parallel or sequentially is not important because other universes are inaccessible. The universe is by definition "all that there is." And this is the tautology that Hawking and Mlodinow fall into: To say that anything that could possibly happen actually does happen in alternative universes, is an unassailable position. For example, it is a tautology to say that I write this sentence or I do not write this sentence. To say that I write this sentence in one universe and do not write this sentence in another universe, explains nothing. Saying that both events happen but in different universes is wordplay, not physics.

Hawking and Mlodinow cite the implausible values for the fundamental constants in physics as evidence for their anthropic argument. It is a great mystery in physics as to what determines the values for the fundamental constants. The basic forces in nature and the elementary particles that form all matter possess intrinsic properties that to date have no theoretical explanation. The electron, which is a fundamental particle that determines how atoms interact chemically, has an intrinsic mass, electric charge, magnetic moment, and angular momentum. These values are measurable, and because an electron has no discernable size or internal structure, they essentially define the particle.

What is especially striking is that all electrons are identical. Nature does not make defective electrons. Apparently every electron that there is, ever was, or ever will be, has the exact same physical properties. Electrons are identical to the point of being indistinguishable from each other. It is impossible to ever label or tag an electron, and the fact that no single electron can ever be distinguished from any of the others in the universe has profound consequences when formulating the physical laws that govern electrons.

The precise values for the physical attributes of an electron are among the fundamental constants in nature that can only be measured. No theory accounts for their values, but it appears that these values must be set very close to what they actually are in order for our species to have evolved. Because the "M-theory" that Hawking and Mlodinow advocate allows for many possible universes, each with different fundamental constants, they contend that all these universes exist and we just happen to be the observers in a universe with fundamental constants that allow us to observe.

In other words, M-theory doesn't explain the values of the fundamental constants. It just says that if you roll the dice an infinite number of times, a universe with our fundamental constants will eventually appear. That is not a theory in the scientific sense of the word because it doesn't predict anything about the actual universe we observe.

Future Theories

Physicists have long hoped that a unified theory of all the forces in nature (Theory of Everything) will predict the values for the fundamental constants. In other words, the mathematics would predict the existence of particles, such as electrons, and the mathematical solutions would provide numerical results for an electron's physical attributes that would agree with what we know about the electron.

Such a theory remains elusive so let me make my own tautological statement. A future Theory of Everything will either predict the values for the fundamental constants or it will not. If it does, physicists will find the theory extraordinarily elegant, and theologians will say that God intended our existence by establishing physical laws at the moment of creation that allowed us to evolve. If the theory does not predict the values for the fundamental constants, physicists will keep puzzling on the issue and theologians will say that God intended our existence by choosing values for the fundamental constants that allowed us to evolve.

Either way scientists and theologians will agree that God is a hypothesis that cannot be tested. There comes a point in theology where you just have to believe that the universe has a higher purpose and meaning, even if that meaning is not readily discernable. There comes a point in physics where you have to say: "that is just the way things are" because explanations through causation have to stop at some point.

My own view is that humans might not be evolved enough to comprehend a Theory of Everything. There is no reason to believe that the human brain is the pinnacle of evolution because there is no reason to believe that the evolution of intelligence will not continue long into the future. On an evolutionary time scale the human species, *Homo sapiens*, has not been around for that long. Modern humans have only existed about 100,000 years, an insignificant amount of time compared to the hundreds of millions of years that evolutionary processes have shaped species on the planet. What might brain structures and intelligence look like 100 million years from now?

As I write this paragraph my dog lies patiently at my feet waiting for me to get up and do something of interest, such as work in the garden where she can enthusiastically contribute by chasing the various critters that inhabit our yard. My endless fascination with pixilated patterns of light on a computer screen has no meaning to her. I sometimes say to her that if she could do calculus, or edit and proof my writing, she could do work that would be of real use to me. She listens to me attentively, as she does for everything I say, wags her tail, and maintains her vigil.

Of course, I could talk to my dog all day about advanced calculus, unified theories of physics and their theological implications, and she would listen attentively and understand nothing. We know that this is not the fault of the dog. A dog does not possess the brain structures to process the concepts needed for language, mathematics, or theology. Nor does a dog have the life span humans require to learn advanced concepts in all these subjects.

On the other hand, dogs do possess brain structures that I lack and intelligences that I cannot comprehend. Their sense of smell and their ability to discriminate and glean information from rich mixtures of the faintest odors is an intelligence as beyond my ability to imagine possessing as my knowledge of math is beyond theirs.

But those facts about dogs and people leave open the possibility that far into the future, another species, with a more advanced brain structure, might have similar things to say about humans. Will they say that the species, *Homo sapiens* of the Holocene epoch, figured out many important concepts in physics, but lacked the brain structure needed to understand the math required for the Theory of Everything?

A central tenet of Christianity is that God created humans in God's image. As a result the human striving to understand the natural world (God's creation) is a quest to know God. It also follows that how humans treat other humans is a reflection of our relationship with God.

But all around I see humans creating God in the image of humans. Much of the evil done in the name of God, evil that atheists cite to disparage theists, arises not from believing in God, but from anthropomorphizing God. Humans have created innumerable images of God that for most part depict God as acting and thinking like humans. However, the sheer scale and grandeur of the universe is evidence that a creator God is unimaginably extravagant and inventive. I would be careful about concluding that humans are the endpoint in the creative process.

And, I would also be careful about promoting education programs focused only on STEM. Ultimately, to be engaged and productive, human beings need and seek meaning in their lives—a topic discussed in Chapter 8. Meaning is found outside of science and requires engagement with the questions that arise in the humanities, which should be an essential part of any education program.

Having it Both Ways

The February 2012 report to the President of the United States issued by the President's Council of Advisors on Science and Technology (PCAST) referenced earlier provided five general recommendations and respective rationales for transforming education in STEM fields [11]. The recommendations are:

1. Catalyze widespread adoption of empirically validated teaching practices.
2. Advocate and provide support for replacing standard laboratory courses with discovery-based research courses.
3. Launch a national experiment in postsecondary mathematics education to address the math preparation gap.
4. Encourage partnerships among stakeholders to diversify pathways to STEM careers.
5. Create a Presidential Council on STEM Education with leadership from the academic and business communities to provide strategic leadership for transformative and sustainable change in STEM undergraduate education.

I support all of these recommendations; they are consistent with arguments that I have advanced in this book. However, the report is telling for its focus. The opening sentences are:

> "Economic projections point to a need for approximately 1 million more STEM professionals than the U.S. will produce at the current rate over the next decade if the country is to retain its historical preeminence in science and technology."

On the third page the report states:

> "In addition to the need for more STEM professionals, there is also a national need for more workers with some STEM training. These "STEM capable" workers are able to use knowledge and skills from STEM fields but work in areas that are traditionally considered non-STEM fields. The ranks of the STEM capable workforce are expanding as this skill set comes to represent an increasingly valued commodity in many fields."

In other words, businesses would benefit, and the economy as a whole would prosper, if more people in the available workforce possessed STEM skills. More and more occupations require the skill set that scientists possess—that is facility with mathematics, computers, electronic equipment, testing and debugging hardware and software. Appendix D of the report documents the expanding need for STEM skills in many occupations not usually thought of as being science or technology oriented.

The benefits achieved from having a workforce able to think like scientists—that is, ask questions, evaluate and weigh evidence, reach scientifically valid conclusions, and present them clearly—are not a focus of the report because these abilities are not high on the educational priority lists of politicians and policymakers.

In fact, for all the emphasis on STEM education of late, I rarely hear of or read about how the quality of one's life can be enhanced by becoming scientifically literate. The benefits of STEM education are almost always presented as economic. I believe the reasons for this are:

• People want the economic benefits of scientific discoveries, except when those discoveries are inconvenient or clash with narrow economic interests.
• People want scientists to ask questions, except when those questions make them uncomfortable or call attention to truths that no one wants to face.
• People celebrate the innovations of nonconformists and the prosperity they bring, while at the same time they demand an educational system that requires conformity and adherence to the belief that everyone must be held accountable to quantifiable arbitrary standards.

As a result, the motivation politicians and policymakers have for wanting scientists and the motivation of scientists are at odds. The politicians and policymakers have a fundamental misunderstanding of what science is about that again arises from willful ignorance. Many political, corporate, and religious leaders who set and fund education policies engage in repeated attacks on science while at the same time they reap the economic benefits that science has brought. The examples of the Kansas State Board of Education and BP manipulating science to serve political and corporate agendas are not isolated incidents.

Emails obtained by *Bloomberg Business* show that, despite his denials, Harold Hamm, the CEO of Continental Resources, wanted earthquake scientists at the University of Oklahoma dismissed and pressured the dean to do so [34]. Hamm even offered to sit on a search committee to fill vacancies because he felt a representative from the oil and gas industry should be included in hiring decisions. The trigger for Hamm's outrage is that the scientists are studying the link between the nearly 400-fold increase in earthquakes in Oklahoma to oil and gas exploration and recovery.

Florida Governor Rick Scott, who criticized students in liberal arts programs like anthropology, has denied widespread reports of an unwritten policy since he took office that bans state officials from using the terms "climate change" and "global warming" in emails and reports [35]. What cannot be denied is a 2012 law passed in North Carolina that bans the use of scientific predictions of future sea-level rise in formulating state policies on use and development of lands in coastal areas. The state of Tennessee, site of the Scopes trial in 1925 [36], passed a law in 2012 that allows public school teachers to teach creationism and to deny climate change in their classrooms [37].

However, in the realm of cognitive dissonance it would be hard to outdo Jeb Bush. In a single interview, he said that the science on climate change is "convoluted" and called the scientists "really arrogant." Then he went on to say: "I think as conservatives we should embrace innovation, embrace technology, embrace science." [38] This all from a man who first said that he is "not a scientist" when it comes to climate change.

The misuse of science by the same people advocating that more students study science is an attempt to have it both ways. Our education system reflects a disconnect between the stated goal of educating more scientists and an understanding of what that actually means. As a result, what is presented as science in school is often not really science.

I began this chapter by noting the national trend of disparaging liberal arts degrees in favor of STEM degrees. But that is perhaps the greatest misunderstanding of all. *A university science degree is a much-maligned liberal arts degree.* It is no accident that in the traditional organization of a university, arts and sciences are grouped together in the same college. The primary focus of all degrees in arts and sciences is how to think and express one's self. A scientific investigation begins with an idea in the form of a question, continues with the gathering and weighing of evidence, and concludes with publications that present novel insights.

A scientific investigation often has a technical component, which means that practitioners must develop mathematical and laboratory skills. These technical skills have economic value. But scientists are not technicians and are not necessarily motivated by interests in technology. The willful ignorance of these facts about scientists has resulted in an ineffective and dysfunctional approach to science education and peril to our society as a whole. Our economic and environmental wellness is dependent on continued progress in science. We cannot afford to have authentic science education repeatedly disparaged in favor of a more convenient authoritarian facsimile and to have the scientific method routinely manipulated in order to advance feel-good public relations.

References

1. Anthony P. Carnevale, Jeff Strohl, and Michelle Melton, *What's It Worth? The Economic Value of College Majors* (Washington, DC: Georgetown University Center on Education and the Workforce, 2015). https://cew.georgetown.edu/report/whats-it-worth-the-economic-valueof-college-majors/.
2. Anne Fisher, "Choosing a College Major? Read This First," *Fortune*, May 7, 2015, http://fortune.com/2015/05/07/choosing-a-college-majorread-this-first/.
3. Melissa Korn, "College Majors Figure Big in Earnings," *Wall Street Journal*, May 7, 2015, http://www.wsj.com/articles/college-majors-figure-bigin-earnings-1430971261.
4. Akani Otani, "College Majors that Make the Most Money," *Bloomberg Business*, May 7, 2015, http://www.bloomberg.com/news/articles/2015-05-07/here-are-the-college-majors-that-make-the-most-money.
5. Mandi Woodruff, "Students Pick Dumb Majors Despite Pay Gap," *Business Insider*, November 9, 2011, http://www.businessinsider.com/students-pick-dumb-majors-despite-pay-gap-2011-11.
6. Gus Lubin, and Robert Johnson, "College Students Need to Look at These Charts Before Deciding on a Major," *Business Insider*, November 21, 2011, http://www.businessinsider.com/majors-pay-the-most-2011-11?op=1.
7. "A New System of College Rankings – Invitation to Comment," U. S. Department of Education, accessed December 19, 2014, http://www2.ed.gov/documents/college-affordability/framework-invitation-comment.pdf.
8. Barack Obama, "Remarks by the President on Opportunity for All and Skills for America's Workers," GE Energy Waukesha Gas Engines Facility," Speech in Waukesha, Wisconsin, January 30, 2014, accessed May 1, 2018, https://www.whitehouse.gov/the-pressoffice/2014/01/30/remarks-president-opportunity-all-and-skills-americas-workers.
9. Patrick McCrory, Radio Interview with Bill Bennett, January 29, 2013. http://media.townhall.com/townhall/bennett/GovMcCrory1.29.13.mp3.
10. Rick Scott, Radio Interview with Mar Bernier, October 10, 2011. http://www.care2.com/causes/dont-know-much-about-anthropology-rick-scottcriticizes-the-liberal-arts.html.
11. President's Council of Advisors on Science and Technology, *Engage to Excel: Producing one million additional college graduates with degrees in science, technology, engineering, and mathematics*, Report to the President (Washington, DC: Executive Office of the President, February 2012), 3. Accessed May 1, 2018, https://files.eric.ed.gov/fulltext/ED541511.pdf.
12. Christopher Drew, "Why Science Majors Change Their Minds (Its Just So Darn Hard)," *New York Times*, November 4, 2011, http://www.nytimes.com/2011/11/06/education/edlife/why-science-majors-change-their-mind-its-just-so-darn-hard.html?pagewanted=2&_r=2&emc=eta1.

13. Alfie Kohn, *No Contest: The Case Against Competition* (New York: Houghton Mifflin, 1992).
14. G. Aad et al. "Combined Measurement of the Higgs Boson Mass in pp Collisions at √S = 7 and 8 TeV with the ATLAS and CMS Experiments," *Physical Review Letters* 114, (2015): 191803. This article from the LHC collaboration had 5154 authors.
15. Nancy Kober, *Reaching Students: What Research Says About Effective Instruction in Undergraduate Science and Engineering*, Board on Science Education, Division of Behavior and Social Sciences and Education (Washington, DC: National Academies Press, 2015).
16. Laura Snyder, "The Philosophical Breakfast Club," Filmed June 2012 at TEDGlobal, Edinburgh, Scotland. Video, 12:54. http://www.ted.com/talks/laura_snyder_the_philosophical_breakfast_club?language=en.
17. "College of Family and Consumer Sciences," University of Georgia, accessed May 1, 2018, http://www.fcs.uga.edu/college/history.
18. Aaron White, "The Debate Over Evolution in Kansas Schools 2005," The Pluralism Project at Harvard University, accessed May 1, 2018, http://pluralism.org/reports/view/106.
19. "The real process of science," Understanding Science, University of California Museum of Paleontology, accessed May 1, 2018, http://undsci.berkeley.edu/article/0_0_0/howscienceworks_02.
20. "A science checklist," Understanding Science, University of California Museum of Paleontology, accessed May 1, 2018, http://undsci.berkeley.edu/article/whatisscience_03.
21. Mario Livio, *Brilliant Blunders – Colossal Mistakes by Great Scientists That Changed Our Understanding of Life and the Universe* (New York: Simon & Schuster, 2014).
22. Royston M. Roberts, *Serendipity: Accidental Discoveries in Science* (New York: Wiley, 1989).
23. Don Ringe, *In Search of Ancient Astronauts*, Directed by Harald Reinl, Hosted by Rod Sterling, (Alan Landsburg Productions, Original air date: January 5, 1973).
24. Erich von Däniken, *Chariots of the Gods? Unsolved Mysteries of the Past* (New York: Putnam, 1968).
25. Seth Mnookin, *The Panic Virus: The True Story Behind the Autism-Vaccine Controversy* (New York: Simon & Schuster, 2012).
26. Ben Raines, "BP buys up Gulf scientists for legal defense, roiling the academic community," *The Press Register*, July 10, 2010, http://blog.al.com/live/2010/07/bp_buys_up_gulf_scientists_for.html.
27. Leonard Sax, *Boys Adrift: The Five Factors Driving the Epidemic of Unmotivated Boys and Underachieving Young Men* (New York: Basic Books, 2009).
28. Ricardo Hausmann, Laura D. Tyson, and Saadia Zahidi, *The Global Gender Gap Report 2011*, Appendix D, Table D9 (Cologny/Geneva Switzerland: World Economic Forum, 2011). http://www3.weforum.org/docs/WEF_GenderGap_Report_2011.pdf.

29. Thomas A. Diprete, and Claudia Buchmann, *The Rise of Women: The growing gender gap in education and what it means for American schools* (New York: Russell Sage Foundation, 2013).

30. Richard Whitmire, *Why Boys Fail: Saving Our Sons from an Educational System That's Leaving Them Behind* (New York: American Management Association, 2010).

31. Stephen Hawking and Leonard Mlodinow, *The Grand Design* (New York: Bantam, 2012).

32. A fun trivia question to ask people: What happened on October 22, 4004 B. C.? Few people know that the creation happened around 6 P.M. on the evening of that day. At least that was the finding of a 17th century Irish bishop, James Ussher, who did an extensive textual analysis of the bible and worked out its entire chronology from the birth of Jesus Christ on backwards to the moment of creation in Genesis. (Although the October 22 creation date is according to the proleptic Julian calendar, not the Gregorian calendar used today.) https://en.wikipedia.org/wiki/James_Ussher.

33. Kenneth Miller, *Finding Darwin's God: A Scientist's Search for Common Ground Between God and Evolution*, (New York: Harper Perennial, 2007).

34. Benjamin Elgin, "Oil CEO Wanted University Quake Scientists Dismissed: Dean's E-Mail," Bloomberg Business, May 15, 2015, http://www.bloomberg.com/news/articles/2015-05-15/oil-tycoon-harold-hamm-wanted-scientists-dismissed-dean-s-e-mail-says.

35. Tristram Korten, "In Florida, Officials Ban Term 'Climate Change'," FCIR: Florida Center for Investigative Reporting, March 8, 2015, accessed May 1, 2018, http://fcir.org/2015/03/08/in-florida-officials-ban-term-climate-change/.

36. The Scopes trial in 1925 in Dayton, Tennessee was a staged trial that challenged a state law at that time that forbade the teaching of evolution in public schools. John Scopes, a substitute teacher, agreed to incriminate himself so that the law could be tested in an actual court case. The trial attracted intense national publicity as famed lawyers Williams Jennings Bryan who argued for the prosecution and Clarence Darrow who argued for the defense, came to Dayton to face off in the courtroom. Scopes was found guilty and fined $100, but the verdict was later overturned on a technicality. https://en.wikipedia.org/wiki/Scopes_Trial.

37. House Bill 368/Senate Bill 893, "An Act to amend Tennessee Code Annotated, Title 49, Chapter 6, Part 10, relative to teaching scientific subjects in elementary schools." General Assembly of the State of Tennessee (2012). http://www.capitol.tn.gov/bills/107/bill/hb0368.pdf.

38. Ashley Killough, "Jeb Bush rails against 'intellectual arrogance' in climate change debate," CNN, May 20, 2015, http://www.cnn.com/2015/05/20/politics/jeb-bush-climate-change/.

Part III

The Threat to American Democracy

6

False Choice: Pseudoscientific Narrative

Early in the morning of Monday August 27, 2012, 15-year old Robert Gladden Jr. packed his bag for the first day of his sophomore year at Perry Hall high school in northeast Baltimore County. In it he placed the parts of his father's gun that he had disassembled the night before, 21 rounds of ammunition, and a bottle of vodka. He arrived at school and attended his first three classes. At 10:25 AM he went to the cafeteria for lunch, opened his backpack and showed some of the friends the gun parts inside, advising them to leave. When two of these students did get up to leave and were confronted by teachers, one student said, "I can't talk right now," hurried away, and left the building, and the other student obeyed and returned to the cafeteria. Neither student said anything to the teachers about the weapon. Gladden excused himself to go to the bathroom, where he re-assembled and loaded the gun. He then tucked it under his shirt and returned to the cafeteria. Standing in the room crowded with dozens of students, he pulled the gun out, lowered the barrel and opened fire [1].

Gladden intended that morning to kill as many people as he could. We know that from his words recorded on video during a police interrogation later that day, as well as from the full recording of his confession posted online [2]. In the conversation with Baltimore County police detectives, Gladden, in an eerily calm manner, describes in chilling detail his motivations and actions that day. He brought 21 rounds with him because that was all the ammunition his father had in the house. He planned on using it all with the last round saved for him. Suicide had been on his mind for years and he had a suicide note in his pocket. In it he wrote: "Lifes (sic) just not something I enjoy, I hate people. I was just gonna off myself but then realized that, I'd rather make a point." In the police interview he said the shooting was "to make a point. That the world is a fucked-up place." In his words, he wanted to "off" as many people as possible before killing himself.

School shootings have become tragically common in America. The words "Sandy Hook," "Columbine," and "Virginia Tech," are part of the national vocabulary and bring to mind horrific images of grisly mass murders. The damage inflicted by these mass killings reverberates through the families and communities affected and radiates outward. The pain is permanent and can never be fully healed. The dozens of lesser-known shooting events that differ primarily in lower casualty figures also destroy families and communities. Recently, I attended an active shooter teacher workshop. I learned some useful survival and defense strategies for the event that an active shooter is ever on my campus or enters my classroom, but my colleagues and I left the session muttering about the tragic fact that teacher training now includes this topic.

Just as disturbing, however, is the response of many adults to mass shootings. In the aftermath of these events, guns-rights activists flood the airwaves and drown out the discussion on an appropriate public response with uncompromising, emotionally engaging narratives that leave no room for compromise. There is absolutely no willingness to have a meaningful public discussion on the issues of guns and violence in America. No serious discussion of modifying or expanding existing laws regulating guns to improve public safety.

Gun advocates regard any law regulating the sale of guns, no matter how reasonable or benign, as an intolerable infringement on their civil rights, and they go to extreme measures to demonstrate this. In the aftermath of the 26 murders at Sandy Hook Elementary School, sales of assault rifles and high capacity ammunition clips actually soared as gun enthusiasts rushed to buy these weapons simply because many fellow citizens said they shouldn't be able to buy these kinds of weapons. Reasonable suggestions for background checks to screen out the mentally disturbed were denounced as "inconveniencing" and placing an "unnecessary burden" on law-abiding gun buyers. Some organized groups, such as Open Carry Texas [3] flouted their legal entitlement to own and carry assault weapons. Members staged demonstrations in which they converged simultaneously on a public business while openly carrying assault rifles, forcing national corporations such as Starbucks [4] and Target [5] to explicitly ask people not to openly carry firearms in their businesses because of the discomfort it causes many of their customers.

Ostensibly, we send children to school, in part, to learn how to transition from their youthful self-centeredness to the mature understanding of their relationships to others that will be expected of them as adults. This includes an understanding that, in the adult world, rights come with responsibilities.

Constitutional rights in particular, we teach students, have limits. Laws that benefit the whole of society will be personally inconvenient at times; an individual's needs and desires are not all that matters because other people exist too, people with different perspectives, different circumstances, and different legitimate goals. Consequently, compromise is a necessary part of any negotiation in our democracy. However, these core values of responsibility, perspective, and compromise—values that adults say they want schools to teach children—are often openly violated in public by these same adults.

Public discourse concerning gun violence is one example. The arguments for unfettered, unregulated, universal, instant access to any kind of gun ring with self-righteous indignation. They represent a self-centered immature way of thinking that has become all too common on many issues. In an ideal educational setting, this kind of thinking is the opposite of what we should value and teach our children in schools. But instead of reasoned debate and compromise, what occurs for gun violence, and many other issues, are "educated" adults constructing emotionally engaging narratives, often dressed up with pseudoscience, that present false choices purposely intended to thwart any real progress on difficult societal problems.

The Dark Side of Storytelling

The debate on guns is another example of the technique of using emotionally engaging, pseudoscientific narratives to construct self-serving false choices. Arguments surrounding gun violence are actually pseudoscientific by design because Congress intentionally suppresses data on gun violence. Over two decades ago, scientists at the Centers for Disease Control and Prevention (CDC) suggested that gun violence should be treated as a public health problem. Congress responded in 1996 by passing the Dickey Amendment, which effectively cut off funding for CDC research on gun violence. Worried that other researchers might start investigations of their own, Congress followed up in 2003 with the Tiahrt Amendments, which forbade federal agencies from sharing gun data with researchers or the general public. Massive data suppression and inhibition of independent research renders the science that exists on gun violence unreliable. It removes some of the essential elements for doing science described in Chapter 1. Congress has abetted the purveyors of pseudoscientific narratives surrounding guns by mandating willful ignorance.

In Chapter 2, I discussed the sales adage: "Facts tell; stories sell." It succinctly sums up the scientific fact that narratives constructed in the form of a story are a much more engaging and memorable means of persuasion than bullet points on a Powerpoint slide. Stories sequence events on a timeline with a clearly marked beginning, middle and end, and they link cause and effect in a way that is easy to understand and helpful in remembering. The protagonists and antagonists are usually easy to identify (unless it's a mystery genre and then figuring that out is part of the fun). Good storytellers don't give out plot and character details all at once, but instead tantalize their audience by revealing one tidbit at a time. The sense of anticipation created, wanting to know what will happen next, is the secret to keeping the audience engaged. It is the reason reviewers use "spoiler alerts" to warn potential audience members that their enjoyment of a story might be reduced by knowing too much beforehand.

Stories are so powerful that any how-to guide on marketing, or public speaking, or non-fiction writing will advise the presenter to use stories. I am using this technique to write this chapter. In setting its background, I could have started with a bulleted list that summarizes statistics on school shootings and casualty figures. But I know that numbers tend to be numbing. Instead I chose to present a narrative of one particular school shooting. In the narrative, I included highly specific details that engage all the senses. The "bottle of vodka," the snippet of dialog "I can't talk right now," and the "reassembling the weapon in the bathroom," create an emotional response by placing the reader on the scene. I am also using the storyteller's technique of delaying gratification. You are wondering what happened at Perry Hall after Robert Gladden opened fire and you anticipate that, if you keep reading, I will eventually reveal the outcome. I did drop one teaser by indirectly revealing that Gladden survived the shooting. How else could he have given a confession afterwards? You also suspect that I will eventually reveal the reason I am profiling this particular school shooting, out of the dozens that I could have chosen. You are correct on those suspicions.

In fact, the technique of narrative non-fiction, particularly for popular histories and biographies, is widely used by writers. The technique is so effective that many of my college students have a difficult time distinguishing fiction from non-fiction. A novel completely imagined by its author and a documented, factual account of a historical event presented using the narrative structure of a novel are often difficult for students to distinguish. And therein lies the dark side of storytelling. Stories remove all the messiness from real life and distill complicated events, people, and motivations into heroic struggles of good versus evil. By framing all debate on public issues in terms of stories, polarization and gridlock is assured. The fact is few people ever see themselves as villains. The villains in your story are most likely the heroes in theirs. Remarkably, competing stories may sequence the same events, but never actually intersect. Instead, the audience is called on to make a choice between conflicting narratives. This is often a false choice because usually elements of truth are found in both and reasonable compromises are available. To overcome these obstacles, it is necessary to learn to "re-frame" stories. By that I mean to take a standard narrative, and after substituting different actors and issues, look for any logical contradictions that ensue.

Reframing Stories

For example, consider the Second Amendment, which is an almost sacred text to organized gun advocacy groups such as the National Rifle Association (NRA). For all the hype surrounding the Second Amendment, it should be noted that the word "gun" never appears, nor does the word appear anywhere else in the Constitution. The Second Amendment states: *A well regulated militia, being necessary to the security of a free state, the right of the people to keep and bear arms, shall not be infringed.* The plural noun "arms" includes a great variety of weaponry of widely varying lethality. Bayonets, pistols, rifles, machine guns, grenades, mortars, missiles and thermonuclear bombs are all "arms." The government can and does regulate the ownership and sale of arms. In fact, with the exception of guns and knives, individuals cannot privately own most kinds of armaments and deploy them in their self-defense. You cannot mine your lawn to keep away trespassers, aim a mortar at your neighbor's house if you feel threatened, or mount an anti-aircraft battery on your roof. People do not have a constitutional right to own any "arms" that they desire. The singling out of guns as being different from all other types of arms, and somehow exempt from any regulations defies the wording of the Second Amendment.

I am a believer in Second Amendment rights. I believe that people should be able to privately own guns for hunting, shooting, and personal protection. I believe that military-grade armaments should be born by citizens with proper training in the military—or a "well regulated militia" as the amendment states. I see no conflict with my support of the Second Amendment and my support of laws to regulate military-grade weaponry, which should include assault rifles. But in the narrative promoted by groups such as the NRA, any regulation of ownership of any kind of gun is a denial of Second Amendment rights to all. In the NRA narrative, anyone who supports any kind of reasonable regulation of guns is perceived as a threat to all gun owners. In the false choice they present, gun rights are either absolute or non-existent. I know of no other right enumerated by the Constitution that is granted, completely unfettered with no regulation and no commensurate responsibility.

In fact, using many elements of the gun rights narrative leads to logical contradictions the moment it is "re-framed." For example, consider the organized groups of demonstrators that showed up at a Starbucks openly carrying assault rifles. Photographs of these demonstrations primary show white persons, mostly males, with no obvious religious or ethnic affiliations [6].

Now imagine a group of darker-skin men with assault rifles all wearing Muslim garments and speaking Arabic arriving at the same Starbucks. I think it's safe to say all the baristas and customers would flee in fear and a massive heavily armed police response would ensue.

Imagine a group of young black men with assault rifles. Actually, this scenario does not have to be imagined. A single black man with an object that *might* be a gun can provoke dangerous levels of fear. In August 2014, police fatally shot John Crawford III, a 22-year old black man, inside an Ohio Walmart after he picked up an air rifle from a store shelf to examine for possible purchase. Immediately, fearful customers called police. Store surveillance video contradicted police claims that Crawford pointed the toy gun at them or anyone else; moreover, Ohio is a state that allows open carry of weapons anyway. No police were charged in Crawford's killing [7].

A similar killing happened 3 months later in November 2014, also in Ohio. Police fatally shot 12-year old Tamir Rice, a black child playing with a toy gun in a public park. A fearful bystander had called police. Again surveillance video contradicted police claims that Rice was given a chance to drop the weapon; rather, he was gunned down within two seconds of the police arriving [8]. No police were charged in Rice's killing [9].

Consider a different element of the gun rights narrative—that an armed citizenry is necessary for protection from government tyranny. Gun rights advocates claim that without guns in homes the government would abuse its power and citizens would have no defense [10]. But these advocates appear oblivious to the fact that this situation has already occurred. The United States has a highly militarized police force at all levels—local, state, federal—that routinely storms private homes using unnecessary military-style assault tactics on often mistaken or false pretenses. Many innocent civilians have been killed or injured in these kinds of raids, rarely resulting in any police accountability. Journalists who have chronicled the militarization of the policing in America, [11] and bloggers who cover police abuses of civil rights have no shortage of examples of armed home invasions by police on flimsy or fraudulent pretenses [12].

An armed citizenry has led to an arms race with police, not greater respect for civil rights and private property. The instances whereby homeowners have turned the tables and killed policemen raiding their homes hardly seems like a desirable outcome or solution to the problem. Demilitarization of the police needs to happen through the political process, not by armed confrontation with citizens.

Now consider substituting a different right into the narrative—say a First Amendment right instead of the Second Amendment. Imagine a group of people converging on a Starbucks to publically assert their First Amendment rights by publically viewing pornography on the wi-fi network. I think it's safe to assume that the store would unplug the network and ask them to leave.

The fact is all First Amendment rights come with social limitations—people cannot express themselves, or assemble, or worship anyway they please without social sanctions for conduct deemed excessive or outrageous—and they also come with legal limitations. Just as we have numerous laws defining, regulating, and limiting First Amendment rights, the same is true of Second Amendment rights. In addition to laws regulating military weaponry, the varying gun laws in most states and municipalities reflect our tradition of federalism in the United States. NRA head Wayne LaPierre in Senate testimony called on the government to "enforce the thousands of gun laws already on the books." [13] But his call to action is an admission that gun laws exist and that the government has a right to create and enforce them. In addition, the NRA's first reaction—it was later recanted—to open carry demonstrations criticized them as socially inappropriate. The initial NRA statement: "using guns merely to draw attention to yourself in public not only defies common sense, it shows a lack of consideration and manners." [14]

Clearly the gun rights narrative presents a false choice. All sides agree that there should be limits—both legal and social. And, once that premise is agreed upon there is no reason not to have a discussion on defining and enforcing reasonable laws. Balancing public safety and individual rights is part of living in a democratic society.

False Choices for Financing Education

But when it comes to the safety, maintenance, and operation of our schools, the gun rights narrative isn't the only pseudoscientific false choice foisted on the public. Consider the issue of levying taxes to pay for education. Government funding of education is often framed in terms of a false choice in order to serve corporate and political interests that have nothing to do with education.

Consider the state where I live—Maryland. The state has a history of promoting state-sanctioned gambling activities in order to fund its government.

In 2008, the formerly anti-gambling governor Martin O'Malley became pro-gambling when faced with a large state budget deficit brought about by the financial crisis in the United States that year. The governor and the state legislator went to the voters with a ballot initiative that if passed, would legalize casinos with slot machines. The pitch to the voters—revenue from slot machines would be allocated towards the funding of K-12 education because the money would be directed to the Education Trust Fund (ETF). And so, in November 2008 nearly 59% of Maryland voters approved legalizing slot machines.

In the years that followed hundreds of millions of dollars from casino revenues began flowing to the ETF, which was used to replace state funding cuts. No enhancement in education spending resulted. The entire pitch to voters had been nothing but an accounting gimmick. Soon afterwards, the casinos were unhappy with only operating slot machines and felt that to stay competitive in an increasingly tight gambling market it would be necessary to also offer table games. In 2012 a ballot initiative to legalize table games went to the voters. The pitch: money from table games would go to education.

During the weeks leading up to the November 2012 vote, I found the TV commercials in favor of legalizing table games painful to watch. Many of them featured teachers pleading with voters to support legalized gambling because the additional revenue would provide more educational opportunities for children. I wondered how children watching the commercials would process them. Would they worry that there might not be enough classroom supplies or textbooks if neighbors couldn't lose money on roulette? Would they worry that their teachers might lose their jobs if mom and dad couldn't play blackjack? Politicians also appeared in these commercials promising that this time the law made sure that gambling money would only be used for education—an assurance that was also an admission that, despite the promises four years earlier, the slot machine revenue did not enhance education funding [15].

Personally, I am rather libertarian on the issue of recreational gambling. I rarely play slot machines because I find them boring, but I don't object to anyone else playing them. I am an avid poker player. I find poker a fascinating game and I am a regular at the poker tables in several casinos in the northeast. I think poker should be a legal activity. However, my recreational choices, and those of others, should have nothing to do with funding education.

Again, let's re-frame the issue and imagine some different TV commercials in support of an alternative gambling proposal. Instead of a teacher in a classroom substitute a state lawmaker in an office. Imagine a member of the state legislature, standing by a desk, looking directly into the camera and saying: "Lawmaking is time and labor-intensive work with a need to pay for office staff, supplies, travel, and research. Money is tight, but if you vote yes on the new gambling proposal, all the additional revenue generated will go directly to pay the salaries and benefits for lawmakers and their office staff. Don't worry that the money from gambling might be used for other purposes, like education. The money must be used to support the work of your governor, and state senate and house representatives, because that's the law."

Of course, there will never be such a commercial, let alone such a proposed law. Politicians believe that state sponsored gambling is only acceptable to the public if the revenue that results furthers the government's loftier goals, such as education. No politician would suggest gambling to financially support the government's mundane or unpopular activities. Try to imagine a law to expand gambling as a means to pay the salaries of the state's tax auditors. It's not possible. Politicians would never pay for education first and then propose that voters approve the use of gambling revenue to pay their own salaries and office staff expenses. They know that proposition is a losing bet.

The table games initiative did pass. I can now enjoy poker here in Baltimore rather than trek to Atlantic City. But did it increase funds available for education? In May 2013, shortly after table games went live in the Maryland casinos, a *Baltimore Sun* editorial noted that state casino gaming revenue decreased from $28.2 million in the last month of slot machines to $26.1 million for the first month of slots plus table games, while the casino's share of the revenue increased from $14.7 million to $19.3 million [16]. As the editorial noted: "The addition of blackjack, poker and roulette has shifted wagering from the kind of gambling where the state gets a big cut (slots) to one where it gets much less."

This outcome should have been predictable if the table games proposal had been given some thought. Casinos do not magically create money, as many politicians seem to believe. In contrast to many other economic activities that create wealth, gambling does not. Gambling is a zero-sum game because the gambler's net loss is the casino's net gain. There is a finite amount of money available for recreational gambling. When table games appeared, the casinos didn't take in significantly more money. Instead the finite amount was partitioned between the table games and the slot machines. Compared to slot revenues, casinos must keep a larger fraction of the table game revenues in order to stay in business because table games are much more expensive to operate.

However, the allure of using state-sanctioned vice to fund education is just too seductive for politicians to pass on. Two years later in 2014, a Maryland state delegate, Heather Mizeur, mounted a surprisingly strong, although ultimately unsuccessful, challenge in the Democratic primary for governor to the party favorite, Anthony Brown. The centerpiece of her campaign: a proposal to legalize marijuana and use the additional tax revenues to pay for education [17, 18]. During the primary campaign, I had an opportunity to have breakfast with Heather Mizeur along with a group of other people and ask questions in person. I asked her why proposals to legalize a vice, like hers for marijuana or the earlier gambling proposals, were always tied to education funding, and not some other service that the government provides. I pointed out that it is always an accounting gimmick because money for education is never increased when these proposals pass. These kinds of proposals are always false choices. She acknowledged the validity of my question, but explained that her campaign's polling had shown that linking marijuana legalization to education funding made the proposal, and her campaign, much more attractive to voters. Sadly, this poll's finding says more about voters' decision-making processes than it does about Heather Mizeur's.

Aftermaths

In January 2017, the CEO of the Baltimore City School District announced plans to layoff hundreds of employees—including many teachers—in order to close a $130 million budget shortfall [19]. The Horseshoe casino in downtown Baltimore had been enormously successful since its 2014 opening—generating more than $200 million for the ETF. However, from 2014 to 2017 state funding for the Baltimore city schools had actually *decreased* because no changes to the state formula for funding schools had ever been made [20]. As a result, excess money in the ETF was being used for state government expenditures not related to education. After all, regardless of their origin, all dollars are created equal.

And, sadly, mass shootings at schools, businesses, and workplaces continue unabated with no meaningful discussion of how to prevent and limit the carnage. Coverage in the national media for each shooting is simply proportional to the number of casualties. I suspect most of my readers are unfamiliar with the Perry Hall shooting because it was not a mass casualty event and, as a result, produced only a few paragraphs in the national news the next day. Despite Robert Gladden's intentions, "Perry Hall" is not in the national lexicon today, in the way that the words Sandy Hook, Columbine, and Virginia Tech, are. The reason is the kind of weapon that Gladden had access to. He did not come to school that day with an assault rifle or a semi-automatic handgun and multiple high-capacity ammunition clips. The weapon he took from his father the night before was a double-barreled Western Field shotgun with 21 individual shells for ammunition.

When Gladden opened fire, the first round struck 17-year old Daniel Borowy in the back, grievously wounding him. An alert and courageous teacher, Jesse Wasmer, charged and tackled Gladden. In the struggle that ensued the gun discharged a second time into the ceiling. More adults piled on and within seconds they had Gladden subdued without further injuries. Borowy was rushed to the hospital in critical condition.

The Perry Hall high school shooting demonstrates that the kinds of weapons disturbed individuals have access to makes a huge difference in the lethality of their murderous rampages. Had Gladden's father owned an assault rifle with high-capacity magazine clips the outcome would have been much different that day. The ability to spray the crowded cafeteria with 30 bullets in a matter of seconds would have resulted in multiple deaths and any teacher who tried to intervene would have been killed instantly. The words "Perry Hall" would today bring to mind horrific images of bloody carnage and senseless death in the same way that the words "Sandy Hook" and "Columbine" do. Senators, House Representatives, and gun advocates and lobbyists, who claim that *all* guns should be treated equally under the law and that *no* gun regulations should exist, are demonstrating willful ignorance of the differences between various kinds of guns.

Despite his status as a minor—15 years of age at the time of the shooting—Robert Gladden Jr. was charged as an adult with attempted first-degree murder. When the Sandy Hook massacre happened on December 14, 2012, he was in a Baltimore County jail. Afterwards he stated in a recorded call from the jail with a cousin: "You know what school I wish I went to? Sandy Hook Elementary." In February 2013 Gladden pleaded guilty and was sentenced to 35 years in prison. The sentence went way beyond the state guidelines of 20–30 years. In handing down the stiffer sentence, the judge called Gladden's comments about the Sandy Hook massacre "unforgivable" [1, 21].

Daniel Borowy survived and recovered from his wounds. His mother says that Daniel, who has Down's syndrome, does not fully comprehend what happened. Less than two months after the shooting, on October 7, 2012, Daniel Borowy joined Jesse Wasmer on the field at Oriole Park at Camden Yards. Before a sell-out crowd and national television audience for an Oriole post-season game, Wasmer threw out the ceremonial first pitch—a public acknowledgment of his heroism during the shooting [22].

Schools Are Not Cultural Islands

Of course, it could be argued that schools should only be focused on academics and that teaching values is best left to families and churches. A personal stand on an issue that I might consider self-centered and immature may be moral, courageous, and principled in another person's narrative. In this view, teachers should restrict their instruction solely to academic skills and avoid injecting their personal values and biases into discussions. The role of the teacher should only be to instill and uphold academic standards.

The primacy of academic standards is one education issue on which there is apparently bipartisan agreement. Standards-based curricula, such as the recent Common Core, and school accountability through standardized tests are issues on which there is broad agreement across much of the political spectrum. Schools are called on to be "rigorous" and children are admonished that schoolwork must come before sports and leisure activities. However, the consensus on the primacy of academic standards apparently applies only within the confines of classrooms. Adults conveniently exempt themselves from the academic rigor, standards, and accountability that they want enforced on children and teachers.

Outside of classrooms, public discourse has been turned into a sport for the entertainment of the masses. There is no longer any pretense of serious discussion to solve communal problems. Instead all issues are framed in terms of an "us versus them" competition. Sports, like stories, entertain and do so for similar reasons. Sporting events feature heroes battling villains. The heroes must outwit and outlast the opposition in order to reach a triumphant ending that is often in doubt. Most competitions have a narrative arc that can be recounted in story form by the media and the fans.

Like stories, sports can be uplifting and bring communities together through a shared experience. But, there is also a dark side to turning everything into a contest. No problems are ever solved. Sports are by definition repetitious. Year after year, generation after generation, games such as baseball, football, basketball, and others unfold in accordance with the same timeless rules and rituals. The outcomes of the individual games and playing seasons are morally neutral. Good "sportsmanship" is admired—that is playing by the rules, doing one's best, striving for excellence, being gracious in defeat and victory—but from a moral viewpoint it doesn't matter who wins or loses so long as everyone plays by the rules. This moral neutrality allows people to cheer for their favorite players and teams without having to justify their reasons.

Grading Politicians

But when politicians and corporate leaders debate and weigh issues, the final decision is not morally neutral. There are often serious problems impacting the livelihoods and well being of millions of people that need to be solved. In the process of turning every debate on an issue into sport, and resorting to repetitive, unproductive patterns of action, academic standards are routinely mocked by many of the same people who make a big show slamming teachers and schools. Do they really expect our children to value what they do not? The purpose of education is to instill the academic standards necessary to debate and resolve issues in a productive manner. Consider typical public discourse and how adults would fare in various subjects if held to the same standards as school children.

English: Debates in Congress frequently include politicians taking the floor to denounce proposals as being "politically motivated" and to accuse colleagues of "playing politics" or of acting to "gain a political advantage." Actually, a politician is a person who practices politics. These kinds of accusations are as trite as saying that I, a physicist, practice physics. In fact, most of the rhetoric in Congress is either trite or platitudinous. Everyone supports eliminating government waste, reducing the deficit, improving education, punishing criminals, and so on. Saying that you are for these things does not contribute in any meaningful way to public debate. This kind of content-free use of language would receive an F in English class.

Math: During the 2010 election, the Republicans made great fanfare with a "Pledge to America," [23] in which they outlined their plans to cut taxes while reducing the deficit. Did they understand the difference between addition and subtraction? At the same time, President Obama announced plans to cut the deficit in half by the end of his term. Did he understand that any non-zero deficit represents an additional accumulation of debt, and that half of a very large number is still a large number? Neither side produced numbers for deficit reduction that made any sense—and this is a math problem involving simple arithmetic, not advanced calculus! Yes, both parties promised that their policies would fix the disparities between the positive and negative numbers by promoting "jobs and economic growth." But math also teaches that extremely rapid growth is unsustainable, a fact demonstrated twice in recent history by economic implosions in dotcom and real estate. As I write this, in 2017, U. S. debt continues to accumulate at an alarming rate.

Reading: A disturbing cultural attitude has developed in regard to reading. When in agreement with the writer people say, "that's the truth," and when in disagreement people say, "that's biased." Actually, all writing is biased. In school, it is taught that a written piece should have a point of view, an intended audience, a central argument and factual evidence supporting the argument. It is the reader's job to render judgment on the validity of the argument and the relevance and weight of the evidence. But, if we stop reading after encountering a central argument that we don't like, and never consider the evidence for it, we stop learning. It is imperative to read viewpoints different from our own, and give them careful consideration even if we still decide to disagree. It is intellectually dishonest to dismiss everyone we disagree with as biased and laud all those we agree with as sources of truth.

Indeed, the trait of intellectual honesty, which is so vital to academic discourse, is the one most absent in public debate. An intellectually honest person constructs arguments based on facts, not by demonizing people who hold opposing viewpoints. Relevant facts that contradict an argument are acknowledged and addressed, not purposely omitted or distorted. Pursuit of the truth is the goal, not validation of personal beliefs.

But when public discourse is framed as an "us versus them" contest, facts become almost irrelevant. Politicians and pundits argue for their sides by cherry-picking facts and twisting arguments in ways that would never be acceptable in an academic setting. Students who write and debate in the manner of today's politicians and pundits would receive failing grades.

A New Genre of Comedy

In fact, intellectual dishonesty has become so pervasive in public discourse that it has given rise to an entire genre of comedy programming. Comedy Central's *The Daily Show* and the now discontinued *Colbert Report* mock intellectual dishonesty using a simple comedic formula. Lest you think that these comedy shows are irrelevant, many of my college students tell me that this is the only news they watch—not an unreasonable choice given that the news offered by the major networks has degenerated into prurient tabloid journalism. And what the students see on these comedy shows is not a flattering portrait of the adult leaders in our society.

These shows have a steady and inexhaustible supply of comedic material. The formula is simple: a video is played showing a politician taking a stand on an issue, followed by a video of the same politician taking the opposite stand on the same issue. The comedian then cracks jokes that play on the cognitive dissonance.

For example, in a skit on the *Daily Show*, an actor dressed as a professional wrestler parrots Democratic arguments made against Senate filibusters while the party enjoyed majority status in the Senate. The same wrestler switches persona to parrot Democratic arguments made in favor of filibusters when the party had minority status [24]. The message is clear: senators are as sincere as the wrestlers seen on TV.

On the *Colbert Report,* Sarah Palin is shown calling for White House Chief of Staff Rahm Emmanuel to resign because he used the word "retard" in a meeting. Audio is played from Rush Limbaugh's radio show in which he makes repeated use of the word "retard" followed by Sarah Palin's defense of Limbaugh's use of the word [25].

Night after night this goes on. Congressional Democrats promise "ethics reform" in one video, while in the next video these same Democrats refuse to acknowledge their own ethical violations. Republican indignation over deficit spending is juxtaposed with Dick Cheney's claim made when he was vice-president that "deficits don't matter."

Journalists are also lampooned. A telling moment about our culture came in Jon Stewart's interview with MSNBC financial journalist Jim Cramer on *The Daily Show*. Cramer defended his poor stock picking advice by claiming that the CEOs of the failed companies that he recommended lied to him. When Stewart suggested that he not take at face value what CEOs say, Cramer responded with a bizarre defense. He said: "I'm not Eric Sevareid. I'm not Edward R. Morrow. I'm a guy trying to do an entertainment show about business for people to watch" [26]. In short, Cramer defended himself by asserting that he needs to entertain an audience that would tune him out if his talk became too technical.

The irony of this exchange is breathtaking. A comedian is asking relevant questions while a journalist pleads that he doesn't ask questions because he needs to entertain.

The fact is our public discourse is so rife with intellectual dishonesty that the politicians and pundits are fooling no one. The humor in these shows is that the people being lampooned apparently believe their own pronouncements. It is like laughing at an inept magician, whose tricks are obvious to everyone but himself. This transparent intellectual dishonesty is not lost on young people; they see calls for higher educational standards for what they are: self-aggrandizement for adults, not concern for children. In fact, many politicians openly denounce educated people as "elitists" while at the same time demand more education for our youth.

Schools cannot be cultural islands. Our government and corporate leaders clamor for higher educational standards, increased accountability for teachers, and more students trained in math and science. But it is clear that these same leaders advocate policies in ways that would not meet the barest minimum standards for a passing grade in any academic subject, and are quick to dodge accountability for themselves. We do not tolerate intellectual dishonesty from our children in our schools. But it is apparently tolerated and promoted everywhere else. Educational standards cannot be improved until adults begin to model the education values that they loudly espouse.

Dismembering Literature to Avoid its Truths

Stories are powerful for a reason. Some truths can only be revealed through narrative. No amount of explanation or analysis will ever be more clear and lucid than the works of great literature in revealing the complexities of the human struggle and the timeless truths of what it means to be human. Unfortunately, school curricula have a way of discouraging love of literature by taking powerful stories and dismembering them into lists of facts to remember and be tested on. Consider the following sample test question for the novel *1984*.

Reread the following sentences from the excerpt.

"The patrols did not matter, however. Only the Thought Police mattered."
According to details in the excerpt, what is the most logical reason that the patrols do not "matter" but the Thought Police do matter?

A. People are already accustomed to helicopters flying near their windows, but the idea of Thought Police is recent and unfamiliar.
B. People are pleased to have helicopter patrols keeping everyone safe, but they don't see how the Thought Police keep them safe.
C. People can see when the patrols are snooping but cannot ever know exactly when the Thought Police are snooping.
D. People know that the helicopters appear only in a few winter months but the Thought Police are active most of the year.

--- Sample question aligned with Common Core State Standards from a Grade 8 Literature Mini-Assessment on the novel *1984* by George Orwell [27].

The question requires students to carefully parse the details of the text, but it has little relevance to the fundamental truths about the human condition that the story reveals.

The novel *1984* by George Orwell is a frequently assigned middle/high school text [28]. Published in 1949, it portrays a dystopian vision of the future in which a totalitarian government controls all facets of its citizens' lives. The instrument for control is fear. A massive surveillance program—"Big Brother"—that monitors a person's every action, a state of endless war, a continual rewriting of history to make the past consistent with whatever present the government decrees, distortions of language—"doublespeak"—as an instrument of thought control, all of these combine to create an interminable sense of fear that keep the masses in their places and the government in power. Holding power is the government's only goal. It has no interest in solving problems or working towards a better future for its citizens because doing so would lessen the ubiquitous fear and threaten the government's hold on power.

Another dystopian novel of the first half of the twentieth century—*Brave New World* by Aldus Huxley published in 1932—depicts a competing vision of totalitarianism that employs different, although equally disturbing, methods of control [29]. In this dystopia, a small group of "world controllers" rule a single "World State" and control all aspects of their subjects' lives from artificial breeding in "hatcheries and conditioning centers" to a planned death at age 60. The instrument for control of the population is pleasure. The masses—lower castes—are bred for low intelligence and provided menial jobs commensurate with their limited abilities, along with sufficient food, housing, and "soma" rations. Soma is a drug used to keep everyone in a peaceful state of bliss with no ambition or desire for self-improvement or advancement. Meanwhile the upper castes are provided a materialistic and hedonistic lifestyle in which they revel in drug-induced euphoria and sexual pleasure. Education consists of conditioning citizens to accept their place in the social structure and avoid critical thinking, scientific inquiry, serious literature, or any individual initiative. This program of control is effective because no one is dissatisfied.

To summarize, in Orwell's dystopia people are taught what to think; in Huxley's they are taught not to think. As Neil Postman in his 1985 book *Amusing Ourselves to Death* put it:

> "What Orwell feared were those who would ban books. What Huxley feared was that there would be no reason to ban a book, for there would be no one who wanted to read one. Orwell feared those who would deprive us of information. Huxley feared those who would give us so much that we would be reduced to passivity and egotism. Orwell feared that the truth would be concealed from us. Huxley feared the truth would be drowned in a sea of irrelevance." [30, p. vii]

Postman then went on to argue that it is Huxley, not Orwell who was right.

"As Huxley remarked in Brave New World Revisited, the civil libertarians and rationalists who are ever on the alert to oppose tyranny *"failed to take into account man's almost infinite appetite for distractions."* [30, p. viii]

Postman presents a compelling case that Huxley's vision is the future. His analysis is especially prescient given that he wrote it before the World Wide Web, smartphones, Youtube, Facebook, downloadable music, text messaging, and all the other sources of unending distraction that render masses of people oblivious to their political, social, and natural environments. He also wrote before anti-depressants became some of the most widely prescribed drugs in America, and prior to the surge of prescription drugs for school children to mollify various hyperactive and attention-deficit behaviors deemed incompatible with the classroom environment. Prescription drug use in America has become eerily reminiscent of Huxley's fictional "soma."

I would argue that both Orwell and Huxley are alive and well, but reside on opposite sides of the current political spectrum. The political right is oblivious to how Orwellian they have become. Right wing politicians and media serve up a constant drumbeat of fear and bogeymen. From al-Qaida and its offshoots, to ISIL, to Iranian mullahs, to North Korean nuclear weapons, to illegal immigrants pouring over our borders, we are surrounded by existential threats from all manners of evildoers bent on our destruction. The fear is used to justify massive government surveillance programs that would have been the envy of organizations like the Soviet KGB or the East German Stasi. In addition, the United States has slid into a condition of perpetual, open-ended warfare, with frequent calls for new military interventions—Libya, Syria, Iran. Military jargon has become laced with Orwellian doublespeak: "servicing the target" for bombing, "collateral damage" for killing innocents, and so on. Rather than learn from past mistakes, the political right rewrites history to suit its current narratives—think of the constantly evolving justifications for the Iraq war—and it aligns with fundamentalist religious groups that seek to use the force of law to impose tight control on people's behaviors so that all private actions will align with narrow and self-contradictory interpretations of religious texts.

The political left is oblivious to how much like Huxley they have become. The rhetoric from the left is suffused with a denial of human agency. People don't make decisions, but are conditioned by their upbringings and environments. Obesity is a "disease," sub-prime borrowers are "victims of predatory lenders," problem gamblers have "addictions," and female sex workers are "prostituted women." Government must act as a protector, using full force of law if necessary, to limit the availability of bad choices—supersized soft drinks, payday loans, Internet gambling, paid sex, and so on. Speech is limited not by fear of imprisonment, but by a suffocating political correctness that can end a career and result in quick social ostracism for an offhand comment deemed flippant or insensitive, even if made in private conversation. Language must be cleansed of words that acquire negative stereotypes—crippled, retarded, and so on. Sensitive topics must come with "trigger warnings," to avoid exposing fragile egos to damaging psychological trauma. Everyone has a right to work in an environment free from exposure to any language or expression that they deem personally offensive. Of even more consequence, it is acceptable for people to be too busy and distracted to engage in public life. In the 2012 presidential election, only 57.5% of eligible citizens in the United States exercised their most fundamental civil right—to vote [31].

There are some truths in both the narratives of the political right and left. There really are bad people who mean to do harm to the United States and it citizens. Intelligence gathering is necessary if the government is to make informed decisions. Environments exert a strong influence on people. Many compulsive self-destructive behaviors have medical causes. But both sides engage in the storyteller's penchant for exaggeration. Both are oblivious to the darker side of their programs.

The novels *1984* and *Brave New World* are often assigned in schools, but rather than focus on the essential truths being spoken, the curriculum is all about facts that can be gleaned from the texts and tested. The tests will provide proof that "education" took place. Then the adults can ignore the truths and sit safely in their bubbles armed with the test data in case any questions are raised about the efficacy of the "education" their children received. No one will be asked to step back and examine their personal narratives, to ask if they are logically consistent, factually correct, or might just intersect at some points with competing narratives.

The Orwell and Huxley narratives are both still relevant because even though they appear mutually exclusive they exist side-by-side in our current society. It is perhaps why neo-conservatives and neo-liberals find agreement in the faux education that the culture of standardized curricula and testing is foisting on our children. Being taught what to think and being taught not to think amount to the same thing—neither condition is representative of a real education, nor do they model the educational values our schools are called on to teach. Both conditions benefit the ruling elites and erode our democracy.

References

1. Jessica Anderson, "Text messages show Gladden warned of bringing gun to school," *Baltimore Sun*, March 15, 2013, http://www.baltimoresun.com/news/maryland/baltimore-county/bs-md-co-gladden-20130315-story.html#page=1.
2. Confession of Perry Hall High School Shooter Robert Gladden, *Baltimore Sun*, March 16, 2013, http://www.baltimoresun.com/news/maryland/baltimore-county/perry-hall/bs-md-gladden-sentencing-20130225-story.html, video, 12:55, accessed May 1, 2018, https://www.youtube.com/watch?v=fKcDyDa6pGQ.
3. Open Carry Texas is a non-profit 501(c) 4 organization that advocates for the open carry of firearms in Texas, accessed May 1, 2018, http://www.opencarry-texas.org/.
4. Stephanie Strom, "Starbucks Seeks to Keep Guns Out of Its Coffee Shops," *New York Times*, September 18, 2013, http://www.nytimes.com/2013/09/19/business/starbucks-seeks-to-keep-guns-out-of-its-cofee-shops.html.
5. John Mulligan, "Target Addresses Firearms in Stores," July 2, 2014, https://corporate.target.com/article/2014/07/target-addresses-firearms-instores.
6. Photographs accessed August 17, 2015, http://www.opencarrytexas.org/events.html.
7. Elahe Izadi, "Ohio Wal-Mart surveillance video shows police shooting and killing John Crawford III," *Washington Post*, September 25, 2014, video, 00:53, accessed May 1, 2018, http://www.washingtonpost.com/news/post-nation/wp/2014/09/25/ohio-wal-mart-surveillance-videoshows-police-shooting-and-killing-john-crawford-iii/.
8. Full surveillance video release of Tamir Rice shot by police, video, 07:51, accessed May 1, 2018, https://www.youtube.com/watch?v=sdAYPQd1H1A.
9. Updates on the status of the investigation on the killing of Tamir Rice can be accessed at: https://en.wikipedia.org/wiki/Shooting_of_Tamir_Rice.
10. Wayne LaPierre, *Guns, Crime, and Freedom*, (Washington, DC: Regnery Publishing, 1994).
11. Radley Balko, *Rise of the Warrior Cop: The Militarization of America's Police Forces* (New York: Public Affairs, 2013).
12. See blogs chronicling police misconduct and brutality: accessed May 1, 2018, https://www.washingtonpost.com/people/radley-balko, accessed May 1, 2018, http://thefreethoughtproject.com/category/cop-watch/police-brutality-cop-watch/.
13. Wayne LaPierre, CEO of the National Rifle Association, Testimony before U. S. Senate Judiciary Committee on January 30, 2013, video, 10:21, accessed May 1, 2018, https://www.c-span.org/video/?c4344412/wayne-lapierres-opening-statement.
14. Doug Stanglin, "NRA view on guns in café campaign angers Texas group", *USA Today*, June 4, 2014, http://www.usatoday.com/story/news/nation/2014/06/03/texas-open-carry-nra-firearms-in-restaurants/9908271/.

15. Elizabeth Janney, "Despite Campaign Promises, Casinos—Not Schools—Are Big Financial Winners," *Maryland Patch*, June 22, 2014, http://patch.com/maryland/owingsmills/despite-campaign-promises-casinosnot-schoolsare-big-winners-financially.
16. "The state busts: How Maryland is losing money on table games," Editorial, *Baltimore Sun*, May 7, 2013, http://articles.baltimoresun.com/2013-05-07/news/bs-ed-slots-20130507_1_maryland-live-casino-table-games-gaming-control-commission.
17. Heather Mizeur, "Marijuana Legalization: A Comprehensive Plan to Legalize and Regulate Marijuana in Maryland," accessed August 17, 2015, http://www.heathermizeur.com/marijuana.
18. John Wagner, "Maryland gubernatorial hopeful Heather Mizeur to propose legalization of marijuana," *Washington Post*, November 19, 2013, http://www.washingtonpost.com/local/md-politics/maryland-gubernatorial-hopeful-heather-mizeur-to-propose-legalization-ofmarijuana/2013/11/19/32338a2e-50d4-11e3-a7f0-b790929232e1_story.html.
19. Tim Prudente, and Erica L. Green, "Baltimore City schools CEO looks to deep staff cuts to close $130 million budget gap" *Baltimore Sun*, January 27, 2017, http://www.baltimoresun.com/news/maryland/education/k-12/bs-md-ci-school-budget-cuts-20170126-story.html.
20. Luke Broadwater and Erica L. Green, "Casinos prosper; Schools do not," *Baltimore Sun*, January 22, 2017, http://digitaledition.baltimoresun.com/tribune/article_popover.aspx?guid=6aff6b1f-95b3-4666-9ccb-15716c23e1d0.
21. Jessica Anderson, "Perry Hall High School shooter Gladden gets 35 years in prison," *Baltimore Sun*, February 25, 2013, http://articles.baltimoresun.com/2013-02-25/news/bs-md-gladden-sentencing-20130225_1_robert-w-gladden-daniel-borowy-kathleenwatkins.
22. Photograph of Daniel Borowy and Jesse Wasmer throwing the ceremonial first pitch at Oriole Park at Camden Yards on October 7, 2012 retrieved from: http://darkroom.baltimoresun.com/2013/05/oj-brigance-first-pitch-als-night/bba-alds-yankees-orioles-2/.
23. Republicans in Congress, "Pledge to America: A new governing agenda built on the priorities of our nation, the principles we stand for and America's founding values," Republican Party, accessed August 16, 2015, http://www.gop.gov/resources/library/documents/solutions/apledge-to-america.pdf.
24. Jon Stewart, "Jon Stewart Enlists Mick Foley To Compare Politics To Professional Wrestling," Huffpost, filmed in New York, NY on May 16, 2010, video, 09:32, http://www.huffingtonpost.com/2010/03/16/jon-stewart-enlists-mick_n_500487.html.
25. Stephen Colbert, "Sarah Palin Is A F—king Retard," Huffpost, filmed in New York, NY on April 11, 2010, video, 05:12, http://www.huffingtonpost.com/2010/02/09/colbert-sarah-palin-is-a_n_454744.html.

26. Jon Stewart, "Exclusive – Jim Cramer Extended Interview, Part 1," Comedy Partners, filmed in New York, NY on March 12, 2009, video, 05:47, http://www. cc.com/video-clips/fttmoj/the-daily-show-with-jon-stewart-exclusive---jim-cramer-extended-interview-pt--1.

27. "Grade 8 Literature Mini-Assessment, Excerpt from 1984 by George Orwell," Student Achievement Partners, accessed May 1, 2018, http://achievethecore.org/page/921/1984-by-george-orwell-mini-assessment.

28. George Orwell, *1984* (London: Secker & Warburg, 1949).

29. Aldous Huxley, *Brave New World* (London: Chatto & Windus, 1932).

30. Neil Postman, *Amusing Ourselves to Death: Public Discourse in the Age of Show Business* (New York: Penguin, 1985).

31. "2012 Voter Turnout Report," (Washington, DC: Bipartisan Policy Center, 2012), http://bipartisanpolicy.org/library/2012-voter-turnout/.

7

School Choice: The Tautology of the Market

The use of "data-driven" metrics to define educational outcomes, the corruption of K-12 math education, the shilling of science education as a means to enhance corporate profits, the de-professionalization of teaching, and the abandonment of any pretense of intellectual honesty in the public arena all have a common purpose: to promote a narrative that education is in a state of crisis and must be reformed. The proposed solution, often advocated by the same groups that have constructed the crisis narrative, is a business model of education. These groups—private think-tanks, education reform advocates, corporate foundations, and their political allies—posit that the "crisis" in education would be remedied if schools were forced to operate like businesses and succeed or fail as market conditions permit.

The code words for this education reform agenda are "school choice" and "privatization." The logic is simple and seductive. In a market economy, consumers benefit from competition. If education is reduced to a commodity provided by corporate entities (aka schools), then the consumers (aka students/parents) will choose the best providers. Competition will force substandard schools to close and reward the successful schools with more students. Of course, a market economy is profit-driven: the investors and operators of the corporations (in this case, schools) primary motivation to succeed is potential profitability.

This in fact has become the view of many students, parents, corporations, and politicians, that education is purely a financial investment with payoffs in the form of increased future earnings for the students and greater profits for their future employers. And why shouldn't the principles of market economics be allowed to operate for education as it does other arenas of our daily lives? Consumers get to choose banking services, cell phone plans, restaurants, and

© Springer International Publishing AG, part of Springer Nature 2018
J. Ganem, *The Robot Factory*, https://doi.org/10.1007/978-3-319-77860-0_7

online shopping sites, and they benefit from this ability to choose. Investors choose which of these businesses they will finance with their scarce capital resources, and they will cut off funding if consumers flee because of unmet needs. The "free market" apparently works well for consumer goods and services, so why not turn education over to the market?

In addition, the wealthy have always had school choice. There are and always have been high-priced private schools from pre-school through college to which parents with sufficient financial resources can send their children. Students at these schools usually meet the reformers' criteria for successful educational outcomes: they do well on standardized tests and obtain high-paying jobs upon graduation. Curiously, these successful outcomes often occur without a profit motive or return on investment, since most traditional private schools are non-profit corporations.

The fact that many private schools perform very well without generating a profit is one clue that markets might not be a causal force for successful educational outcomes. This chapter illuminates the opposite—examples of profit-driven schools with poor outcomes—as evidence that markets are not a panacea for improving education. As I will demonstrate in this chapter, the logic and evidence for the effectiveness of market-based educational reform is highly questionable.

Free Markets: An Untestable Hypothesis

Proponents of market-based education reform, and privatization in general, tend to imbue the "free market" with near magical qualities. It is an "invisible hand" that channels the inherent selfishness of individuals into a collective force with unlimited creative power. This of course requires that the market be allowed to operate "freely." Do not try to find the "invisible hand" and guide its movement or it will cease to be. It has a kind of quantum indeterminacy; it is only there if you are not looking. If too many questions are asked about how the market works, or if too many attempts are made at regulation, its magic powers will be destroyed and failure will ensue.

Some proponents of the "free market" ascribe to it God-like abilities and frame their arguments in moral terms. These worshipers of the market even go so far as to believe that interfering with its workings is immoral. Many self-identified Christians conflate Jesus' teachings in the Gospels with market-based economic principles and free-market capitalism. For example, ministries that preach the "Prosperity Gospel," have millions of adherents in the United States. This theology—that promoters claim is Christian—teaches that God rewards the faithful with personal wealth [1]. By equating financial success with religious faith, capitalism and Christianity become intertwined in the minds of its true believers.

Nonetheless, however lofty the language the underlying assertion of free market advocates is always the same—public services will be improved through privatization because of the introduction of a profit motive. Problems that resist solution by the public sector will magically go away as individuals and companies seek to maximize profits and enhance their wealth.

Moral Hazards

What is often overlooked is an important distinction between the multitude of private markets that provide consumer goods and services and the privatization of public services. In consumer-driven markets private money is exchanged with private providers. All participants in the transaction have skin in the game. Alternatively, when public services are privatized, public money is transferred to private entities, which results in a very different kind of market dynamic with the government assuming most of the risk.

The difference between these two situations is stark. For the private consumer markets, the government might regulate the activities and provide a legal framework for enforcing contracts and settling disputes, but it is not ordinarily a party to the transaction. Exceptions occur when the government provides guarantees or insurance to facilitate private transactions— government-backed loans for home buying or student financial aid are examples. This is well known to result in "moral hazards," conditions in which the party receiving the guarantee can behave in a reckless or even dishonest manner because all risk is assumed by the government. The great recession of 2007–08 that was precipitated by massive fraud in government-backed mortgage securities is a large-scale example of the consequences of moral hazards.

When the government privatizes public services moral hazards are built in from the start. We have countless examples of private contractors of all types— medical, military, prisons, etc.—cutting deals with government agencies. These deals are often at the least ethically questionable; often they are based on outright lies and deceits. This precedence makes it rather difficult to assert that privatization of public services is somehow inherently more moral than the government providing these services.

Behaviorist Fallacies in the "Business Model"

In addition, the kind of "business model" that education privatization advocates envision usually relies on principles from behavioral psychology (behaviorism)—that is, carrot-and-stick incentives. "Pay for performance" is a common mantra. As I document in prior chapters, the primary motivation for implementing various tests and assessment metrics is the doling out of rewards and punishments to teachers, students, and schools. The assertion that outcomes are improved when people react to rewards and punishments rather than pro-act out of intrinsic motivation relies fundamentally on behaviorism. Conflating market economics with behaviorism is common; many businesses use behaviorism in the form of raises, performance bonuses, awards, and so on to manage employees.

Often overlooked, however, is the now substantial body of research that shows that behaviorism does not work well in business environments. In fact, research shows, schools and businesses might both be better off if they abandoned behaviorism. Markets might appear to follow behaviorist principles—doling out monetary rewards and punishments to the businesses that are most successful in meeting demand. But the individuals whose collective actions create the market have much more complicated motivations than pure behaviorism can describe. Businesses and schools that fail to understand this will not be as successful as those that do.

Most importantly, the conflation of behaviorism with market economics is part of a larger misunderstanding of cause and effect. Markets neither create nor innovate; only people can do those things. The demand for many "must-have" products today—automobiles, photocopiers, personal computers, cell phones—followed their inventions. Consumers did not want these products prior to their existence. It is a fallacy to believe that consumer demand somehow resulted in these inventions. Consider the practice of "marketing," which is basically the art of convincing consumers to want a product or service that they didn't know they wanted. There would be no need for marketing if demand were entirely consumer driven. In a similar manner, privatizing public education and doling out monetary rewards and punishments to the teachers and schools based on testing metrics cannot *cause* positive changes in educational practices. Change only comes about when teachers and schools *act* differently, not simply because they are compensated differently.

The market-based approach to improving education outcomes is a simple and attractive solution to a complex problem. This chapter demonstrates the fallacies of many of its assertions—assertions that are based on untested assumptions and a lack of compelling evidence. Indeed, the entire "free market" dogma is one such untested assumption. There are no "free markets" anywhere, nor have there ever been at any time or in any place. The concept of "free market" is practically meaningless. At the same time, there will always be markets, whether the government intervenes in them or not.

The hypothesis that the "free market" is the best of all possible economic systems has never been tested. Proponents of market-based education reform, and "free markets" in general, are instead serving up another tautology. The tautology of the market is: When the market is allowed to operate freely, we get desirable outcomes; when there is market intervention, we get undesirable outcomes.

This is an untestable hypothesis because desirability is always defined in terms of the self-interest of some particular individual, or organization and no market ever operates completely unaffected by government rules and regulations. Therefore, the hypothesis can never be falsified. Anytime there is an outcome that is costly to someone's self-interest it can be blamed on market intervention because there is always market intervention. Conversely, anytime there is an outcome that benefits someone's self-interest it can be said that market forces prevailed because there are always market forces.

Markets: Meaning, Politics, and Morality

Like the word "science" discussed in Chapter 5, the "market" is a universally understood word that no one seems able to define. Sources as diverse as dictionaries, economic textbooks, and philosophers all provide different explanations and definitions. Although it may be presumptuous of me to attempt my own, for the purposes of this discussion allow me to share my definition of a market.

> *When the number of exchanges between buyers and sellers for a particular product or service is sufficient for mutually understood trade practices and price structures to emerge, there exists a market for that product or service.*

My definition is akin to the concept of mutually understood languages; I consider both languages and markets to be naturally occurring social phenomena that result from the fact that people are both highly individualized and highly social beings. Market conventions, like language conventions, will emerge spontaneously whenever and wherever there are enough people to form social structures. Moreover, the conventions will continuously evolve in response to changing conditions.

Anytime there is sufficient demand for a product or service that suppliers are willing to meet, a market will emerge. As naturally occurring social phenomena, markets are difficult to eliminate. If you don't believe me, just try getting rid of a market that you don't like. The U. S. government has spent decades and hundreds of billions of dollars waging wars across the globe, imprisoning millions of people, and confiscating enormous sums of money in an effort to eliminate the market for certain drugs. It has not worked. The market for illegal drugs is still functioning. Likewise, the "world's oldest profession" is called that for a reason. The market for sex is not going away anytime soon, no matter how many resources law enforcement agencies allocate to arresting sex workers and their customers.

The fundamental condition that creates a market—buyers and sellers for a product or service—holds whether or not the government sanctions or regulates the transactions. It is certainly true that government regulation affects prices and availabilities for products and services. However, the participants constantly adapt to the prevailing government policies and the markets carry on—even if the prevailing policy calls for elimination of the market. It requires a great expenditure of effort and resources on the part of the government to completely shut down a market. Markets are phenomena that resist being forcibly stamped out.

Politics and Markets

The question isn't whether or not there should be a particular market, but rather what are the rules for that market and who decides them? Compare the market for recreational marijuana in Colorado to one in the state in which I live, Maryland. In Colorado, recreational marijuana is a legal product, but its sale and distribution is tightly controlled and regulated by the state government. In Maryland, at the time of this writing, the drug is illegal for recreational use and the state actively prosecutes sellers and users. (Medical marijuana is being legalized and regulated in Maryland.) Which of these markets is "freer"? Is it the market that operates under the tight control of the government, or the one that operates in opposition to the government? And what about the morality of marijuana use? Is it immoral to use marijuana in Maryland, but moral in Colorado?

A libertarian might argue that marijuana sales and usage are none of the government's business, period, and that the rules of the market should be decided only by the buyers and sellers. But all markets, whether for drugs or anything else, have wider social implications. As a result there will always be regulations such as permits, zoning ordinances, health and safety codes, licensing requirements, various business subsidies and so on. In addition, there will always be taxes because most markets cannot operate effectively without tax-based, government-provided infrastructure—roads and bridges, airports, law enforcement, national security, and government-backed currencies, for example.

In the *Travels of a T-shirt in the Global Economy* economist Pietra Rivoli examines the operation of the global markets involved in the manufacture, sale, and eventual disposal of an ordinary cotton T-shirt sold in the United States. Rivoli starts with the growth of the cotton in Texas, continues to textile manufacturing in China, follows with the re-importation to U. S. retailers, and, after it is worn for a time, concludes with its donation to the Salvation Army. After investigating the operation of the markets involved in each stage of the T-shirt's life, Rivoli discovers that in her T-shirt's journey around the globe it encountered very few free markets.

> "While my T-shirt's life story is certainly influenced by competitive economic markets, the key events in the T-shirt's life are less about competitive markets than they are about politics, history, and creative maneuvers to avoid markets. Even those who laud the effects of highly competitive markets are loathe to experience them personally, so the winners at various stages of my T-shirt's life are adept not so much at competing in markets but at avoiding them." [2, p. x]

The lesson from the T-shirt's life story is that economics is inseparable from politics. It is the political process that determines the rules under which the market will operate. The market will exist one way or another, but the workings of the market will depend on whether the government decides to directly participate in it, subsidize it, regulate it, actively persecute it, or engage in some convoluted combination of all these approaches. The "invisible hand" of the market, is in fact more like the hands of the man behind the curtain in the *Wizard of Oz*. Someone is always acting behind the scenes. We might call it market regulation when we approve, or market interference when we disapprove, but it is always active intervention by the government in the buying and selling processes.

My claim—that the government determines the rules of the market—is not new, radical, or even contested. No one believes in free markets. I repeat, no one, not the most conservative Republicans, not the most ardent Libertarians, not the most passionate pro-business advocates believe in free markets. Show me any person claiming that the government should not intervene in markets, and I'll show you a position or policy advocated by that same person that calls for government intervention in a market. In fact, when it comes to products and services sold legally in the United States, there are no "free markets" of any kind. And so most of the assertions about the benefits of "free markets" that advocates make have never been tested.

Morality and Markets

Advocates of market-based solutions to problems also wrap their arguments in the language of morality. The alleged optimum efficiency of "free markets" is extrapolated to become an argument for their moral superiority. The belief that the market, when left completely alone, will solve social problems on its own, is espoused by advocates of "laissez-faire capitalism," and is derided by their opponents as "market fundamentalism," which is a quasi-religious faith in the almost supernatural power of unregulated markets [3].

The alleged moral superiority of free markets has resulted in some rather curious bedfellows. Consider the deep influence of the ideas of Ayn Rand on members of the political and religious right. Ayn Rand is an unlikely hero for those on the right of the political spectrum. She was a Russian Jew, who in 1926 at the age of 21, emigrated to the United states. A committed atheist, she opposed all forms of religion, and rejected all claims of knowledge obtained outside of the senses, such as divine revelation. She supported abortion rights and opposed the Vietnam War and the draft. She condemned homosexuality, but called for the repeal of all laws against it. To her, valid knowledge arose only from sense perceptions and human reason.

Rand promoted her "philosophy" of objectivism through fiction and non-fiction writings, including speeches. In her words, the essence of "objectivism" is "the concept of man as a heroic being, with his own happiness as the moral purpose of his life, with productive achievement as his noblest activity, and reason as his only absolute." [4] In other words, her beliefs are the antithesis of Jesus' teachings in the Gospels.

Although never taken seriously by academic philosophers, Rand has gained enormous popularity in fundamentalist Christian circles. Specifically, she provides a moral rationalization for selfishness; in her system of thought, the greatest good is accomplished when everyone acts according to his or her rational self-interests. Voila! Free-markets arising from inherent human selfishness and becoming a moral force in their own right. This trick allows some self-identified Christians to embrace Ayn Rand's beliefs without experiencing any cognitive dissonance. Christian fundamentalism and market fundamentalism somehow become one and the same.

However, it does not take much in the way of observation to see that there is nothing particularly moral or immoral about the existence of a market. There are all sorts of markets that many people find morally offensive and want eliminated. In addition to the aforementioned markets for sex and for certain kinds of drugs, the government does not allow markets for human organs, labor from undocumented immigrants, or child labor. Paradoxically, in many of these cases the market itself, and not the activity, is deemed morally offensive. Donating a kidney is seen as noble and altruistic, but selling one is considered abhorrent. Sex between consenting adults is considered a private activity; however, when cash is exchanged it is considered a matter of public interest and the participants are subject to government sanctions. Voting is exercising a basic civil right and demonstrating responsible citizenship, but buying and selling votes is corrupt. Many drugs can be bought and sold legally with a prescription from a doctor, but the buying and selling of the same drugs is illegal without one.

Philosophers have grappled with the paradox that a product or service can be moral, while at the same time a market for the same product or service is considered immoral. In *Why Some Things Should Not Be For Sale: The Moral Limits of Markets,* [5] philosopher Debra Satz examines the ethics of what she terms "noxious" markets for things like human organs, or services like child labor. She argues that markets cannot be detached from the broader social contexts in which they operate, and that for a society to be democratic it must regulate markets in order to mitigate some of the inherent inequities that they produce.

I would argue that as naturally occurring social phenomena, markets are amoral. Speaking of markets in moral terms makes about as much sense as imbuing the phenomena of electricity or gravity with moral authority. Traditional libertarianism makes the mistake of extrapolating from the individual to the collective. Markets are emergent social phenomena that result from the independent actions of many individuals in much the same way that the macroscopic properties of water emerge from the many individual molecules of H_2O.

Therefore, I believe that it is possible to concede to libertarians the dignity of the individual, the sanctity of human agency, the right to make our own choices and direct our own lives, but still call for collective action to limit the destructive social impacts caused by completely unfettered markets. There will always be disagreement on what constitutes a "noxious" market and how much autonomy an individual should have. But in my view democracy is an ongoing process that attempts to balance the rights of individuals with the needs of society as a whole. Whenever the balance tips too much in one direction or the other—either trampling individual rights or neglecting the common good—democracy is imperiled.

Education Markets: The Higher-Ed Debacle

Education markets have always existed. You can choose to pay to send your child to a private school; you can choose to pay to attend school yourself. As I noted earlier, attendees of private schools tend to have high test scores and go on to lucrative jobs after graduation, both of which comprise education reformers' definition of successful educational outcomes. But the question remains: do free agents making choices in the educational marketplace *cause* those successful outcomes? Will introducing a profit motive for the education providers result in further improvements?

In fact, this experiment has already been tried in the field of higher education. For-profit colleges and universities experienced an explosion of growth in the 1990s and 2000s due to the advent of widespread access to the Internet, the steep rise in tuition at traditional colleges and universities, and the increased premium on earnings that college degree recipients command in the labor force. Heavy marketing in print and on television made institutions like Strayer University, Corinthian Colleges, and the University of Phoenix household names. The ads targeted non-traditional students, primarily adults already in the workforce looking to improve their career prospects and earning power.

Traditional colleges and universities have multiple inefficiencies that appear ripe for competitors to exploit in the marketplace. These institutions typically have bloated administrative costs, too many resources devoted to non-educational activities like athletic facilities and landscaping, and many costly labor-intensive teaching practices such as small seminars and laboratories. Moreover, at many prestigious universities teaching undergraduates isn't even the primary mission—much of the labor and capital resources go to research activities instead. With these obvious constraints on the traditional higher education model, it would stand to reason that a corporation focused on delivering high-quality undergraduate instruction and educational experiences could promise a successful business plan and almost certainly grab significant market share.

At least that is how Wall Street viewed the potential of for-profit higher education. Stock prices of exchange-listed for-profit colleges and universities soared in the early 2000s. However, an investor who bought shares of these companies around 2010—early in the most recent bull market for stocks—would come to regret that investment. In June of 2010, shares of Strayer Education sold for near $240. Five years later, in June of 2015, they sold for $55. Apollo Education Group, which operates the University of Phoenix, sold for $46 per share in June 2010; five years later the price was $13. The stock price for ITT Educational Services went from $80 per share in June 2010 to

$4 in June 2015. Education Management Corporation sold for $20 per share in June 2010. By June 2015 a share was worth 20 cents. Corinthian Colleges sold for $18 per share in June 2010. On April 27, 2015 it ceased all operations and a week later filed for Chapter 11 bankruptcy, completely wiping out the value of its stock. For comparison, the S & P 500 index went from 1080 to 2100 during this five-year period—a near doubling.

The Change in Financial Aid Rules for Colleges

Examination of the historical stock charts for this group of companies shows that their share values fell off a cliff after June 2010. The price patterns suggest that some catastrophe hit the for-profit higher education industry that year from which it would never recover. Indeed, such an event did occur—the federal government changed the student financial aid rules with the specific intent of ending abusive lending practices at for-profit colleges. A press release from the Department of Education in October 2010 noted that only 11% of higher education students attend for-profit colleges, yet they account for 26% of all student loans and 43% of all loan defaulters. In addition it stated: "More than a quarter of for-profit institutions receive 80% of their revenues from taxpayer financed federal student aid." [6]

Apparently the business model for many of these for-profit colleges consisted of transferring public funds, in the form of federal student financial aid, directly to the executives and stockholders of these corporations. A two-year investigation by a Senate Committee completed in 2012 examined the for-profit higher-education sector in detail for 2008–09 academic year [7]. According to the report:

> "Committee staff estimates that in 2009 when all sources of Federal taxpayer funds, including military and veterans' benefits, are included, the 15 publicly traded for-profit education companies received 86 percent of revenues from taxpayers." [7, p. 3]

The report also found that for 2008–09 more than half the students who enrolled left without a degree or diploma. The reason was that expenditures on instruction were small compared to expenditures on marketing and recruitment. Students became burdened with high debts and in many cases, received a substandard education that did not prepare them for the high-paying jobs that they were promised. The result was that many students defaulted on their loans and saddled taxpayers with huge losses.

To protect taxpayers from incurring further losses, the Obama administration changed the lending rules in 2010 in order to demand more accountability for education outcomes from schools dependent on federal financial aid for students. The schools would be required to disclose their actual graduation rates and their alumni's post-graduation job-placements and earnings to potential students before enrollment. In addition students enrolling in post-secondary education programs would need to hold a legitimate high school diploma before being eligible for financial aid, not a credential from one of the many "high school diploma mills."

The Impact of New Financial Aid Rules on For-Profit Colleges

On the surface, these rule changes appear rather benign. Require that students first complete high school and then inform them of their graduation chances and future job prospects before they borrow money to attend college. How could lending rules so simple and obvious upend the entire for-profit higher education industry?

As the industry unraveled in the years that followed the rule changes, the reasons surfaced. It became apparent that some of these companies never provided legitimate educational services from the onset, so rather than comply with the new lending rules, they responded by gaming the system. Some examples:

- In May 2015, the Securities and Exchange Commission charged the CEO and CFO of ITT Educational Services with fraud for failing to disclose to its investors, and for covering up in its financial statements large losses in its student loan programs. "Our complaint alleges that ITT's senior-most executives made numerous material misstatements and omissions in its disclosures to cover up the subpar performance of student loans programs that ITT created and guaranteed," said Andrew J. Ceresney, Director of the SEC's Division of Enforcement [8].
- In October 2015, a federal judge ordered Corinthian Colleges to pay $531 million in damages to its students [9]. The judgment was in response to a lawsuit brought by the federal government that alleged that Corinthian operated a "predatory lending scheme" and manipulated statistics on job placements in order to recruit students. It is doubtful that the students will see much of that money given that the company is bankrupt and its assets have been liquidated. The U. S. Department of Education appointed a

"special master" to oversee the discharge of the student-loan debt Corinthian students incurred [10].

- A few weeks later, in November 2015, Education Management Corporation decided to settle with the government, rather than take its case to trial, so that it could avoid admission of wrongdoing. The Justice Department alleged the company used aggressive "boiler room" tactics to recruit students who had almost no chance of succeeding in college. The company agreed to forgive loans totaling over $100 million to about 80,000 former students nationwide [11].

Wall Street analysts apparently understood all along where the money came from that justified such high stock prices, because the sell-off began in 2010, the moment the federal money spigot was turned off. According to the market hypothesis—that a profit-motivation spurs innovation—these companies should have responded by remediating the educational shortcomings in their programs. A better product that better served their customers would have kept them in business. However, the for-profit universities did not respond by innovating, or for that matter, even reproducing known models for higher education that historically have worked. When the flow of free money was turned off, the for-profit universities responded with deceptions, retrenchments, and bankruptcies.

The for-profit university boom and bust in many ways mirrored the housing boom and bust that occurred at roughly the same time. In both cases government-backed loans resulted in risk-free private profits for the corporations doing the lending. In both cases the rush for free government money motivated widespread fraud and abuse. A profit motive did not *cause* improved outcomes in higher education in comparison to traditional non-profit institutions. Instead it demonstrated the dangers of the moral hazard created by allowing the risk-free use of public money for private gain. If I were allowed to participate in a betting game in which I could keep all the money I won, but have all my losses reimbursed by the government, I would play that game for as long as I could and for as high a stakes as I could get my hands on.

The Charter School Movement

The for-profit higher education debacle of the recent decade illustrates that market-based approaches to education do not automatically result in innovations and improvements. Nor is a profit-motive causal in producing better educational outcomes. Flooding the higher education system with public money in the form of student financial aid can be beneficial by providing educational opportunities for those who might not otherwise have any, but it can also create moral hazards that lead to corruption that students and the taxpayers must guard against. In this case the "market" did not self-correct the deficiencies in the educational services. Rather, the "market" was part of the problem.

Despite these experiences, or maybe with complete obliviousness to them, many well-meaning advocates for school reform passionately believe that school choice will solve many seemingly intractable education problems—particularly in urban areas. Their reasoning is that if given a choice, parents and students will abandon poor performing schools, thus forcing them to either improve or close. Just as a business that is not meeting the needs of consumers will either have to adapt to attract customers or fail, schools should be subject to the same accountability to the market forces that exist when consumers have choice.

One result of this advocacy has been the movement towards "charter" schools." These are schools that are publically financed, but operate under a different set of rules and regulations than the public schools, and often in competition with them. There is no typical charter school because the laws governing them vary from state to state and from locality to locality. Some charter schools are affiliated with national chains—KIPP, Gulen, and White Hat Management are examples—and others are local institutions. Some are non-profit, some are for-profit, and some are non-profits that contract out the bulk of their services to for-profit corporations. As a result, there is as great a variety in programs and outcomes for charter schools as there is in public schools.

However, the essential idea behind the charter school movement is to provide publicly-funded alternatives for students who are forced to attend low-quality public schools because they cannot afford private schools. Charter school advocates reason that traditional public schools will either improve, if they are to remain "competitive" in the "market" for education that charter schools enable, or they will close because of low enrollments. And in fact in cities such as Chicago, dozens of traditional public schools have been closed as large numbers of charter schools have opened.

Ironically, the original idea behind charter schools was not to improve public schools through competition and market-based economics—the business approach—but rather to spur educational innovations through experimentation and collaboration—which is how science typically works. After serving for over twenty years as the president of the American Federation of Teachers (1974 to 1997), Albert Shanker wanted to figure out how to engage the large number of students who refused to participate in the education process, usually by dropping out of high school or not graduating. Shanker's idea was to assemble a team of teachers to collaborate on designing a new school for these high-risk students. The plan for the new school would require approval of the local school board and the teacher's union, after which it would be granted a "charter" to operate. The teachers in the charter school would be exempt from all of the usual regulations and curricula and would be free to try out new ideas and educational experiments in order to determine what works best for these high-risk students. Shanker's essential idea was collaborative, not competitive. Charter schools would work with the existing public schools, not be in competition with them.

However, advocates of market-based approaches to education reform soon realized that the charter school model was the perfect vehicle for advancing their agenda. They embraced charter schools as a way of providing publicly-funded school choice in areas with low-performing public schools. They lobbied for state laws that allowed charter schools to compete with and in many cases replace public schools, and permitted the private, and even for-profit operation of charters, and the employment of non-union teachers. In a strange twist, an idea conceived by the head of a union became a means for attacking and undermining his union, and his vision for public education. As the charter school model morphed into something very different than his original vision, Shanker went on to denounce it.

The Impact of Charter Schools

The use of charter schools to diminish the power of teachers' unions and to funnel public money either directly, or indirectly, to private corporations has made evaluation of their effectiveness a highly charged political issue. As a result it is difficult to find any consensus, or even get an unbiased study, on educational outcomes for charter schools. Advocates argue that charter schools should have fewer regulations and opponents argue that there should be more. For example, the Website for The Center for Education Reform has an interactive map that rates each of the 50 states by a "Parent Power Index" that factors in the specifics of each state's charter school laws. In 2015, Ohio ranked rather high—#8 overall—and the index stated:

> "Ohio has an average charter law but could improve its place by allowing all types of schools to open across the state." [12]

However, the Website for the Center for Public Education, cited studies of wide variations for student achievement in Ohio charter schools as being attributed to its state laws that permitted "multiple authorizers," which allowed "charter organizers to 'shop' for the most advantageous route for approval." [13]

In contrast Maryland ranked very low in the 2015 Parent Power Index—#43 over all—and the index stated:

> "Maryland should be ranked dead last on this scorecard. However, despite the odds being stacked against them, charter schools in The Old Line State shine. Maryland has one of the weakest charter laws in the country because of the enormous obstacles charter applicants face from school boards the minute they show interest. Charters face outward hostilities from boards, are micromanaged, operationally limited, poorly funded and are not even allowed to hire their own principals and staff to ensure success under their model." [14]

However, attempts to change Maryland's charter school law have run into strong opposition from teachers' unions because the current law requires charter operators to pay union wages and abide by union contracts. The unions see the so-called "weaknesses" in the state law as its "strengths." [15]

In other words, the tautology of the market is on full display. State laws that permit greater autonomy for charter schools are embraced by reformers as enabling innovation and derided by advocates of traditional public education as lacking in accountability. The fact that good and bad outcomes occur for both models is not going to change either of these narratives. However, the following conclusions about charter schools can be stated.

• **On average charter schools do no better or worse than public schools.** This is apparent because it is difficult to find any consensus on charter school performance. The one consistency in studies of charter schools is inconsistency. A 2013 study by the Stanford Center for Research on Education Outcomes (CREDO) found that for reading there was no significant difference between charter schools and the local public schools for 56% of the comparisons. For the remainder the differences could go in either direction. For 25% charter schools were significantly better and for 19% they were significantly worse. For math scores the corresponding results were no significant difference in 40% of comparisons, and for the remainder they were significantly better for 29% and significantly worse for 31% [16].

These results are not surprising because charter schools have not solved the education problem. The purpose of charter schools is to teach the same population of students to perform well on the same standardized tests using essentially the same pedagogy and curricula as found in traditional public schools.

There is nothing radically different about the charter school approach to education that would lead to an expectation of radically different outcomes. As another study that surveyed the existing data on charter schools in 2011 and found no discernable benefit stated: "After more than 20 years of proliferation, charter schools face the same challenges as regular public schools in boosting student achievement." [17]

• **Partisanship is leading to the same corruption of the scientific method as described in Chapters 3 and 5.** Studies of the effects of charter schools contain elaborate statistical analyses and comparison tests to identify correlations, but few controlled experiments to identify the actual causes for the statistical differences. Anytime there are arguments about statistical significance rather than causes something is wrong. For example, a CREDO report in 2015 analyzing data from 41 urban school districts found that as a whole urban charter schools provided significantly higher levels of growth in reading and math achievement compared to their public-school counterparts [18]. However, a review of this CREDO study published by the National Education Policy Center (NEPC) disputed both its methodology and conclusions [19]. Both the CREDO report and the NEPC review of it have highly technical discussions of statistical methods, but no discussions of controlled experiments to identify specific causes. This is because huge data sets have been collected and are available for statistical analysis, but apparently no one is conducting rigorous experiments. Again, just about any narrative can be constructed with a large enough data set. There are of course ethical issues and limitations with conducting controlled experiments on school children. But just as in medical studies, protocols exist and institutional review boards should be present to oversee them.

• **Moral hazards abound.** The chapter in Diane Ravitch's book *Reign of Error* on "The Contradictions of Charters" documents numerous examples of private charter school operators enriching themselves at public expense through ethically questionable contracts and legal loopholes for which they personally lobbied [20]. The Website *Cashing in on Kids* has an ongoing blog that calls out corruption and shady management practices by operators of charter schools across the country [21]. There is no shortage of abuses for the blogosphere to publicize. This is not surprising given the abuses that occurred in the higher education industry when public money was available for private profit. There is no reason to expect that diverting public money to for-profit K-12 schools will not enable the same bad behaviors.

"School Choice" Is Often False Choice

Like the for-profit higher-education debacle, the charter school movement is another example that highlights the perils of a tautology of choice: simply having choice in a competitive market, and a profit-motive for the school operators, are not *causal* to better educational outcomes. In fact the entire school choice concept as it is currently promoted rests upon a logical fallacy. Advocates of school choice often conflate legitimate consumer choices with false choices. Consider these choices. Would you prefer buying a large sedan or a minivan for transporting your family? Would you rather eat out tonight at the local sports bar or order Chinese take-out and watch the game at home? Would you rather save money on your cross-country flight with a low-cost no-frills airline or splurge with an airline that provides in-flight meals and movies? These are all legitimate choices that you and millions of other consumers routinely make and the market responds to.

Now consider the following false choices. Would you rather buy a car that complies with all government-mandated safety standards or a car with serious defects that might cause an accident that could kill you or a family member? Would you rather eat out at a restaurant that passes local health inspections for safe handling of food or one that was the source of a recent outbreak of food-borne illness that sickened hundreds of people? Would you rather fly an airline that complies with all government and industry standards for the maintenance and operation of its airplanes or one that had a recent crash attributed to a combination of faulty equipment and poor training of its pilots?

Suppose these dangerous options were heavily marked-down in price and the consumers informed of the risks and voluntarily sign liability waivers. Should the market still be allowed to determine the availability of these choices? The answer to this question has for the most part been no. With a few exceptions—cigarettes for example—products known to be dangerous or defective are kept off the market. Consumer choice is not the preferred mechanism for regulating health and safety.

Yet, "school choice" arguments are typically framed in terms of false choices. Would you rather send your children to a school that is poorly maintained and literally falling down, or to a school kept in good condition with a fully functioning infrastructure? Would you rather send your children to a school with lazy and incompetent teachers, or to a school where the teachers are committed and highly skilled? Would you rather send your children to a school in which they would fear for their safety, or to a school with adequate security and classroom management practices that maintain order and discipline?

It is no secret that many urban schools are in disarray and exemplify the wrong side of these "choices." It is shameful that any children are attending these severely dysfunctional schools whether by force or by choice. What this means is that the causes of these deficiencies should be identified and fixed. The solution to failing public schools should be to have program reviews, which is a common practice in traditional higher education.

A program review would examine all aspects of a particular school. Are the teachers engaged and using the best available pedagogies, or are they just going through the motions? Is the administration bloated and dysfunctional or is it providing the support necessary for the school to function effectively? Are the children being fed? Is the building falling apart and in need of repair? Are there safety and security issues?

Without identification of the actual causes of dysfunction it is not possible to allocate resources effectively. Why spend money on testing if the building is literally falling down? Does it make sense to spend money on technology in the classroom if the children aren't being properly fed? Will a teacher from Asia know how to do a better job, or should more resources be spent on teacher training, better working conditions and higher wages for American teachers?

Ideally review boards should follow a collaborative process. The teachers, administrators, and parents should all work together to identify what is working, what is not working, and how best to allocate resources to improve outcomes. In practice review boards are often maddeningly frustrating for all involved because frequently recommendations are not followed. No one wants to hear that they are part of the problem, and review boards cannot make resources magically appear. However, unless the actual *causes* for poor educational outcomes are identified and remediated there is no reason to expect that a different school will have better outcomes.

Imagine that airlines operated on the principle of choice rather than convening a review board after an air disaster. Instead of identifying the confluence of failures—of which there are usually many—that resulted in the crash, a new competing airline would start up in order to offer worried travelers a "choice." Its major selling point would be the tautological claim that none of its airplanes had crashed. The older airline would continue flying but with less resources to operate and maintain its planes because it would be forced to offer reduced fares in order to attract passengers. Would you feel safer having this "choice" or would you rather know what *caused* the crash and be assured that the problems were fixed?

The Logical Fallacies Embedded in the "Business Model"

In addition to ignoring causation, advocates for modeling schools after businesses are often oblivious to another failing: they ignore the most recent trends and developments in business management. What are often touted and claimed by education reformers as the principles of the "business model" are in fact refuted by business experts today. Clearly, advocates for running schools as businesses have not read any recent books on business management practices because their thinking appears stuck in the 1950s.

The decades-old dogma underlying this out-of-date "business model" is that workers respond to incentives in the form of monetary rewards and personal recognition. The reasoning goes like this: Without the right incentives workers simply won't be motivated to produce, and so management should focus on aligning worker incentives with the goals of the company. Pay for performance is the mantra. High-performing employees, usually defined as those generating the most profit for the company, should receive high rewards. This practice will motivate them to continue with their superior productivity and encourage lower-performing employees to do more.

This style of management is deeply rooted in the assumptions behind classical economics and behavioral psychology (behaviorism). The underlying assumption of classical economics is that people are rational actors in the marketplace, with "rationality" defined as always acting according to their best financial interests. Behaviorism assumes that people respond entirely to external stimuli by seeking to enhance pleasure and avoid pain. These appear to be reasonable assumptions. But, if you were starting a business, you would be wise not to apply these principles to its operation.

Research over the past five decades in the field of "behavioral economics" has shown that humans are not always rational actors in the market. People routinely act in ways that are counter to their economic self-interests. They are, according to the book title of a popular treatment of the subject, "predictably irrational." [22] In fact many common marketing practices exploit the predictable ways in which people act counter to their financial self-interests. Additionally, behaviorism has been shown to be an overly simplistic view of human motivation. Behaviorist control techniques might be effective for training your dog, but workers are not pets, and treating them as such will only improve their productivity under very specific circumstances. For many jobs, particularly ones that require creativity, the carrot-and-stick stimuli that exemplify the behaviorist approach may do the opposite.

Despite the preponderance of research against a behaviorist model, the management practices of most schools, from the administrators to the teachers to the students, reek of behaviorism. As documented in Chapters 2 and 3, every action performed is assessed, scored, graded, and ranked with proportional rewards and punishments doled out. A student's entire self-worth can hinge on his or her grade-point average. Teacher contracts now have clauses that base pay on student test scores. Administrators are rewarded based on metrics such as graduation rates, college admissions, and whether their schools are making adequate yearly progress (AYP).

Yet, examples of actions that defy the assumptions of behaviorism and classical economics abound in schools. Students intentionally fail courses, exhibit disruptive behavior, and even drop out of school—all actions that are irrational if their goals are to better their economic positions in the future. Teachers are not always motivated by money—a fact discussed in Chapter 8—and often do not respond to financial incentives because if money was their primary goal they probably wouldn't be teaching. And what about the examples of the administrators cited in Chapters 2 and 3, who responded to the "carrot" incentives by falsifying test scores? Is their behavior rational according to the assumptions of behaviorism and classical economics? It might be, but the fact is we expect the adults in charge to adhere to ethical norms at all times regardless of the punishment/reward structures in place.

The Failure of Behaviorist Incentives

Evidence that behaviorist principles do not work in schools has been accumulating for decades. As far back as 1993, Alfie Kohn published *Punished by Rewards: The Trouble with Gold Stars, Incentive Plans, A's, Praise, and Other Bribes*, in which he challenged the prevailing wisdom that incentives are the most effective means for motivating students in schools and workers on the job [23]. Kohn challenged both the effectiveness of such means of control and the morality of such a system, in essence calling out behaviorism as an unacceptable method of manipulating people that damages interpersonal relationships more than it elicits cooperation. By 1993, there were already plenty of research studies in the literature to support Kohn's arguments.

Evidence continues to accumulate that "incentivizing" people isn't the most effective means of management, and in the modern economy, it can actually be counterproductive. Ironically, the business literature has moved past such practices, while advocates of applying behaviorist principles to managing educators appear stuck in a decades-old past in which businesses were primarily engaged in manufacturing, which is not the economy of today.

In 2009 Daniel Pink published *Drive: The Surprising Truth About What Motivates Us* [24]. In it he identified three essential elements of genuine motivation: autonomy, mastery, and purpose. People want to direct their own lives (autonomy), continuously improve their skills and abilities to do things that matter (mastery) and serve meaningful causes that benefit more than the individual (purpose). Pink presented research findings that showed that businesses and organizations that provide people with opportunities to meet these deep psychological needs have far more productive workers than those that use carrot-and-stick reward and punishment practices.

Since Pink's work additional books on management practices have echoed his findings and challenged the traditional reward structure. One need only read the titles to know that these books attack behaviorist management practices. There is *Carrots and Sticks Don't Work: Build a Culture of Employee Engagement with the Principles of RESPECT™* by Paul L. Marciano, Ph.D., published in 2010 [25]. There is *Why Motivating People Doesn't Work … and What Does: The New Science of Leading, Energizing, and Engaging,* by Susan Fowler published in 2014 [26]. There is *The Optimistic Workplace: Creating an Environment That Energizes Everyone,* by Shawn Murphy published in 2015 [27]. Peruse any of these books and you will find that building healthy relationships and creating a sense of purpose are common themes. Of course, people need to be paid if they are to work, but if you want the high levels of achievement that only come about with an engaged workforce, people must believe that their work matters—that what they do means something to others. People are inherently social beings. Relationships with one another more than matter, they make us human.

In a sense Pink's challenge to the traditional business reward structure should be obvious. I know of few people who live their lives strictly according to the assumptions of classical economics—that is seeking to maximize their financial position in every decision that they make. Examples abound of people choosing to forgo greater income or asset accumulation in exchange for "qualify of life" benefits. Stay-at-home moms and dads might trade earnings and career advancement for more time spent with their young children. People might turn down lucrative job offers for work that they could do but would not enjoy. People might choose to reside in a particular geographic location because of family, or climate, or recreation opportunities, rather than take a higher paying job in a less desirable place to live. Necessarily different for every person, these "quality of life" benefits cannot be quantified, yet are very real and an important part of most major financial decisions.

In addition, adults, and most children for that matter, know when authority figures are attempting to control them with punishments and rewards, rather than seeking to engage them in the achievement of mutually beneficial goals. At the bottom of the economic ladder, people might have no choice but to go along with manipulative reward structures. But once people have choices, many will seek out work that they find more meaningful over work that pays more. For example, it has already been documented in Chapter 5 that no one would choose early childhood education as a career if money were the sole motivating factor. However, many people do choose this career because they enjoy working with young children and find deep meaning in teaching the next generation. Ironically the primary reason for education is to enable greater freedom of choice so that people can pursue careers in which they find their greatest sense of purpose and passion. Commanding students to become educated, but only in fields that make the most money misses the point. An education is intended to expand opportunities, not narrow them.

Money as a Motivating Factor Is Misunderstood

Part of the misunderstanding about the role of money as a reward is the assumption that money motivates people and that motivation is causal in improving people's ability to perform. But this is a fallacy akin to the magical thinking examined in Chapter 3 that "setting expectations" will improve teaching. Motivation is necessary, but simply being motivated will not improve a person's performance any more than saying that you expect more from them. Improvement at any skill requires a regimen of study, deliberate practice, and reflection. Honing valuable and difficult-to-acquire skills requires a commitment to and time for ongoing self-improvement.

Money, motivation, and high expectations do not improve skills. Money can certainly motivate someone to use a skill that he or she already possesses. But there is a difference between performing at a level already achieved— work that a person already knows how to do—and performing work at a higher level or a new kind of work altogether. Money can be causal for the former, but it cannot cause the latter. If my employer sent me a big bonus check tomorrow, it would be appreciated and motivate me to keep working, but it would not cause me to wake up the next morning suddenly knowing how to do my job a whole lot better.

Developing skills also requires resources in addition to practice time. My scientific training required work in laboratories equipped with expensive measuring devices. Programmers need access to computers, engineers need materials to build things, historians need access to books and libraries, musicians need instruments, and athletes need practice facilities and equipment. In the private marketplace, businesses usually require some form of capital investment to get started. Marketable products and services cannot be conjured out of nothing. Again, student or employee motivation will not substitute for required resources in schools or in businesses.

Using money to incentivize people often gets cause and effect backwards. In many cases money is not the cause of, but rather the result of success in the market. Organizations of any kind that seek only to maximize profits are often dysfunctional. Watch the documentary *The Smartest Guys in the Room* [28] about the collapse of Enron for an extreme example of what happens to a company when all that matters to the leadership and the workers is money. No one at Enron understood the products or services being sold, only that the goal was to make lots of money for the company and drive its stock price ever higher. In contrast, Steve Jobs built the most valuable company in the world— Apple Computer—by focusing relentlessly on creating superior products and services. His wealth was a byproduct of his success, not the reason for it.

Markets Increase Inequalities

However, what success in the marketplace, and the money generated as a result do lead to are inequalities. Money is a form of leverage. It can be invested to generate more opportunities in the market, and as a result, more money. It is in the nature of markets to amplify inequalities. There is nothing inherently wrong about that fact, but it should be acknowledged, particularly in the education market, because turning education over to the market will increase inequalities, not lessen them as many people believe. Market-based education reform will make inequalities worse. In fact, this has already happened.

For example, consider the Obama administration's "Race to the Top" education initiative [29]. States willing to adopt education policies promoted by the U. S. Department of Education competed for federal grants to fund education programs. But a competition, by definition, produces winners and losers. The majority of states that applied for Race to the Top funds were unsuccessful in securing funding. Among the states that did receive funding were Maryland and Massachusetts, states already known to have strong public education systems. On the *U. S. News & World Report* 2015 rankings of states with the "best" high schools these states ranked 1 and 4 respectively [30]. States not receiving Race to the Top funds included Mississippi and Alabama, states already known to have weak public education systems. On the same *U. S. News & World Report* list these states ranked 49 and 50 respectively.

In Chapter 2, I question the use of opaque formulas fed with suspect data to define "best," as is done by *U. S. News & World Report*. Many excellent schools would rate poorly using these kinds of formulas (Chapter 8 has more on this topic). However, education policymakers take these formulas seriously and allocate resources to school accordingly. As a result, the rich become richer and the poor become poorer.

For example, if you look at the rankings of these same four states by average median household income from the years 2011–13 the ordering would be Maryland (1), Massachusetts (6) Mississippi (50) and Alabama (45) [31]. As is well-known, educational attainment closely tracks income levels at the local level—wealthy suburban schools have better outcomes than poor urban schools. After all, in most localities schools are funded by property taxes, which means that schools in wealthier neighborhoods typically have more money, and the families they serve also have more money to invest in educating their children. That same effect happens at the state level when all the results are aggregated. Not surprisingly there is a strong correlation between a state's median household income and rankings of the quality of its high schools. Of the 10 states that top the median household income list, 5 also appear in the top 10 on the *U. S. News & World Report* list of best high schools. Of the 10 states that are at the bottom of the median household income list, 4 also appear in the bottom 10 on the *U. S. News & World Report* list.

Competition in a marketplace for education strengthens the link between wealth and education outcomes rather than weakening it. This, of course, leads to increased inequality. The states that already have the best-funded education systems are being awarded more money. States lacking in funds for education are falling further behind. As a report from a coalition of civil rights groups noted:

"The implementation of the Race to the Top Fund's grant process highlights our concerns about an approach to education funding that relies too heavily on competition: only fifteen states and the District of Columbia were on the short-list in the first round to be "eligible" for possible funding. These finalist states contain only 37% of the students in the United States eligible for free and reduced lunch. Only 14% of the students in the finalist states are Hispanic compared to 26% in the non-finalist states. Overall, 74% of Hispanic students live outside finalist states. While 53% of Black students in the United States are in the finalist states, losing 47% of the Black students places a huge economic burden on the country." [32]

If anything, the vast education inequalities in the United States that result from wide disparities in family incomes demonstrate that we already have an education system which operates too much like the "business model" desired by free market advocates and dismissed by current business management research. The current approach to education is only working for those with the income and wealth needed to access adequate education opportunities. In addition, the "business model" that advocates envision is one from the distant past. It is education "reform" that doubles-down on out-of-date business practices which the business world abandoned decades ago. We need less of market-based economics and behaviorist business practices in education, not more. Education should be an equalizer by enabling all students, regardless of socio-economic background to reach their full potential. The "business model" subverts the power of education to equalize. This presents a great danger for all of us.

As I stated earlier, markets are naturally occurring social phenomena that are unavoidable. It is difficult, if not impossible, to eliminate market forces in any organized social structure. But rather than worship them, we should regard market forces as we do any of the other forces in nature—like electricity—and harness and manage them for our collective benefit, rather than allow them to run unfettered and destroy us.

The Paradox of Wealth

"For the body is not one member, but many. If the foot says, "Because I am not a hand, I am not a part of the body," it is not for this reason any the less a part of the body. And if the ear says, "Because I am not an eye, I am not a part of the body," it is not for this reason any the less a part of the body. If the whole body were an eye, where would the hearing be? If the whole were hearing, where would the sense of smell be?"

I Corinthians 12: 14-17

Imagine that you are by far the wealthiest person in the world. Your net worth tops that of Bill Gates and Warren Buffet combined. You have used your vast resources to fulfill a life-long ambition—becoming the first person on Mars. Strapped into your custom-built rocket, the engines ignite and your journey into space begins. Your co-pilot, seated next you, has also dreamed of this journey. He has worked in aviation all his life for middle class wages, and has a net worth that is a tiny fraction of yours. What will it be like when you arrive on Mars? Will the vast wealth disparity cause problems because you and your co-pilot will expect different standards of living? In this scenario, it is easy to speculate that it will not. Once you leave planet Earth, your differences in income and accumulated wealth will become meaningless. You and your co-pilot will be economic equals on Mars for the simple reason that there will be no goods or services to purchase.

Wealth is entirely a social construct. It is not possible for an individual to *be* wealthy. When we say that someone is wealthy, we mean that person has greater access, relative to other persons, of the goods and services that society produces. If there is no society to produce the goods and services, then the concept of wealth has no meaning. This simple fact seems to be forgotten. A prevalent attitude is that the wealthy earned their good fortune, and the less well-off should work harder if they want more money, instead of complaining about rising levels of economic inequality. But what is overlooked in all the shouting is that, paradoxically, the people who have the most to gain from ensuring some measure of economic equality and social justice are the wealthy.

In modern times wealth depends on a functioning society in which all members have some minimum level of well-being and life satisfaction, because most wealth is contractual in nature. People no longer "possess" the majority of their assets as they might have in the past. In biblical times when wealth was measured in acres of land, or sacks of grain, or heads of cattle, the wealthy possessed their assets. Today ownership of land is granted by a deed filed at the county courthouse, and few people use their land to produce their own food. Bank and brokerage accounts have become digital creations. Through direct deposit and online bill pay services, the exchange of wages for work, and money for goods and services is accomplished by toggling bits inside computers. Stock trading is entirely electronic. Companies don't even bother issuing paper stock certificates as was done in the past. What is called "cash" is nothing more than pieces of paper issued by the government that are no longer redeemable for precious metals. Even gold, a so-called universal currency, is traded on the expectation of what goods and services it can buy. Other than jewelry, few people have any practical uses for the shiny yellow metal. Without a society that recognizes, honors, and enforces all these contracts, most of what we call "wealth" would vanish.

Producing Goods and Services Requires Networks and Infrastructure

What wealth buys is also contractual in nature and depends on a functioning society. Many of the most sought after goods and services require the combined and coordinated efforts of millions of people to produce, operate, and maintain. Consider smartphones, automobiles, or airplanes. None of these devices can be conjured out of the ground from their elemental constituents by a single person. No single person even knows or understands all that is required to build and make these devices work; rather what is required is the sustained efforts and expertise of millions of people. In fact, without a vast infrastructure in place the devices themselves would be completely useless. What good would a smartphone be without a network? What use would an automobile have without roads, gas stations, and mechanics? Where would an airplane go if there was only one airport in the world? The functionality of these networks depends on millions of people, all working collaboratively, responsibly, and in good faith.

Once on a flight, I found myself sitting next to an off-duty airline captain who was taking an open seat to return to his home. When he learned that I was a physics professor, he talked to me about his college experiences majoring in physics. We then had an engaging discussion about the physics of airplanes. I realized that as a person responsible for educating future pilots and aeronautical engineers, I was also part of the network needed to fly the plane we were on.

We rarely think about all the workers—public and private—needed to fly a plane: the designers, engineers, and builders, the pilots and crew members, the baggage handlers, fuel truck operators, and ticket agents, the air traffic controllers, TSA workers, FAA inspectors, and maintenance workers, the airport administrators and bus drivers, the software programmers, and the many other jobs that would take too much space to list. If you are a person with enough money to purchase a plane ticket, it is in your self-interest to see to it that all of these people have a decent standard of living and adequate healthcare, because you depend on them more than they depend on you. Simply having money isn't going to build and fly a plane safely to a place that you want to go.

Service networks require millions of people, all of whom need to be fed, housed, and cared for when sick. In communities where disparities of wealth have become extreme, it becomes problematic to provide basic services—such as education. In Santa Clara, California the starting salaries for teachers in the public schools range from $45,000 up to $105,000 depending on education and experience. The county is also home to Apple Computer, Google, and dozens of other high technology companies. As a result, the median price of a single-family home in the county is about $1 million. This is far beyond the price range that someone living on a teacher's salary can afford, causing many teachers to leave [33]. San Francisco, where median home prices are in excess of $1 million, faces the same problem. To attract teachers, the school district is building homes and apartments that it can rent to teachers at below-market prices [34]. Communities in which teachers cannot afford to live will soon not have any teachers.

High housing costs in places like San Francisco and New York City exist because these are attractive, vibrant communities for people to live and work. But that vibrancy, and with it the investments in homeownership in these cities, will be threatened if the people providing basic services go away. Home prices have always depended on the neighborhood much more than the size or condition of the house. But a neighborhood is a community of people, not a location on a map. The 2007–08 housing bust painfully illustrated this fact. Neighborhoods that had high rates of foreclosures became places that attracted squatters, not middle class families. In surroundings filled with overgrown yards, fetid swimming pools, and unmaintained homes, those left behind because they could afford their mortgage payments found that their homes were worthless anyway. Many who could afford to stay, walked away, which further exacerbated the disintergration of these communities. In many instances banks foreclosed on homes, evicted the owners, and then abandoned the properties once it became apparent there was no re-sale value. Bank "walkaways" became a source of blight in many of these cities and towns.

Widening Inequality Threatens our Democracy

What can happen on a micro level with neighborhoods can also happen on a macro level with entire societies. By all measures income inequality in the United States has increased since the 1970s, a circumstance that is virtually unique among developed countries. Economist Timothy Smeeding summed up the trend in 2005 when he wrote:

> "Americans have the highest income inequality in the rich world and over the past 20–30 years Americans have also experienced the greatest increase in income inequality among rich nations. The more detailed the data we can use to observe this change, the more skewed the change appears to be... the majority of large gains are indeed at the top of the distribution." [35]

Testifying before Congress in 2005 Alan Greenspan stated when asked about growing income inequality:

> "As I've often said, this is not the type of thing, which a democratic society—a capitalist democratic society—can really accept without addressing."

That testimony, and Smeeding's comment, occurred before the collapse of the housing market in 2007–08 and the onset of the great recession, events which made income inequality even greater. The U. S. Census Bureau reported a record 46.7 million Americans living in poverty in 2014 (14.8% of the population). The rate was 2.3% points higher than before the great recession [36].

Greenspan is of course concerned because history is rife with examples of extreme economic inequality preceding social catastrophes. Consider monarchist France prior to the French Revolution, the southern states in the United States prior to the Civil War, the Weimar Republic in Germany prior to the rise of the Nazis, Zimbabwe prior to Robert Mugabe's dictatorship. In all of these cases the poor did not benefit from the ensuing social and economic collapse, but the wealthy lost everything.

Rising income inequality threatens the income, assets, and well-being of the wealthy. There are no societies without wealth disparities, but there are limits as to how much inequality can exist before the society ceases to function. We would be wise not to test those limits. In writing about what is at stake in rethinking our education system, Tony Wagner and Ted Dintersmith write:

> "As the ranks of the chronically unemployed youth swell, the rift between the unrelenting rich and the disenfranchised rest will rip our society apart. We will fail as a country, not because other nations defeated us, but because we defeated ourselves." [37, p. 59]

The wealthy have benefited the most from markets, but they also have the most to lose if markets can no longer function. Just as science has its limits, so too do markets have their limits. In *The Wealth of Nations,* political and economic philosopher Adam Smith wrote the following famous and oft-quoted line.

> "It is not from the benevolence of the butcher, the brewer, or the baker that we expect our dinner, but from their regard to their own interest." [38]

This statement is usually interpreted very narrowly, with "their own interest" being understood purely in the mathematical sense of maximizing their financial positions. This kind of "greed is good" thinking, exemplified by the Gordon Gekko character in the movie *Wall Street,* has become all too prevalent.

But what is often not noticed is that the butcher, brewer, and baker all need each other. If butcher were the most highly paid profession, and that motivated everyone to become a butcher, we would not have any bread or ale. Moreover, the butchers would lack buyers for their meats. We need an expanded understanding of self-interest that goes beyond the purely mathematical act of counting and comparing sums of money and encompasses nurturing the complex web of human relationships necessary for our survival.

The elevation of the maximization of money and the maximization of test scores to the status of end goals arises from the same defective line of thinking—using "scientific measures" to define what is meaningful. As explained on the limits of science in Chapter 5, science cannot address questions of meaning. There are no mathematical measures or formulae for what makes a meaningful life. Humans can define meaning but that definition must exist outside of science and beyond any quantitative measures. Historically, definitions of meaning have varied greatly across time and place, but they have always encompassed the quality of the relationships that we have with each other. It is willful ignorance to pretend that relationships are much less important than numerical measures of individual achievements. Individualism, when carried to an extreme, becomes a denial of our essential humanity.

References

1. Kate Bowler, *A History of the American Prosperity Gospel* (New York: Oxford University Press, 2013).
2. Petra Rivoli, *The Travel of a T-Shirt in the Global Economy: An Economist Examines the Markets, Power, and Politics of World Trade* (New York: John Wiley & Sons, 2005).
3. George Soros, *The Crisis of Global Capitalism: Open Society Endangered* (New York: Public Affairs, 1998).
4. Ayn Rand, *Atlas Shrugged*, 35th Anniversary Edition (New York: Dutton, 1992), 1170–1171.
5. Debra Satz, *Why Some Things Should Not Be For Sale: The Moral Limits of Markets* (New York: Oxford University Press, 2010).
6. U. S. Department of Education, "Department of Education Establishes New Student Aid Rules to Protect Borrowers and Taxpayers," Press Release, October 28, 2010, http://www.ed.gov/news/press-releases/department-education-establishes-new-student-aid-rules-protectborrowers-and-taxpayers.
7. Health, Education, Labor and Pensions Committee, United States Senate, "For Profit Higher Education: The Failure to Safeguard the Federal Investment and Ensure Student Success," Report issued July 30, 2012, https://www.gpo.gov/fdsys/pkg/CPRT-112SPRT74931/pdf/CPRT-112SPRT74931.pdf.
8. Securities and Exchange Commission, "SEC Announces Fraud Charges Against ITT Educational Services," Press Release, May 12, 2015, http://www.sec.gov/news/pressrelease/2015-86.html.

9. United States District Court Northern District of Illinois Eastern Division, "Consumer Financial Protection Bureau Plaintiff, v. Corinthian Colleges Inc. d/b/a Everest College, Everest Institute, Everest University, Everest University Online, Everest College Phoenix, Everest College Online, WyoTech, and Heald College, Defendant," Case No. 1:14-cv-07194: Default Judgment and Order, October 27, 2015, http://files.consumerfinance.gov/f/201510_cfpb_default-judgment-and-order-corinthian.pdf.

10. U. S. Department of Education, "Education Department Appoints Special Master to Inform Debt Relief Process," Press Release, June 25, 2015, http://www.ed.gov/news/press-releases/education-department-appoints-special-master-inform-debt-relief-process.

11. U. S. Department of Justice, "For-Profit College Company to Pay $95.5 Million to Settle Claims of Illegal Recruiting, Consumer Fraud, and Other Violations," Press Release, November 16, 2015, http://www.justice.gov/opa/pr/profit-college-company-pay-955-million-settle-claimsillegal-recruiting-consumer-fraud-and.

12. "How Much Parent Power Do You Have? Parent Power Index 2015, Ohio," Center for Education Reform, accessed December 23, 2015, http://parentpower-index.edreform.com/parent-power-index/print/OH/2015.

13. "Charter Schools, Finding out the facts: At a glance," Center for Public Education, accessed July 27, 2015, http://www.centerforpubliceducation.org/Main-Menu/Organizing-a-school/Charter-schools-Finding-out-the-facts-At-a-glance.

14. "How Much Parent Power Do You Have? Parent Power Index 2015, Maryland," Center for Education Reform, accessed December 23, 2015, http://parentpower-index.edreform.com/parent-power-index/MD/2015.

15. Liz Bowie, "New effort underway to change Maryland charter schools law," *Baltimore Sun*, January 20, 2015, http://www.baltimoresun.com/news/maryland/education/bs-md-charter-study-20150120-story.html.

16. Edward Cremata, et al., *National Charter School Study* 2013, (Stanford, CA: Stanford University, CREDO Center for Research on Education Outcomes, 2013), http://credo.stanford.edu/documents/NCSS%202013%20Final%20Draft.pdf.

17. Matthew Di Carlo, "The Evidence on Charter Schools and Test Scores," Policy Brief, (Washington, DC: Albert Shanker Institute, 2011), http://www.shankerinstitute.org/sites/shanker/files/blog/2011/12/CharterReview.pdf.

18. *Urban Charter School Study Report on 41 Regions* 2015, (Stanford, CA: Stanford University, CREDO Center for Research on Education Outcomes, 2015), https://urbancharters.stanford.edu/download/Urban%20Charter%20School%20Study%20Report%20on%2041%20Regions.pdf.

19. Andrew Maul, "Review of *Urban Charter School Study* 2015," (Boulder, CO: University of Colorado, National Education Policy Center, 2015), http://nepc.colorado.edu/files/ttr-urbancharter-credo.pdf.

20. Diane Ravitch, *Reign of Error: The Hoax of the Privatization Movement and the Danger to America's Public Schools* (New York: Alfred A. Knopf, 2013).
21. "Cashing in on Kids," In the Public Interest, accessed May 1, 2018, http://cashinginonkids.com/.
22. Dan Ariely, *Predictably Irrational: The Hidden Forces That Shape Our Decisions* (New York: Harper Collins, 2008).
23. Alfie Kohn, *Punished By Rewards: The Trouble With Gold Stars, Incentive Plans, A's, Praise and Other Bribes*, 2nd ed. (New York: Houghton Mifflin, 1999).
24. Daniel Pink, *Drive: The Surprising Truth About What Motivates Us* (New York: Riverhead Books, 2009).
25. Paul L. Marciano, *Carrots and Sticks Don't Work: Build a Culture of Employee Engagement with the Principles of RESPECTTM* (New York: McGraw Hill, 2010).
26. Susan Fowler, *Why Motivating People Doesn't Work … and What Does: The New Science of Leading, Energizing, and Engaging* (San Francisco: Berrett-Koehler Publishers, 2014).
27. Shawn Murphy, *The Optimistic Workplace: Creating an Environment that Energizes Everyone* (New York: AMACOM, 2015).
28. Alex Gibney, director, *Enron: The Smartest Guys in the Room*, (Dallas, TX: 2929 Entertainment and HDNet Films, released April 22, 2005), video, 1:50:00.
29. "Race to the Top Funding Program," U. S. Department of Education, accessed February 14, 2016, http://www2.ed.gov/programs/racetothetop/index.html.
30. Robert Morse, "How States Compare in the 2015 Best High Schools Rankings," *U. S. News & World Report*, May 11, 2015, http://www.usnews.com/education/best-high-schools/articles/how-states-compare.
31. "Table H-8B. Median Income of Households by State Using Three-Year Moving Averages: 1984 to 2013," United States Census Bureau, accessed February 14, 2016, https://www.census.gov/hhes/www/income/data/statemedian/.
32. "Framework for Providing All Students an Opportunity to Learn through Reauthorization of the Elementary and Secondary Education Act," Lawyers Committee for Civil Rights under Law, NAACP, NAACP Legal Defense and Educational Fund, Inc., National Council for Educating Black Children, National Urban League, Rainbow PUSH Coalition, and Schott Foundation for Public Education, Schott Foundation, July 2010, http://schottfoundation.org/resources/civil-rights-framework-providing-all-students-opportunity-learn-through-reauthorization-el.
33. Lillian Mongeau, "Is Silicon Valley Driving Teachers Out?" *The Atlantic*, July 21, 2015, http://www.theatlantic.com/education/archive/2015/07/silicon-valley-housing-tough-on-teachers/399071/.
34. Jill Tucker, "To attract teachers, school districts get into the housing business," *San Francisco Chronicle*, October 26, 2015, http://www.sfchronicle.com/bayarea/article/To-attract-teachers-school-districts-get-into-6591925.php.

35. Timothy Smeeding, "Public policy, economic inequality, and poverty: The United States in comparative perspective." *Social Science Quarterly* 86, (December 2005): 956–983. https://www.jstor.org/stable/pdf/42956021.pdf?seq=1#page_scan_tab_contents.

36. Carmen DeNavas-Walt, and Bernadette D. Proctor, U. S. Census Bureau, Current Population Reports, P60-252, *Income and Poverty in the United States*: 2014, (Washington, DC: U. S. Government Printing Office, 2015), http://www.census.gov/content/dam/Census/library/publications/2015/demo/p60-252.pdf.

37. Tony Wagner and Ted Dintersmith, *Most Likely to Succeed: Preparing Our Kids for the Innovation Era* (New York: Simon & Shuster, 2015).

38. Adam Smith, *An Inquiry into the Nature and Causes of the Wealth of Nations*, Edited by S. M. Soares. (Lausanne: MetaLibri Digital Library, May 2007), Book I, Chapter II, p. 16. Accessed May 1, 2018, https://www.ibiblio.org/ml/libri/s/SmithA_WealthNations_p.pdf.

Part IV

Rethinking Education

8

The Paradox of Education in the 21st Century

Education, as it is generally understood, is the process of acquiring knowledge and skills. Prior generations have understood knowledge to be important facts that are memorized and recalled, and skills to be abilities to perform useful and valuable actions. However, in the 21st century information age an educational paradox confronts us. Knowledge is abundant, nearly free, and can be accessed without memorization. Ubiquitous smartphones allow instant access to almost all the facts that humans have accumulated. In addition, many skills that were once highly valued—the preparation of tax returns, the writing of many standard legal documents, the drafting of architectural drawings—are performed by relatively inexpensive software packages. The trend is for computers to become faster with more powerful software, which means that more and more work that in the past required a knowledgeable and skilled human will in the future be automated.

Nonetheless, as I documented in Chapter 2, the value of an education across many quality of life dimensions is increasing. How is it that educated people are becoming increasingly better off, while at the same time, much of the valuable work traditionally performed by educated people is being off-loaded to computers? Are there additional dimensions of education beyond the acquisition of knowledge and skills that contribute to our understanding today of what it means to be educated?

To start, we must begin to move beyond the argument that education is simply the acquisition of certain attributes in order to succeed in the modern economy. These arguments fall short because they view education solely in terms of knowledge and skills that can be tested and ignore many dimensions that cannot be easily quantified.

© Springer International Publishing AG, part of Springer Nature 2018
J. Ganem, *The Robot Factory*, https://doi.org/10.1007/978-3-319-77860-0_8

Consider the Common Core, an example of a recent attempt at enumerating the essential attributes of an education. Gaining relatively widespread acceptance, the Common Core is a list of standards that children should meet in order to be "college and career ready." [1] Upon closer examination the Common Core standards are simply lists of facts to memorize and skills to master. The lists read like product specifications in a robot factory. Robots might be an expected product of the 21st century; however, the factory approach to education harkens to an economic model that is obsolete. The Common Core is a backward facing approach to education reform. It is the latest incarnation of the deficit model of education.

In this Chapter and the next I will argue that children are not robots to be programmed, but autonomous human beings capable of meaningful relationships with others. Education reform should not look to models that arise from our industrial past, but rather to the power of education to change our relationships. What I call "change-focused" education is happening all around us. We only need to stop being willfully ignorant and look. This is the dimension of education beyond knowledge and skills. The power of education to radically change our relatedness to each other and to our environments is why the authentically educated enjoy such an enhanced quality of life.

Back to the Future

One of the dim memories I have from pre-school is being taught to write my name. My parents, aunts, and uncles all called me Joey, so I signed all the work I did in pre-school "Joey Ganem." But each time I did this the teacher corrected me. Your name is "Joseph" she would admonish me and then change the spelling of my name.

This battle went on for many months, and the reason I resisted had nothing to do with my preference for a signature. I simply could not write the letter "s." Each time I tried it came out as some random squiggle that I knew wasn't the way a real "s" should appear. So, to compensate for my inability to write the letter "s," I simply avoided writing any words containing that letter, including the formal version of my first name. I did not want to admit this deficiency to my teacher because I had no trouble writing the other 25 letters in the alphabet. My struggle with the letter "s" became a hidden embarrassment.

One day in pre-school, I figured out how to write a legible "s," and soon afterwards it became easy for me. Whole new dimensions of written language opened up for me. I could now conjugate verbs, make plurals and possessives, and finally write my name in the teacher-approved way. The long-running battle I had with my teacher over my signature ended. I began signing my name "Joseph Ganem," which is still my formal signature today on official documents and checks.

I tell this story to illustrate a number of points about educating children.

- A child's reason for acting a certain way might not have anything to do with the motives the teacher thinks the child has. I'm sure the teacher thought I was just being stubborn.
- Children really do want to please their teachers, and when they can't, they can be very resourceful in hiding deficiencies and knowledge gaps, particularly if they are embarrassed.
- A small thing, like not being able to write a legible "s" could easily be mistaken for a huge language deficit. It is quite possible that an adult could have concluded that I didn't recognize verb conjugations, plurals, and possessives if I never used them in writing, or that I couldn't understand spoken instructions from the teacher to correct the spelling of my name.
- Language development in children is not a linear progression. As soon as I could incorporate words with the letter "s" in them, I made a significant—albeit discontinuous jump—in the sophistication of my use of written language.

Now let's time-travel my little preschool self to the future. Had I grown up in the modern educational system, I would never have had a chance to fail third-grade math because my difficulties with the letter "s" would have caused me to fail pre-school. In May 2015 Maryland state education officials reported that test results showed that only 47% of the state's preschoolers were ready for kindergarten, compared to 83% who passed the test the year before [2]. The kindergarten readiness test assesses the extent to which preschoolers have the language and math skills needed to succeed in kindergarten.

Of course the drastic drop in kindergarten-readiness between 2014 and 2015 wasn't the result of an abrupt, catastrophic decline in the cognitive abilities of Maryland preschoolers. Instead it resulted from a re-definition of kindergarten readiness. As state education officials explained, the drop in readiness was the result of new assessments that were aligned with the new Common Core standards. One official, Rolf Grafwallner, the assistant state schools superintendent for early childhood development, offered this explanation:

"Those numbers represent just how much different these standards are. We saw a vast difference in the skills the children needed to have to be successful in kindergarten." [2]

What are these new skills now expected of kindergarteners? Some of the stated expectations are so bizarre that they strain credulity. For example:

"Students will be expected to know the difference between informative/explanatory and opinion writing by the time they enter kindergarten ... " [2]

As I mentioned in Chapter 6, my college students often struggle with the difference between fiction and nonfiction, as well as the difference between fact and opinion writing. In my attempts to figure out how a standard this ludicrous could creep into pre-school expectations, I have discovered that language to this effect actually does appear in the Common Core standards. The language arts writing standards for kindergarten state:

"Use a combination of drawing, dictating, and writing to compose opinion pieces in which they tell a reader the topic or the name of the book they are writing about and state an opinion or preference about the topic or book (e.g., My favorite book is...)." [3]

Followed by:

"Use a combination of drawing, dictating, and writing to compose informative/explanatory texts in which they name what they are writing about and supply some information about the topic." [4]

Presumably if kindergarteners are going to compose "opinion pieces" and "informative/explanatory texts," they need to understand the difference between these two forms of writing. And to think, at that age I had trouble writing words with the letter "s" in them.

The idea of testing preschoolers' academic abilities for kindergarten-readiness sounds like a *Saturday Night Live* skit where hyper-competitive parents attempt to secure spots for their children in elite private preschools that cost more than some colleges. But just as the line between reality and parody in politics has blurred (remember Chapter 6?), that same line has become blurred in public education. New curriculum standards in Maryland now demand that kindergarten be an academic experience in which children are held to high standards, rather than a socialization experience that allows children to learn through play.

In Chapter 4, I explain that much of the K-12 math curriculum has been developmentally inappropriate for many years. Instead of remedying this deficiency, the Common Core doubles down on it and infuses the entire K-12 curriculum with developmentally inappropriate instruction and expectations.

The Common Core sets educational standards that are not aligned with even the most basic facts of human development. Educational attainment is part of human development; fundamentally this is a biological process that cannot be sped up. We cannot wish away our biological limitations because we find them inconvenient. Children will learn crawling, walking, listening, talking, toilet training, all in succession at developmentally appropriate ages. Analogous progressions in development will occur in academic subjects as children mature.

I also mention in Chapter 4 the widely influential Bloom's Taxonomy that recognizes multiple learning domains—cognitive, affective, and psychomotor—that children must master. For skills that require performing a physical task, what Bloom's Taxonomy classifies as the "psychomotor domain," it is understood that children will only learn when they are physically and developmentally ready. No one expects four-year olds to type fluently on a computer keyboard, play difficult Chopin etudes on the piano, prepare elaborate meals in the kitchen, or drive a car because four-year olds clearly lack the physical dexterity to do any one of these activities. They are still working on gripping crayons and not bumping into things on the playground.

Therefore, the willful ignorance displayed about the development of skills in what Bloom calls the "cognitive domain," is stunning. The Common Core is blind not only to the progression of normal child development, but also to natural variations in the rate that children develop. It is expected that all children should be at the same cognitive level when they enter kindergarten, and proceed through the entire K-12 curriculum in lockstep with one another. People who think that all children can learn in unison, have obviously never worked with children with special needs, or the gifted and talented, or taught in a classroom—any classroom.

Demanding that children be taught to developmentally inappropriate standards for language and math comprehension is not a harmless experiment. This exercise in futility wastes the time of teachers and students, and unethically sets all of them up to fail. It exacerbates the very problems—achievement gaps between various racial and ethnic groups—that the new curriculum is supposed to fix. The Common Core does this by focusing on deficiencies, rather than on the implications—and opportunities—of individual development. Like its predecessors, the Common Core, with its emphasis on "standards" is a "deficiency-based" model for education. The effort put into developing the Common Core has been in listing and agreeing upon a standard body of knowledge and skills that all students should possess. A student lacking in one of the attributes from the list is deemed deficient and needing to be brought up to the standard.

The Deficit Model of Education

The failure of deficiency-based models for education has been recognized for a long time. In 1997, Richard R. Valencia articulated the history, characteristics, and flaws of deficit thinking in education practices [5]. He rightly called out research by "deficit thinkers" as pseudoscience. [5, p. 6] Even back then, well before the "No Child Left Behind Act," Valencia described high-stakes testing as a "modern form of education oppression driven by deficit thinking." [5, p. 5].

In a more recent work, *Dismantling Contemporary Deficit Thinking* [6], Valencia continues to call out much of the pseudoscience that advocates for deficit models of education cite when foisting their pedagogies on the poor and marginalized. Fundamentally, deficit thinking is characterized by a "blame the victim" mentality that views poverty as a result of character flaws and moral failings. Normal differences between human beings are considered pathologies. According to Valencia, poor students, students of color, English language learners, and basically anyone not from the predominate white culture are deemed deficient and substandard. Equally disturbing, argues Valencia, is that many of the teaching methods used to remediate these students are based on racial and ethnic stereotypes.

Valencia exposes tautologies in the pseudoscience behind deficit thinking similar to ones already encountered in this book, such as the erroneous conclusion that ethnic groups with low high school completion rates must not value education. This is a tautology because values must be measured independent of the observation of low-completion rates before they can become an explanation for low completion rates. In other words, the sole piece of evidence for making the claim that ethnic groups with low high school completion rates do not value education is the low completion rates. The circularity of this argument is so obvious it is dizzying. Valencia finds that the standards-based approach to school reform, with its focus on the symptoms of school failure rather than the causes, is riddled with such deficit thinking and is fundamentally bankrupt.

Personally, I would like to teleport all the monolingual native English-speaking policymakers advocating for more standards to a first-grade class in China and make them students for a year. I'd like to see how well they would do meeting the standards there. My guess is that they would be deemed deficient and in need of remedial work. Policymakers need to reframe their thinking and focus on strengths rather than weaknesses. A student who is learning English as a second language might be bringing down school test scores, but that same student is on track to become bilingual, which will be a major asset as an adult, not a deficiency. Not to mention the volumes of research indicating that learning another language creates more—not less—pathways in the brain for cognitive development and higher order thinking.

An approach to education based on standards invariably results in checklists being brought out and omissions noted, rather than accomplishments cited. The significance of student abilities is always second in consideration to gaps on the checklist. Unfortunately, it is a universal human truth that the list of abilities that an individual possesses will always be much shorter than a list of abilities that same individual lacks. Education when framed in this manner becomes a futile undertaking.

This way of thinking about education arises from the past, from a manufacturing-based economy when the purpose of schools was to prepare the next generation of factory and office workers. Like the interchangeable parts assembled into products, the workers also needed to be interchangeable. Educational standards mirrored part and product specifications in order to meet this need. A high school graduate had to fit into a "slot" in the company in the same way that each part had to fit in place on the assembly line. Expressions such as "trying to fit a square peg into a round hole" have their origin in this economic past.

However, economic realities of the 21st century render both the factory and the factory model of education obsolete. Education needs to re-focus on promoting the development of the individual over the course of a lifetime. Teaching should not be about correcting deficiencies in relation to a standard; it should be about effecting positive *change* in relation to a student's present abilities.

The fact is there are many students in the school system for which meeting Common Core standards will be a futile undertaking. But these students benefit immensely from school because they learn a great deal. They and their teachers should not be deemed failures because that learning is not aligned with the standards. There are also students at the other end of spectrum who arrive in school already exceeding the Common Core standards. They and their teachers should not be deemed successes by their mere presence. These gifted students should be challenged to perform better.

Optimal Engagement in Learning

All students should be challenged to perform better no matter where their abilities fall in relation to the Common Core standards. In school there exists two kinds of boredom: (1) knowing everything that is going on (2) knowing nothing about what is going on. Students tune out in either circumstance. To fully engage students there needs to be optimal challenge. Learning takes place at the boundary between what students already know and the next step into the unknown. If students never step beyond what they already know they will never learn. But asking for giant leaps isn't good either. It results in being overwhelmed and shutting down.

In his classic work *Flow: The Psychology of Optimal Experience,* the psychologist Mihaly Csikzentmihalyi describes the conditions present when a person is completely immersed in an activity and performing at peak level—a mental state that he terms "flow." [7] Essential to achieving a state of flow is balance between the challenge and the skill level the activity requires. A person with a high degree of skill performing an activity with little challenge will be apathetic or bored. In contrast a person with a low skill level performing an extremely challenging activity will be worried or anxious. The sense of timelessness brought about by complete engagement in an activity—"flow" in Csikzentmihalyi terminology—will only occur when the challenge is commensurate with the skill the person possesses.

Learning is most effective when a student achieves a state of flow. But obviously that balance between challenge and skill will vary between students. A model for education that focuses only on deficiencies defined by universal standards rather than finding optimal challenges for unique individuals will not result in effective learning.

The failure of deficiency-based education models like the Common Core to recognize the diversity of human experiences and abilities that students bring into school is a deficiency in our entire approach to education. Moreover, it is a flaw we can no longer afford. The 21st century world we live in is changing too fast.

Human lifespans now vastly exceed the lifetimes of established companies, institutions, and technologies. As a result, it is impossible for an education system to provide students with a knowledge and skill base sufficient for a meaningful and productive adult life. Any list of standards, such as the Common Core, that are "aligned to the expectations of colleges, workforce training programs, and employers," is guaranteed to be obsolete before implementation. Society and workplaces are simply changing too fast.

A rethinking of education is needed that focuses on the development that each student experiences in the learning process. Not only will what I call "change-focused education" be more productive and satisfying for teachers and students, it will better prepare students for a lifetime of continuous learning that is now necessary to cope with our rapidly changing world.

Change-Focused Education

Defining success in terms of mandated standards fails to acknowledge that students who are deemed deficient might be learning the most, while students meeting the standards might be learning the least. As I mentioned in the preface, learning is fundamentally a biological process—neural circuits must be formed in the brain. There are limits to how much anyone can learn in a defined period of time. Take language acquisition for example. According to the U. S. State Department it takes about 600 hours of study for an English speaker to learn Spanish and over 2000 hours to learn Chinese [8]. For English language learners, studies have shown it takes 4 to 7 years to master academic English, which is the level of proficiency required for university study [9].

Clearly for language, or any other academic subject, there are limitations on rates of knowledge acquisition. This suggests that instead of evaluating students in terms of their *level* of knowledge, they should be evaluated on their *rate* of knowledge acquisition. Of course assessing a rate of change requires knowing the level from which each individual student began. This requires the formation of teacher-student relationships and deferring to the judgment of the teachers, which is inconvenient for reformers who want accountability in the form of business-related metrics based on universal and uniform standards. However, investigators who have made the effort to directly observe teacher-student interactions in "underperforming schools" often observe substantial and meaningful amounts of *change* in overall student development.

Mission High in San Francisco

Over four years, from 2010 to 2014, the journalist Kristina Rizga spent an extensive amount of time observing classes and interviewing students and teachers at Mission High, a school with low test scores in San Francisco, CA. She wanted to understand the racial and income gaps that persist in American schools and make recommendations on how to close these gaps. Her four-year immersive experience in the high school became the basis for her book *Mission High: One School, How Experts Tried to Fail It, and the Students and Teachers Who Made It Triumph* [10].

Like many urban schools, Mission High is large (950 students). Most of its students are from poor families (75%), and it has a high concentration of English language learners (38%). The school is extremely diverse (the majority of students are either Latino, African-American, or Asian-American).

Schools with these kinds of demographics usually do have low test scores. But what Rizga discovered surprised her. The low test scores gave a misleading picture of the quality of education students received. Students genuinely liked going to school at Mission High and 84% of the 2010 graduating class were accepted to college despite it being labeled a "low-performing" school.

Rizga learned the difference between standardized tests and teacher-written tests. The purpose of standardized testing is to expose gaps in students' knowledge. But the teachers wrote tests that allowed students to demonstrate what they do know and in doing so, allowed them to build confidence and a desire to learn more. In addition, Rizga discovered that standardized tests don't measure many of the most important components of a quality education—critical thinking, intrinsic motivation, resilience, self-management, resourcefulness, and relationship skills—but teachers using human judgment could assess these components and help students strengthen them. Over the long run, these non-cognitive skills that the standardized tests don't measure can matter more to a student than the cognitive skills—memorizing, recalling, formal reasoning—that the tests do measure.

Rizga provides in-depth profiles of the principal, three teachers, and four students. She introduces us to Maria, who as a child fled to California after gangs brutally raped, tortured, and murdered the aunt she lived with in her native El Salvador. Maria begins ninth grade at Mission High not speaking any English, but is expected to take the same standardized tests as everyone else after just one year. However, Maria is resilient, fiercely determined, learns to write insightful essays, and upon graduating receives acceptances from five colleges.

We meet Pablo, a native of Guatemala, who is coming to the realization that he is gay. He reveals his sexuality to his mother at the end of his sophomore year. After his mother kicks him out of the house, it is a teacher who Pablo calls on for help. Mr. Hsu, a math teacher, provides him with extra clothes, a meal, gives him a ride to a friend's house and helps him file a report with Child Protective Services. Pablo goes on to become a leader in the Gay-Straight Alliance at Mission High.

There is Jesmyn, an African-American student whose family is forced to move between different government-run housing projects. At her previous schools, she received mostly D's and F's. But after transferring to Mission High, Jesmyn learns to write well, pulls up her grades, and becomes the first member of her family to attend college.

As Rizga interviews the teachers, they make it clear that they don't view their students in terms of the "deficit model" of education. Instead of seeing the home languages and cultures of their students as deficits, this school and these teachers celebrate them as foundations to be built on. The goal of teaching is to add to the cultural backgrounds the students have, not replace them. In addition, they know that acquiring proficiency in academic English takes at least four years of intensive study. English fluency doesn't happen the moment a student arrives in school.

The teachers stress that they do not see their students in terms of grades and test scores, but as individuals with value regardless of their academic performances. As the English teacher Ms. McKamey explains:

> "Seeing every student as an intellectual is different than having high expectations. It's about an equal partnership. As a teacher, I do know a lot more than my students, but I don't own their intellect." [10, p. 109]

Nor are the test scores measures of the teachers' self-worth. At Mission High the teachers have developed a culture of accountability to each other through collective reviews of student work and coaching from respected senior colleagues. While politicians and philanthropists argue that test scores should be used to evaluate teachers, McKamey notes that this is not what motivates them:

> "I have never heard teachers talk about evaluations or bonuses as something that motivates them improve. What teachers talk about is the feedback they get from students, parents, and peers they respect." [10, p. 204]

Patterson High in Baltimore

Journalists who take the time to embed in similar urban public schools report similar observations. In 2015, *Baltimore Sun* reporter Liz Bowie and photographer Amy Davis spent an extensive amount of time inside Patterson High School in eastern Baltimore. Patterson has a diverse and vibrant student body with approximately 1100 students in total, and about one-third of the students are children of recent immigrants who collectively speak 24 languages. Their award-winning three-part newspaper report—"Unsettled Journeys"—provided moving portraits of these teenagers from around the world—many of them refugees from wars who had witnessed horrific acts of violence—and their struggles to learn a new language and culture in a short amount of time [11].

Profiled is Narmin from Baghdad, whose father was kidnapped and his home bombed because he worked for Americans. She must cope with recurring nightmares from the trauma. Narmin remains in close touch with her sister and boyfriend who are still in Iraq by texting them constantly with the details of her day. Narmin becomes close to Tom Smith, a teacher who has for many years taught English to new immigrants. In addition to teaching her English, Smith encourages Narmin to forge a new life in America, and counsels her when a health crisis befalls her best friend. Narmin stays in school and is on track to graduate.

There is Monique, who spent her childhood in a crowded refugee camp in central Africa. At age 16, she arrives at Patterson unable to even read or write in her native language of Sango, for which there is only one interpreter in another part of the city. Her inability to communicate makes her socially isolated and at times lost in a figurative sense—not being able to make sense of the school work—and in a literal sense—getting on the wrong school bus or going to the wrong classroom. But, by the end of the school year Monique is speaking some English, progressing academically, and making friends.

Most immigrant children are from Central American countries. Many of these children have fled abusive families, gang violence, and extreme poverty. They attend school, but live in legal limbo; without proper immigration documents they can't work and can be deported at any time. There might not even be a custodial parent to hire lawyers and deal with the legal complexities. Despite these crises, the children are expected to learn English and complete high school.

Out of necessity, teachers who work at Patterson become mental health counselors, social workers, and life coaches, despite having no training for these additional roles. But it is clear that strong bonds form between teachers and students. Journalists like Rizga, Bowie, and Davis who have taken the time to meet and interview students and faculty, show that Common Core standards, curricula, and standardized test scores are of minor consideration in comparison to healing from trauma, assimilating into a new culture, forging a personal identity, and building relationships with adult mentors.

Moreover, what they document is the difficulty of learning a new language for immigrant students, a difficulty that may bring down test scores, but that the students overcome with diligence, resilience, and the support of teachers who honor and uphold their backgrounds and cultures. We cannot get around the struggle of language acquisition through a set of standards. What is true about immigrants learning a new language applies to everyone. It is how the human brain works when it comes to language acquisition. No matter how high their expectations, bureaucrats drafting Common Core standards would be unable to meet these same standards if they didn't grow up speaking English.

Change Is Unique to the Individual

At these schools, labeled as failing and threatened with closures because standards technically are not met, what in fact is witnessed is education at its absolute best. The lives of these students are being changed in much greater and in much more profound ways than for many students who do meet the standards. After all, which lives will be changed more by going to school?

- An already college-bound student who arrives at school already exceeding the standards, or a student for whom college is not a goal, and who raises his grades enough to graduate from high school, thus increasing future job possibilities.
- A native English-speaking student who manages to raise her SAT verbal score by 50 points so that she can attend a more prestigious college, or the child of an immigrant learning to speak English so that she can function as a literate adult in her new country.
- A gay student struggling with identity issues who has an accepting and supportive family, or a student coming out as gay in a hostile family who receives support from a caring teacher.
- A student from a safe suburban neighborhood who has not lost close friends and family members due to violence, or a refugee student who has witnessed unspeakable atrocities and with the help of school counselors is healing from post-traumatic stress.

Curriculum standards and testing regimens are motivated by a well-intentioned desire to close achievement gaps that exist between various socio-economic and ethnic and racial groups. There is a belief that by demanding that all children meet a set of rigid and arbitrarily high academic standards, achievement gaps can be closed and economic opportunities increased for all. The apparent reasoning is that if all children receive the same education and are held to the same academic standards, then all children will have equal opportunity to succeed as adults.

However, addressing pervasive economic inequality by pretending that in an ideal world all children are alike isn't a solution. The inequalities that plague our society are inherent in the structure of our global political and economic systems. Curricula and performance standards will not change the underlying pathologies corrupting these structures.

In addition, it is a mistake to conflate unjust economic inequalities that arise from these broken political and economic systems with normal differences in abilities and dispositions among people that arise from being human. Even if all barriers to inequality were broken down, and all children came from safe environments with loving and supportive families, people would still be different from one another and normal human development would still unfold.

Education should be about helping each child, regardless of background or academic readiness, achieve his or her full, unique potential. It should instill not just academics, but also physical, emotional, and social skills, which are also essential for making meaningful contributions to the well-being of our families, communities, and the economy. Differences between people that arise across all skill sets and educational domains are an inherent and valued part of the human experience that should be celebrated in school, not erased. Education, as witnessed at schools such as Mission High and Patterson, is changing lives by embracing the uniqueness of each child and enabling meaningful relationships between the students, teachers and parents.

Beyond the "Business Model"

> "America's business-inspired obsession with prioritizing 'metrics' in a complex world that deals with the development of individual minds has become the primary cause of mediocrity in American schools."
>
> Kristina Rizga
> *Mission High* [10, Preface, p. 8]

To recognize and support change-focused education, it is necessary to move beyond the business model in regards to defining and assessing educational outcomes. The purpose of education is not to produce high-scoring test-takers, nor is it to produce human capital for businesses. The purpose of education is to produce competent, independent adults, capable of functioning in the world beyond the classroom, engaging in productive work, forming meaningful relationships with others, and developing as individuals over the course of a lifetime.

In their book, *Counting What Counts: Reframing Education Outcomes*, Yong Zhao and his collaborators call for a rethinking of education outcomes [12]. Zhao argues that instead of aiming for college and career readiness, the goal for children should be "out-of-parents' basement" readiness. By that he means that the education process should prepare children to become adults who can support themselves financially, be engaged socially and civically, and live independently. An education focused solely on preparing children to be high scorers on math and reading tests leads to conformity and children who are dependent on others for direction, rather than enabling independence by teaching flexible and creative thinking.

He likens the pursuit of ever-higher test scores to the building of ever-bigger statues on Easter Island—an undertaking that eventually led to the collapse of that civilization because basic survival skills were neglected. Zhao writes:

"Ultimately, just like Easter Island ended up a barren island filled with big statues, countries may succeed in raising test scores, but they will likely end up as nations of great test takers in an intellectually barren land; test scores do not count nearly as much as reformers believe for the success of individuals or nations. Moreover they can come at a huge cost." [12, p. 4]

Zhao notes ironies about our approach to education. While the testing emphasis is premised on increasing economic productivity, there is actually no connection between a country's student test scores and its economic output. In addition, many Asian countries with high-scoring students, that education reformers in the United States seek to emulate, are actually moving away from an emphasis on testing because they want the economic benefits of a more creative workforce—like the one in the United States.

Traditional education, Zhao explains, trained people to perform jobs that in the modern economy are performed by robots. To survive in the 21st century, education must prepare creative and entrepreneurial students who will each succeed in their own unique ways. Diversity, which for the standards movement is a nuisance, must be recognized as strength. He believes that the current curricula should come with warning labels about potential educational side effects in the same manner that drug labels have warnings about physical side effects. For example: this reading curriculum may enhance short-term reading scores but might destroy a child's interest in reading.

Zhao sees no way to fix the current model for education and he therefore calls for a "paradigm shift" in which current curricula are abandoned altogether. Rather than fix deficits, education should be rethought so that it focuses on enhancing strengths. Meaningless drill work must be abandoned. All work children do should serve a purpose that is greater than competing for high grades and test scores, goals that are essentially meaningless.

Zhao does view assessment as a necessary part of education, and he is not calling for its abandonment. Rather, he calls for a paradigm shift in educational assessment. Traditional assessment defines a successful outcome as a body of students who are all alike in their accomplishments. All have mastered the same set of skills and knowledge as mandated in the curriculum and all score high on standardized tests. Deviation from the mandated norms—e.g. low test scores, not meeting all curriculum objectives—is evidence of failure. The paradigm shift Zhao calls for is an education "that preserves or even amplifies human diversity," because "modern society needs a diversity of human talents instead of a homogenous workforce with similar skills and knowledge." [12, p.170].

Zhao sees the fact that the United States has never ranked high on international tests while at the same time maintaining a dynamic and prosperous economy as evidence that the "failure" of our education system to produce students who all have the same abilities, might in the long run be highly beneficial to our economy. Countries that have been more effective in raising test scores are actually putting themselves at an economic disadvantage by reducing the diversity of talents in their workforces.

The new assessment paradigm that Zhao envisions would be premised on the fact that every individual is unique and that "enhancement of individual differences has to become a celebrated educational outcome." [12, p.175] Education must become personalized and so must the assessments. Additionally, the assessments must focus on long-term educational outcomes, they must be "authentic" (that is, relevant to real-life), assess both cognitive and non-cognitive skills, and be developed in collaboration with the individual being assessed.

Like Zhao, Tony Wagner of Harvard University in *The Global Achievement Gap* makes the argument that our schools currently prepare students for an economy that no longer exists [13]. According to Wagner, the problem with our education system is not so much that our schools are failing, but rather that they are succeeding at a mission that is obsolete and irrelevant. He notes that "effective communication, curiosity, and critical thinking skills are more than just the desirable outcomes of a liberal arts education … they are essential habits of mind for life in the twenty-first century." [13, p. xxiii] But schools were not designed to teach and cultivate these habits. Wagner articulates seven "survival skills" for success in the twenty-first century economy. These are:

- Critical thinking and problem-solving
- Collaboration across networks and leading by example
- Agility and adaptability
- Initiative and entrepreneurship
- Effective oral, written, and multimedia communication
- Accessing and analyzing information
- Curiosity and imagination

Note that most of these are non-cognitive relationship-building skills. Also note that these skills are critical to the changed-focused education witnessed in Mission and Patterson High Schools. The teachers would not be successful in changing the lives of their students if they did not possess the skill set listed above. Teachers mindlessly parroting a "curriculum" would not be effective. To succeed they must use these kinds of non-cognitive skills to establish relationships with their students.

Rethinking College: Preparing for the Unimagined

Will the change-focused education seen at schools like Mission High and Patterson Park adequately prepare students for college? After all, the stated reason for having standards is to ensure that graduating students are adequately prepared for college—an experience that is now seen as necessary, rather than optional, for future career success. Assessment scores at the K-12 level are intended to certify that students meeting the standards are college-ready. The non-cognitive skills that the reporters observed might be useful in life, but will they help a student graduate from college?

In fact, higher education institutions are also grappling with many of these same issues that are facing K-12 educators. In Chapter 2, I examined the issue of whether colleges should become SAT-optional. Many college administrators don't believe that the SAT is a measure of college and career readiness, while many other administrators—like the vocal alumnus I cited—certainly do. College faculty also have differing views on this issue. There are also many people, in and out of higher education, who argue that the purpose of going to college is for career training and professional preparation, and that colleges will not be able to accomplish that mission if admitted students lack a standards-based K-12 education.

However, I would argue that a college education should also be changed-focused rather than standards-based. It too should focus on developing the foundational skills that Wagner articulates—such as critical thinking and problem solving, collaboration and communication, etc.—skills that are the learning outcomes from the liberal arts. The reason that colleges should not be focused on career training is that the careers of the future are simply unimaginable. How could they possibly be taught? For example, consider my college education from a historical perspective:

In the fall of 1977, when I started college, I arrived with a typewriter to write my term papers—a brand new electric one, which was a step up from my mother's old manual model that I used throughout high school. Phone calls could only be made and received from my dorm room using a rotary dial phone that hung on the wall. Computer courses taught students how to program using punch cards, and there was only one computer on the entire campus that students could use for course work. Someone with the job title of "computer operator" fed programmer-supplied punch cards into the computer and delivered thick stacks of paper output to cubbyholes for the programmer to pick up a half-hour later. Applying for any kind of post-graduation job often meant feeding an application form with two or three sheets of carbon paper through a typewriter and being extra careful not to make a typo because correcting a typing mistake when using carbon paper was tedious and messy.

The world of 1977 is irretrievably gone and with it are many of the jobs and skills needed to survive in that world. Also gone is the world of 1945, the year my father left the Navy and apprenticed to become a printer, a trade that would support him for the next 25 years, until rapid technological change upended the economics of that industry and he decided to switch careers and become a masonry contractor. My grandson, born in 2015, will graduate from high school in 2033 into a world that will be very different than the one he was born into. It is completely impossible to imagine the world of 2065, when he turns 50 years old. There will be all sorts of job titles and industries never anticipated and many of the jobs of today will have gone the way of "computer operators" and "typewriter manufacturers,"—reminiscences of a distant past. It is impossible from today's vantage point to predict which jobs will vanish and what new jobs will exist.

Preparing students for an unimaginable future presents a challenge for educators at all levels. It is clear from this brief historical examination that an education that focuses on "college and career readiness" is a recipe for rapid obsolescence. Yes, students must be prepared to live in the world of today and to do the kinds of jobs demanded by the current economy. But they must also understand the long view of history, the continuity of change, and the never-ending processes of economic creation and destruction.

Future Trends

While the future is unknowable, certain trends cannot be ignored. One trend is that over time, what college-educated "knowledge workers" do has become less and less about knowledge. What it means to be an "expert" today is very different than what it meant to be an expert 30 years ago. A generation ago experts either possessed or had access to specialized knowledge that was not readily available to the general public. Experts could leverage their information monopolies to earn comfortable livings filling apparently secure jobs.

Today, computer programs can now perform routine tasks that in the past required paying experts thousands of dollars. Tax preparers, travel agents, stockbrokers, publishers, and attorneys—just to name a few professions—have had the economics of their industries upended by the wide distribution of specialized knowledge on the Internet, combined with readily available, user-friendly, software packages that automate many of the services these professionals provide.

To survive in the modern economy, professionals must spend less time using their specialized knowledge, and more time managing relationships across multiple dimensions. How different areas of knowledge relate to each other, how different people relate to each other, how different people relate to different knowledge areas, are the issues modern professionals face each workday. In many industries, managing relationships and coordinating activities among diverse groups of people spans the globe.

Colleges are the places where most professionals learned to nurture this vast network of relationships that their livelihoods depend on. It was in college that they learned to work in groups, received mentoring from experienced professors, became exposed to diverse people and cultures, and developed networking skills. I challenge college graduates to reflect on the narrative of their life stories. How much specific content do they remember from their courses? I'm guessing not much. But the people they met, the teachers who taught them how to think rather than just what to know, the mistakes and misjudgments they made, and the successful struggles to understand difficult new concepts—these are the experiences that guide them today.

But students won't get these experiences from going to college if their entire focus is on acquiring professional knowledge that will either be soon forgotten or quickly obsolete. In fact, the short half-life in memory and/or usefulness of most technical knowledge is the reason that I think that the traditional liberal arts curriculum, with its emphasis on developing the meta-skills necessary to become a lifelong learner, is more valuable in the long run.

It is not necessary to go to college to prepare for existing jobs. If a job already exists, it is easy to find out what duties it entails and what skills are needed. Online research combined with online courses can probably provide sufficient training. College is the place to acquire the skill set for the jobs that have not yet been imagined. Consider, for example, the innumerable jobs associated with the Internet, none of which were imaginable a generation ago. I could not have taken courses about the Web when I went to college, because the idea of the Web did not exist. But my college education provided me the meta-skills necessary for adapting when the Web came into being.

The only way to prepare for an unimagined future is to study the timeless subjects found in the liberal arts. In fact, I would argue that the increasingly rapid rate of technological change has made the liberal arts more relevant, not less. Any technical knowledge picked up in college will be obsolete almost immediately. But a solid foundation in writing, history, foreign languages, literature, arts, ethics, social and natural sciences, philosophy, theology, and mathematics will prepare students for a lifetime of learning and communicating.

In his book *Humans are Underrated*, Geoff Colvin argues that in the future, the humanities will be more important than engineering because of the deeply human skills it develops [14]. More and more of the jobs that require technical expertise will be taken over by computers. However, the skills that make us human—empathy, creativity, social sensitivity, humor, storytelling—in other words, the skills that allow us to build relationships with each other, cannot be outsourced to computers. These skills, skills learned from the humanities, will be the ones of value in the future.

Likewise, news analyst Fareed Zakaria in his book *In Defense of a Liberal Education,* states that technology and globalization will make a liberal education more valuable in the future, not less [15]. A skills-based, technical education is "outdated and shortsighted" because technical skills rapidly become obsolete as the jobs associated with them are automated and outsourced. The key value-added skills in the future are the ones provided by a liberal education.

Business writer Daniel Pink argues that in the future, the MFA (Masters in Fine Arts) will be the new MBA (Masters in Business Administration) [16]. He sees MBA graduates as 21st-century blue-collar workers, with the lucrative jobs that they are expecting soon outsourced to overseas workers. In his book, *A Whole New Mind: Why Right-Brainers Will Rule the Future,* Pink argues that while the last few decades of the 20th century rewarded those with technical expertise—those with analytic left-brain minds that could write code and crunch numbers—the future will belong to those with holistic right-brain minds [17].

"These people – artists, inventors, designers, storytellers, caregivers, consolers, big picture thinkers – will now reap society's richest rewards and share in its greatest joys." [17, p. 1]

As we transition from the information age to what Pink calls the "conceptual age," he sees schools moving in the exact opposite direction—trying to perfect education for the industrial age [16]. When he wrote his book over 10 years ago, Pink was not optimistic about education, because cuts to the arts in order to fund the shift to standardized testing did not make sense given the economic trends [16]. His lack of optimism on education practices turned out to be well founded and his predictions of economic trends accurate.

Yong Zhao also sees a creative mindset as being valuable in the future because of the "long tail effect," described by business writer Chris Anderson [18]. Anderson's influential and prescient book argued that in the future rather than sell products to large markets, businesses will sell products to small highly specialized markets. As these niche products multiply, Zhao argues that many apparently useless skills will become useful. A creative workforce with diverse skills and talents will be essential for any business to remain competitive.

These writers are all aware that history will not stop; in fact, it is on fast forward. Yet-to-be-imagined jobs, in yet-to-be-imagined industries will arrive faster than they have in the past. The only way to educate for the unknown is with a solid foundation in the timeless foundational subjects of the liberal arts. It is the only hope for gaining insights into the unity of knowledge and the unity of human experience, insights that will allow future workers to discern and manage the relationships that their livelihoods will depend on.

We are in the midst of a major transformation in the human experience, akin to the invention of the printing press over 500 years ago and the invention of writing systems thousands of years earlier. The Internet is transforming humanity's relationship to its stored knowledge base. In our ancient and ongoing quest for meaning, it appears that in the future, meaning will arise from understanding relationships between disparate knowledge areas and diverse groups of people. An education needs to be as much about preparing for the unimagined future as it is about learning the present.

The Expectations Trap

If the future cannot be imagined, then how should students navigate the bewildering array of choices for majors, minors, special programs, and studies abroad? Students are understandably anxious over making the right choices. This anxiety is often exacerbated by the expectations of parents and family members because student interests and aptitudes are often not aligned with parental expectations for their programs of study. As a result, tension develops between interests and perceived needs.

For students who do go to college, it is an enormous investment of time and money. Parents, who often foot most of the bill, understandably want a tangible return on the investment. From the parental viewpoint, the "out-of-basement readiness" for the adult world that Yong Zhao talks about is the minimally acceptable outcome. Parents do not want "boomerang" kids either, which results in them pushing their children towards careers that are perceived as stable and well paying. To this end, some majors are deemed more "practical" than others. Parents subtly or not so subtly, guide their children towards programs of study in engineering, business, pre-law, or pre-med, while discouraging aspirations to study philosophy, history, or art. The reasoning is that few people make a living as philosophers, historians, or artists, and those that do often struggle financially.

But students pressured into majors in which they have little interest and aptitude are often unengaged and do mediocre work. Their grades suffer as a result. Over the long run, individual grades mean very little. Twenty years later no one will care if a medical doctor's grade in Biology 101 was an A or a C because the course content will not be needed on a daily basis. What, then, do grades actually mean? Good grades imply a commitment to excellence, a trait employers and professional schools highly value. A degree with bad grades in a "practical" subject is useless. Stated aspirations to be a doctor, lawyer, or engineer will not be taken seriously if a student's grades are poor. Therefore, parents and students need to be realistic about expectations. Grades will be much better in a major that the student enjoys.

A few years ago, one of my students entered his third year of college as a biology major. In my advising session with him, I examined his transcript and noted that he had not passed a single science course. He had either failed or withdrawn before failing the first semester courses in biology and chemistry three times each. He still needed to fulfill the one-course distribution requirement for natural science. I told him that even if he passed the first semester of biology, he would need a dozen additional courses for the biology degree, and they would not be easier courses. I asked him what he most enjoyed studying. His response: theater.

"Major in theater," I told him.

"But that's not a practical major," he replied.

"It's not practical for you to fail all these science courses. It's better that you have a theater degree with decent grades than no degree and a slew of F's on your transcript."

He admitted that he hadn't thought about his choice of major in that way. He switched his major to theater and graduated a couple years later.

The High Expectations Trap

This particular student was an extreme case. However, I've seen many students in majors for which they have no real interest or aptitude, but persist nonetheless because their parents refuse to fund their college education unless they study something "practical." These expectations lead to students just getting by in the major of the parents' choice, when they could be excelling in a major of their choice. As a result, there are students enrolled in engineering programs even though they struggle with the math and have no interest in building anything. There are students muddling through business degrees who would be much better served in the long run with a liberal arts degree. It is actually more practical to have good grades in a history major than bad grades in a business or engineering major. Good grades in a history major indicate a capacity to write well and analyze critically, skills valued by employers.

But expectations sabotage students in other ways, too.

I've seen students who are not mature enough to be in college, but go because it is the expected next step after high school. The result is that they are wasting their time and their parents' money. Partying all night and sleeping all day can be done at a much lower cost at home than in college, and the results achieved will be the same.

I've seen exceptionally smart, curious students who should become scientists, but their parents expect them to become medical doctors because of the prestige it will bring to the family. The result is that if you ask these students why they are so passionate about medicine that they intend to devote their life to its practice, they can only express a nebulous desire to "help people." Of course, I can think of many professions that "help people" and are unrelated to medicine. If you intend to become a medical doctor you should have an intrinsic interest in medicine.

I've seen students juggle the demands of double and even triple majors so that they can pursue their interests and satisfy family expectations. The result is a great deal of stress from pursuing credentials that have little meaning in the long run. Employers care more that you have a degree than all the majors and minors that you acquired along the way.

The Low Expectations Trap

Of course, no parent or teacher wants to have low expectations either. Extensive literature, going back decades, documents the pernicious effects of low expectations on student learning and life outcomes [19]. Parents and teachers who believe that their children cannot learn will soon find that they have children who do not learn. Low expectations cloud judgment and obscure objective truth; they keep people from even trying to succeed. This is a fact not lost on politicians who are always "managing expectations" of their own performances—a phrase that is always code for lowering expectations. Politicians intuitively know what many students do—that you can't fail if no one expects you to succeed.

As we have seen in earlier chapters, reformers have seized upon the documented damage from low expectations to claim that raising expectations for teachers and students will fix schools. Or in the words of a memorable phrase frequently used by George W. Bush, it is "the soft bigotry of low expectations" that has been most damaging to student achievement in urban and minority schools. Research into the link between expectations and student achievement has found, not surprisingly, that teachers with low expectations act differently towards their students than teachers with high expectations [20]. It is not the thoughts, but rather the actions that do the damage. However, listen to any principal or high-level school administrator talk about their programs and you will inevitably hear them speak of the "high expectations" they have for their students and faculty.

Motivations in Place of Expectations

It would appear that educational success hinges on calibrating expectations to an appropriate level. If both high expectations and low expectations stunt student achievement and set them up for failure, what is the optimal level? *In my view the optimum level for expectations should be zero.* Teaching and learning should be activities performed for their own sake—or in Csikzentmihalyi's terminology they should be "autotelic" experiences [7]—and should not be performed for external rewards. Instead of thinking in terms of expectations, which are always external pressures on individuals that often lead to resentments, we should think in terms of motivations, which are intrinsic drivers of behaviors.

The goal of education should be to develop and nurture intrinsic motivation in our children so that they develop what Csikzentmihalyi calls autotelic personalities—driven to succeed in the activities that are most meaningful to them. It is when people are intrinsically motivated that they rise to challenges, overcome obstacles, push boundaries, grow and thrive. The state of "flow" that Csikzentmihalyi describes is a psychological state of complete immersion in an activity for its own sake and is best achieved through intrinsic motivation.

It is through autotelic experiences that people find themselves most productive and as a result most happy.

Perhaps the most important advice I received in school was from my doctoral thesis advisor, Richard Norberg, on the day I left graduate school. I had completed and defended my doctoral thesis, finished up with the movers, and packed my car for the drive to my new city and job. I stopped at his office to thank him and say goodbye. His parting words were:

> "Whatever you do in life, do what you enjoy. Don't do what others expect. Your wife, your parents, your children, your friends, your co-workers, will all have expectations. Don't give in to them. Do what you most enjoy."

As time has gone on, my appreciation of this advice has grown. What Norberg meant by "do what you most enjoy" is do the work that is most meaningful to you because then you will be motivated, engaged, and happiest. Giving into expectations is a trap. Parents, administrators, teachers and students all need to let go. Everyone needs to accept that no matter what happens in school the future will always be uncertain. The real value of an education isn't in teaching what is known; it is in preparing students for the unknown. By definition the unknown can never be expected; facing it requires knowing what *motivates* us to do our best.

The Limits of Education

Like science, education also has it limits. It is not a cure-all for every societal problem. Consider this all too-common call for action after a national crisis.

> "Thus, in far too many instances, we entered into financial commitments that we couldn't afford, with terms and conditions that we didn't truly understand, in order to buy things that we really didn't need. If more Marylanders had the benefit of sound financial literacy education, fewer of our friends and family members would be facing the loss of homes and life savings today." [21]

Peter Franchot
Op-Ed, *Baltimore Sun*,
February 10, 2010

Peter Franchot, the comptroller for the State of Maryland, advocated adding financial literacy to the curriculum in Maryland after the 2007–08 financial crisis. He was not successful, mostly because of resistance from the education establishment in Maryland to additional curricular requirements. I am a financial literacy advocate and I agree with Franchot that more financial literacy education should be provided at the K-12 level. I believe that more education on essential life skills improves individual decision-making and outcomes. However, I sympathize with the educational establishment and understand why an apparently well-intentioned proposal to improve financial literacy was rejected. Franchot's reasoning is simply wrong. It contains fallacies about the causes of the 2007–08 financial crisis and, more broadly, about the role of education in society. More education is not the cure-all for societal ills that many advocates claim. There are limits to the kinds of societal problems that education can address.

In fact Franchot's implication that poor consumer choices precipitated the financial crisis is misdirection away from the true cause. The political and financial establishments, of which Franchot is a member, want to draw attention away from their obvious culpability by blaming consumers for the disaster. But consumers did not cause investment banks such as Bear Stearns and Lehman Brothers to be leveraged at multiples in excess of 30 to 1. With that amount of leverage failure is inevitable. Any adult with any experience in any kind of marketplace knows that the normal fluctuations in the value of any asset (stocks, bonds, real estate, commodities, merchandizes, etc.) are much greater than 1 part in 30. Any person or corporation taking on that amount of leverage will be wiped out at some point in time—even if the actual investments are good for the long term.

However, the people who ran these failed companies, and who made financial decisions far worse than average consumers, are the most financially literate and sophisticated members of our society. Would more education have helped them? If Dick Fuld had taken a financial literacy course before graduating high school, would he have allowed Lehman Brothers to become so over-leveraged? If Angelo Mozilo had been taught about mortgages in math class, would he have allowed Countrywide to sell millions of mortgages to people who couldn't afford to pay them back? If Joe Cassano had had a course on the basics of insurance while still in school, would he have bankrupted AIG, the world's largest insurance company, by selling products as inane as credit default swaps?

Obviously, the answer to all the above questions is no. To use a mother's phrase, the architects of the financial crisis all "knew better," and if that is the case, more knowledge is not going to prevent future bad behavior. Financial leaders, despite their extensive knowledge of markets and investments, still made colossally bad decisions. Therefore, it is not realistic to expect that providing more financial education to average consumers will eliminate the kinds of bad choices that many made.

Clearly the simple act of "knowing" is not sufficient to alter behavior; this is the problem with calls for more education whenever there is a national crisis. Financial decision-making is just one example. There are many other bad decisions people make despite being educated to know better. Consider the incidence of smoking in the United States. It has been over 50 years since the release of the 1964 report by the U. S. Surgeon General on the dangerous health effects of smoking. At that time about 40% of the adult population in the United States smoked. Extensive education through schools, public service ads, and warning labels on cigarette ads and packaging have steadily eroded the incidence of smoking so that today about 20% of the adult population smokes—an apparent triumph for educators working in concert with public health officials.

But, 20% is still 1 out of every 5 people, or about 60,000,000 smokers in the United States. Did that many people fail to learn? At the selective private college where I teach, I observe smart, well-educated, students walking around puffing on cigarettes. I doubt that they missed the lessons in school on the dangers of smoking, or are completely blind to the ubiquitous anti-smoking public service ads.

In fact, smoking is a very curious behavioral phenomenon that clearly illustrates the limits of education. The oddity about smoking is that adults do not take up the habit. Almost all smokers begin the habit as teenagers. Even though it is illegal to sell cigarettes to underage persons, and the marketing is ostensibly aimed at adults, without teenagers the tobacco industry would disappear. While there is a strong correlation between education level and incidence of smoking within the adult population, clearly the decision to begin smoking has a maturity component that education cannot completely overcome.

So it goes with alcohol abuse, drug use, unwanted pregnancies, bullying etc. The incidence of these problems is far greater than the ignorance about them. I am certain that only a tiny fraction of the women with unwanted pregnancies are truly ignorant of how pregnancy occurs. Virtually everyone has heard about the dangers of drinking and driving, but alcohol-related car accidents are still significant causes of deaths and injuries. The "war on drugs" has been going on for decades with no end in sight.

Education has made a huge improvement in the quality of life for many people, but it has its limits. As I've already mentioned, education cannot speed up normal human development. In addition, it cannot eliminate normal human drives. Poor decision-making persists even among people who know better. Knowing the right thing to do and actually doing it are two different things. Knowing what to do requires the simple act of remembering. Following through on a course of action is a commitment that requires a physical and emotional investment, and the allocation of time and money to actions that are often counter to innate desires. Education is good at teaching how to remember, but that doesn't necessarily result in committed courses of action.

The irony of the financial crisis, which, again, Franchot blamed on lack of education, is that the failed banks and investment institutions spent millions of dollars on sophisticated marketing campaigns designed to induce consumers into making bad choices. Then these same institutions were shocked, just shocked, that consumers actually bought the toxic financial products being peddled. The bankers then said that future financial catastrophes would be avoided if consumers were better educated and informed on financial decision-making. But if knowledge is the solution, why didn't it work for the bankers? And most importantly, why did the banks spend all that advertising money miseducating consumers?

Knowledge is necessary for sound decision-making, but it is not sufficient. Forcing students to sit through another class and pass another exam will not solve every societal problem. The political and corporate leaders who argue for education as a solution should examine their own assumptions and culpability for the problems they want solved. If "knowing better" didn't work for them, what makes them think it will work for everyone else?

Education has its limits because schools are not cultural islands. You cannot have one set of values for schools and a completely different set for everyone else. You cannot expect schools to educate children while political and corporate leaders inundate children and adults with sophisticated marketing campaigns intended to miseducate. You cannot expect education to produce citizens who make good decisions, while actively encouraging them to make bad decisions.

The Necessity of Purpose and Meaning

Education, like science, has its limits. But, unlike science, education can and should address questions of purpose and meaning because these questions lead directly to motivations. This is perhaps the greatest misuse of math and science in education—using these disciplines to undermine motivation by deliberately stripping education of purpose and meaning.

Filmmaker and mother of three, Vickie Abeles launched a national conversation on the purpose of education with her documentary *Race to Nowhere,* [22] followed by her book *Beyond Measure* [23]. The documentary profiled the pressures on youth brought by developmentally inappropriate expectations and over scheduling. In the film, children describe the extreme pressure they face to "succeed," which they understand to mean get good grades, do well on tests, and participate in extracurricular activities, all as means to attain entrance to prestigious colleges so that they can launch a career. The expectations placed on the children that she profiles are unrelenting and overwhelming, leading to various mental disorders such as anorexia and cutting. Also interviewed are psychologists and medical doctors who explain the damage to children's health and well–being from the disruption of family relationships and sleep patterns as a result of all this frenzied activity.

Abeles argues that parents need to take back control of their children's education from an out-of-control education system and refuse to let school impinge on family time. In addition to academics, the quality of the relationships that children have with their family and friends should also be a priority. Parents need to work with the school system to limit the amount of assigned homework and have their children opt out of tests if necessary. Education should not be about the cramming of content into students' minds for no other purpose than to do well on tests and to gain admission to prestigious colleges. Prepping children for career-readiness is questionable, given that it is impossible to know, at a young age, a child's career aspirations. Abeles' documentary goes so far as to say that the loss of unstructured or family time amounts to a stealing of childhood and argues that children's health and well-being should come first.

Abeles received pushback from people who seem to miss the point. For example, education blogger Jay Mathews, in a *Washington Post* column "Why Vicki Abeles' 'Race to Nowhere' is wrong," cites studies to support the argument that children are on average doing too little homework, not too much [24]. He sees her film as only being relevant to the small minority of students from affluent, success-minded families, not as representative of a majority. On his blog, he and Abeles engage in a back-and-forth on the statistical minutia of various academic studies of how children spend their time.

The point missed is that the current goals of education—good grades, high test scores, resume-building extracurricular activities, college and career readiness—are all essentially meaningless aspirations. How much or how little homework or effort students put in, whether their stress levels are healthy or unhealthy, are all futile topics for discussion if the goals of the process have no meaning. Abeles has an apt title for her film—*Race to Nowhere.* Those who think that parenting is about finding the right amount of activities for their children, and that educating is finding the optimum number of homework assignments are missing the point. Meaning and purpose are more important than knowledge and skills.

Education must serve a purpose beyond pleasing adults, helping the school make AYP, or impressing others with a high-paying career. If those are the only reasons for an education, there is no purpose, and children and parents have a right to rebel against the process. In addition, those who have succeeded at the process and have obtained admittance to an elite college have not necessarily obtained a meaningful goal. College is not an endpoint; it is only an opportunity to acquire the knowledge and skills needed to serve greater purposes. In his book *Excellent Sheep,* William Deresiewicz, a former professor at Yale, provides a scathing analysis of the career-oriented education that the students at elite colleges seek [25].

> "You need to get a job, but you also need to get a life. What's the return on investment of college? What's the return on investment of having children, spending time with friends, listening to music, reading a book? *The things that are most worth doing are worth doing for their own sake.* Anyone who tells you that the sole purpose of education is the acquisition of negotiable skills is attempting to reduce you to a productive employee at work, a gullible consumer in the market, and a docile subject of the state. What's at stake, when we ask what college is for, is nothing less than our ability to remain fully human." [25, p. 79]

I have added the emphasis in the quote because it supports my argument that education should be an autotelic activity for everyone involved. It is clear that Deresiewicz has observed what I and many other professors have observed: scores of emotionally fragile students who are entirely focused on grades and the potential impact of their GPAs on future careers rather than on the experience of learning.

On many occasions I have had students in my office literally in tears over a C on an exam. Students can become so stressed from receiving less than stellar grades that they will often elect to drop a course rather than put in the work necessary to learn the material. Many students, in many courses throughout the university, cannot cope with criticism of their coursework. I don't know how these students are going to cope with life if they never learn to struggle. Because of their need for constant reassurance through good grades they never challenge themselves. A self-worth based entirely on the meaningless praise provided by grades and test scores is hollow and fragile.

When it comes to forming a solid self-image, one founded on more than test scores and GPAs, the children of the privileged elite can actually learn from disadvantaged poor. Sociologists Stefanie DeLuca, Susan Clampet-Lundquist, and Kathryn Edin, conducted 10 years of fieldwork with parents and children living in some of Baltimore's public housing for their book *Coming of Age in the Other America.* [26]. They sought to understand why some children in disadvantaged environments made successful transitions to an adulthood in which they engaged in productive work and formed meaningful relationships, while other children remained products of their environments and entered adulthood disconnected and adrift.

They found that the single most predictive factor in determining whether students stayed either in school or working was the presence of an "Identity Project." They defined an Identity Project as:

"… a source of meaning that provides a strong sense of self and is linked to concrete activities to which youth commit themselves." [26, p. 66]

They found that Identity Projects came in many forms, some stronger than others, but had a commonality in that they:

"… helped some youth avoid associations with delinquent peers and instead forge connections with teachers and mentors." [26, p. 66]

Weak Identity Projects were often activities pursued in private, but stronger, more protective ones linked youth to like-minded peers with shared interests. The most robust forms were Identity Projects that allowed the youth to connect and forge relationships with institutions.

What their research did not find was an explanation for why some youth developed Identity Projects and others did not. From their interviews it appeared that Identity Projects often grew from random encounters that piqued a particular interest. However, many of these Identity Projects developed from extracurricular activities—arts, music, sports, club, youth-groups—the kinds of programs that financially-strapped schools and cities are eliminating in order to focus more on academics and closing achievement gaps.

Closing achievement gaps requires a motivating purpose. What the research on Identity Projects shows is that students find meaning in their lives from connections to other people. It appears to me that these "Identity Projects" are autotelic experiences for the students involved because they find inherent meaning and purpose in them.

Students being challenged to do better must have a stake in the outcome beyond just individual test scores. Raising standards for the poor and marginalized can't just be an elaborate exercise in statistics designed to assuage the guilt of the ruling elites. Politicians and their billionaire donors cannot dictate elevated educational standards, while at the same time using their power to create economic and political structures which ensure that no real opportunities will ever exist for the poor.

I believe that finding a source of meaning as a foundation to a productive and engaged life is a universal human need. The concept of an Identity Project emerged from research on the question of why some of the disadvantaged youth succeed despite tremendous obstacles. I think a related question, which has a related answer is: Why do some of the privileged youth fail? I believe that the answer to this second question would relate to the absence of meaningful goals that Deresiewicz observed in his students. Youth whose identities are determined by numerical measures and nebulous career plans, whose sole aim is to achieve an acceptable rate of return on their educational investment, are those who become emotionally fragile. On the other hand, youth with identities forged by striving, and overcoming the failures along the way, towards the achievement of meaningful goals that connect them to other people develop perseverance.

The data-driven pseudoscientific approach to education that infests American schools at all levels is devoid of meaning. A focus on numerical measures stripped of any context results in pointless debates on which standards should be applied, how much work should be required of students and teachers, and what is an appropriate amount of stress. In fact, nothing of significance can be achieved without hard work and engagement, and stress is an essential part of living. But the goals of the process must have meaning. The education process must, in the end, connect students to other human beings in a meaningful way. Schoolwork needs to have purpose and meaning.

There is a tendency to blame the youth for the dysfunctions that sociologists study and cultural commentators observe. Many people might argue that if some youth from public housing can rise above their circumstances then why can't others? Isn't it their own fault? Many people might watch Abeles' movie and read Deresiewicz's book and say that the privileged young people they profile need to get their acts together and grow up. But blaming youth for societal problems has been going on for ages. The problem with youth is that they are young. A much bigger problem is the adults who drive misguided and inept educational policies; they are old enough to know better.

References

1. "Preparing America's students for success," Common Core States Standards Initiative, accessed May 1, 2018, http://www.corestandards.org.
2. Erica L. Green, and Liz Bowie, "New assessments show half of Maryland's students ready for kindergarten," *Baltimore Sun*, May 19, 2015, http://www.baltimoresun.com/news/maryland/bs-md-kindergarten-readiness-20150519-story.html.
3. "English Language Arts Standards >> Writing >> Kindergarten," Common Core States Standards Initiative, accessed May 1, 2018, http://www.corestandards.org/ELA-Literacy/W/K/#CCSS.ELA-Literacy.W.K.1.
4. "English Language Arts Standards >> Writing >> Kindergarten," Common Core States Standards Initiative, accessed May 1, 2018, http://www.corestandards.org/ELA-Literacy/W/K/2/.
5. Richard R. Valencia, *The Evolution of Deficit Thinking: Educational Thought and Practice,* Stanford Series on Education & Public Policy (New York: Routledge, 1997).
6. Richard R. Valencia, *Dismantling Contemporary Deficit Thinking: Educational Thought and Practice* (New York: Routledge, 2010).
7. Mihaly Csíkszentmihályi, *Flow: The Psychology of Optimal Experience* (New York: Harper & Row, 1990).
8. "Language Assignments to 3/3 LDPs," Foreign Service Institute, U. S. Department of State, accessed May 1, 2018, https://www.state.gov/documents/organization/247092.pdf.
9. Kenji Hakuta, Yuko Gto Butler, and Daria Witt, "How Long Does It Take English Learners to Attain Proficiency?" University of California Linguistic Minority Research Institute, Policy Report 2000–1, January 2000, accessed May 1, 2018, https://web.stanford.edu/~hakuta/Publications/%282000%29%20-%20HOW%20LONG%20DOES%20IT%20TAKE%20ENGLISH%20LEARNERS%20TO%20ATTAIN%20PR.pdf.
10. Kristina Rizga, *Mission High: One School, How Experts Tried to Fail It, and the Students and Teachers Who Made It Triumph* (New York: Nations Books, 2015).
11. Liz Bowie, and Amy Davis, "Unsettled Journeys," Baltimore Sun, Part I – October 30, 2015, Part II – November 3, 2015, Part III – November 6, 2015, http://data.baltimoresun.com/news/unsettled-journeys/splash/.
12. Yong Zhao, et al, *Counting What Counts: Reframing Education Outcomes,* (Bloomington, IN: Solution Tree Press, 2015).
13. Tony Wagner, *The Global Achievement Gap: Why Even Our Best Schools Don't Teach the Survival Skills Our Children Need – and What We Can Do About It* (New York: Basic Books, 2008).
14. Geoff Colvin, *Humans are Underrated: What High Achievers Know That Brilliant Machines Never Will* (New York: Portfolio, 2015).

15. Fareed Zakaria, *In Defense of a Liberal Education* (New York: W. W. Norton, 2015).
16. Danial Pink, "The Coming Right-Brain Economy: Daniel H. Pink Says the MFA Is the New MBA", interview by John O. Harney in *Journal of the New England Board of Higher Education* 20, no. 1 (Summer 2005): 16-17. http://files.eric.ed.gov/fulltext/EJ792609.pdf.
17. Daniel Pink, *A Whole New Mind: Why Right-Brainers Will Rule the Future* (New York: Riverhead Books, 2006).
18. Chris Anderson, *The Long Tail: Why the Future of Business is Selling Less of More* Revised and Updated Edition (New York: Hyperion, 2008).
19. Robert Rosenthal and Lenore Jacobson, *Pygmalion in the Classroom: Teacher Expectation and Pupils' Intellectual Development*, 2nd edition (Norwalk, CT: Crown House, 1992).
20. Claude Goldenberg, "The Limits of Expectations: A Case for Case Knowledge About Teacher Expectancy Effects," *American Educational Research Journal* 29, no. 3 (1992): 517–544.
21. Peter Franchot, "MD students need a course in financial literacy" *Baltimore Sun*, February 10, 2010, http://articles.baltimoresun.com/2010-02-10/news/bal-op.franchot0210_1_personal-financial-literacy-education-week-nation.
22. Vicki Abeles, and Jessica Congdon, directors, *Race to Nowhere: The Dark Side of America's Achievement Culture*, video, 1:25:00 (Lafayette, CA: Reel Link films, 2010).
23. Vicki Abeles, *Beyond Measure: Rescuing and Overscheduled, Overtested, Underestimated Generation* (New York: Simon & Shuster, 2015).
24. Jay Mathews, "Why Vicki Abeles' 'Race to Nowhere' is wrong," *Washington Post*, April 3, 2011, https://www.washingtonpost.com/local/education/why-vicki-abeles-race-to-nowhere-is-wrong/2011/03/25/AFmnRtXC_story.html.
25. William Deresiewicz, *Excellent Sheep: The Miseducation of the American Elite and the Way to a Meaningful Life* (New York: Free Press, 2014).
26. Stefanie DeLuca, Susan Clampet-Lundquist, and Kathryn Edin, *Coming of Age in the Other America* (New York: Russell Sage Foundation, 2016).

9

The Robot Factory

In 1997 humanity was dealt a symbolic blow when a team of researchers at IBM built and programmed a computer—Deep Blue—that won a six-game chess match against the then reigning world chess champion, Gary Kasparov. "The Brain's Last Stand" is how a cover story in *Newsweek* reported the result [1]. Fears were stoked that Kasparov's defeat signaled the onset of a major societal transformation, akin to the industrial revolution of the 18th and 19th centuries, that would result in severe social and economic dislocations. Only this time it would not be machines replacing human labor, but machines replacing human intelligence.

The fear of machine intelligence overtaking humans is even more discomforting than machines replacing human labor. When it comes to physical size, strength, and endurance there is nothing all that remarkable about humans. Plenty of animals are bigger and stronger, can run faster, swim farther, and climb higher. But the human brain is what sets us apart and has allowed us as a species to control our environment, inhabit all reaches of the globe and beyond, and construct the elaborate social and political structures that make modern life possible. Would humans now become irrelevant and be enslaved by their own creations?

Chess is of course just one tiny slice of human intellectual pursuit, but the chess problem fascinated early researchers in artificial intelligence (AI). On the surface the problem appears easy. Nothing is hidden in a chess game; there are none of the random events found in board games that require players to roll dice or draw cards. The object of the game—checkmate—has a clear mathematical definition: all of the pieces move according to precise mathematical rules, and a game is conducted by two players who alternate turns.

© Springer International Publishing AG, part of Springer Nature 2018
J. Ganem, *The Robot Factory*, https://doi.org/10.1007/978-3-319-77860-0_9

The rules are so simple that a six-year old can learn them. Since a computer can accurately project and evaluate many more possible positions going forward from the current position than a human ever can, it should be able to outperform a human chess player. Indeed a computer will always beat a human player who knows only the rules of chess but nothing else about the game beyond that.

But for a computer to beat a skilled and *educated* player the chess problem turns out to be much more difficult than it appears. By "educated" I mean a person who has read, studied, and absorbed some of the extensive literature on the game, who has experience putting ideas in that literature into practice against strong chess players, and who has reflected on those experiences and internalized some understanding of how the game is played at very high levels. Beating an educated chess player with practiced and honed playing skills turns out not to be an easy task. The first commercially available chess computers in the 1970s couldn't even beat an average tournament player. Beating a grandmaster was out of the question, and the thought that a computer would ever beat a world champion seemed utterly unrealistic.

But advances in computer technology progressed at a staggering pace and by the 1990s the strength of the top chess programs running on supercomputers had approached that of a grandmaster. It was just a matter of time before a world champion succumbed and Gary Kasparov just happened to be the champion at that time in history. However, even then the computer's victory was far from certain. The six-game match was tied until the final game—1 win each and 3 draws—when Kasparov became unnerved and self-destructed in the sixth game. IBM, basking in the publicity, refused Kasparov a rematch, shut down the research project, and shipped Deep Blue off to a museum immediately afterwards.

Today, over 20 years later, computer-processing power has significantly increased since Deep Blue, and chess software running on an ordinary laptop computer has no trouble beating a grandmaster. This is not surprising when *all* the advantages a computer has in a game of chess are considered, because there are many more beyond just computational speed and the ability to accurately project and evaluate trillions of positions. For example, human players would perform much better at chess if they shared the following characteristics of a computer:

- Never tired
- Never became upset
- Never became distracted

- Never forgot anything (Grandmasters must accurately commit to memory a large number—tens of thousands—of chess positions and the actions to take in each of them, something a computer can do perfectly for many millions of positions.)
- Never made a mistake (A computer will not make a "mistake" in the human sense of the word that is doing something it knows it should not do. However, a computer will take actions that appear reasonable without fully foreseeing all possible negative consequences—what humans call "misjudgment.")

In other words, according to modern educational standards, a computer fits the profile of an ideal student and could certainly be programmed to do well on standardized tests. These are also the characteristics of the model employee, which is why we feel so economically threatened. However, the dire predictions about the obsolescence of human intelligence have not played out since the Deep Blue experiment. In fact the economic premium for being an *educated* human has increased over the past 20 years—a fact documented in Chapter 2. What are we to make of this paradox?

First, I think that we have been asking the wrong questions and wrongly interpreting the results of experiments with machine intelligence. The questions posed are usually in regards to the implications of computers surpassing human intellectual ability. For example, "If computers can surpass grandmasters at chess, how long will it take for computers to surpass humans at any activity requiring intelligence?" But, I think that this question is backwards. The experiments pitting human chess players against computers actually demonstrate the uniqueness and power of human intelligence. Indeed, a far more interesting question is: "Why can educated humans compete at all against computers in chess? Given all the advantages a computer has, why did it take decades of cooperative research by many humans with high levels of expertise in electronics, programming, and chess, to build a computer that could defeat a single person—the world chess champion?" Obviously human minds must work in different, very powerful ways to overcome all these disadvantages and still be competitive against machines.

Second, and more importantly, being educated is not the ability to perform tasks on various lists of educational standards that often read like product specifications in a robot factory. Those who understand that education is much more than remembering and performing are advantaged in many ways. Leveraging the unique abilities that allow humans, with all their obvious foibles and limitations, to perform stellar intellectual feats is why those with an authentic education enjoy a steadily increasing economic premium in this twenty-first century digital information age. But in our obsession with accumulating large amounts of data, measuring and quantifying, establishing standards and expectations, analyzing costs and benefits, and calculating returns on investments, we have created an educational system mired in training children to essentially be better robots. We should instead educate them to become better humans. But there is a widespread willful ignorance of what it means to be human. Denying many essential elements of our humanity has served the economic self-interests of the elite, but its continuation comes with great risks to everyone.

Performing Versus Understanding

When the older of my two daughters was about five years old, she became aware that the world is a very big place. It became apparent to her that for adults to navigate and find their way in such an unfathomably large space as the world outside our home, they must possess a knowledge and understanding of that space that she lacked. She had a sense of the local environment, the familiar places visited most days—schools, neighbor's houses, stores, restaurants. But, every so often we would all pile in the car and my wife and I would announce that the trip would take most of the day because we were going to her grandmother's house. Off we would go for hours along highways that snaked over mountains, over bridges, bearing left in some places and right in others, past farms and through busy cities, and somehow, we would arrive precisely where we predicted: grandmother's house. Clearly her parents knew something about space and our location in the world relative to all other locations that she did not.

So one day, at the beginning of one of these trips, she asked me: "Dad, how do you *know* how to get to grandma's house?"

I couldn't think of a way to answer the question that would make sense to a five-year old. This was in the days before smartphones and GPS, so I navigated using maps, route numbers, and highway signage. How do you explain to a five-year old that the world is actually finite and can be represented on paper with a kind of drawing called a map? So I took the easy way out and lied.

"Your grandmother is my mother and when I was a child I lived in her house. I remember the house that I lived in, where it is, and how to get back to it."

She didn't challenge or call me out on my lie, at least not at that moment. She climbed in the backseat and off we went from our house near Baltimore, Maryland, to my parents' house over 300 miles away near Albany, New York. After a three-day visit, we decided to visit one of my cousins who lived near

Manchester, New Hampshire, and also has a daughter, Nikki, close in age to my daughter. Off we went again on another long ride over the green mountains of Vermont and through picturesque New England villages. This time my daughter asked: "Dad, have you ever been to Nikki's house?"

A simple yes or no question. Not realizing that I was being set up, I told the truth. "No. Not since Nikki's parents' moved. I haven't been to their new house."

"Dad, how do you *know* how to get to Nikki's house?"

I had been caught in a lie. What to do now? I decided to take the way out favored by politicians—tell a truth that has nothing to do with the question being asked. My response: "I spoke to Nikki's mom on the phone. She told me where their new house is and how to get there."

"But, Dad, if you've never been to Nikki's house before, how are you going to *know* when we get there?"

These are two very profound questions that my daughter was posing. What does it mean to know something? My ability to steer a car for long periods of time, over great distances, make choice after choice from many possible roads to take, and arrive precisely at the destination I intend, demonstrates that I possessed some kind of knowledge and understanding of space that she lacked and I was not explaining. But, the second question is even more profound: How do we *know* when we have arrived at a place that we have never been before? The first question gets at how we understand something. The second question is about what it means to understand something.

These kinds of questions on the understanding and meaning of knowledge have been examined and written about by philosophers and theologians for centuries. There is an entire branch of philosophy—epistemology, the theory of knowledge—that seeks to understand how we acquire and validate what we claim to know. In addition, both philosophy and theology examine questions of meaning and seek to understand our relationships to each other and to higher purposes beyond our individual selves. However, curiously, in modern educational practice, the verb "to understand" has for the most part been banned.

Student Learning Outcomes (SLOs)

School curricula and classroom activities are now organized around "student learning outcomes," or "SLOs" in current educational jargon. An SLO is a statement of the form: The student should be able to (action verb) that leads to an explicit *measureable* result [2, 3]. The emphasis on measureable is mine, because teachers are cautioned not to write SLOs that cannot be measured for assessment purposes. In practice that means the verb in the SLO must be an *observable* action. For example, an acceptable SLO could be: Students should be able to convert fractions to decimal equivalents. The verb "convert" is an observable action and a test could be constructed to measure the ability of students to perform fraction to decimal conversions.

But an unacceptable SLO would be: Students should understand that any fraction with a numerator less than its denominator has a decimal equivalent of less than 1. The verb in this statement "understand" is an action that cannot be observed, which means that understanding cannot be explicitly measured or assessed. In fact, instructional articles for teachers on writing SLOs provide lists of verbs to avoid using, such as understand, develop, appreciate, and apply, because these verbs are not observable, measureable actions [2, 3].

In Chapter 4 on math education, I discussed how educators frequently mistake process for understanding—that just because a student can perform an action, it doesn't mean that the student understands the action. In education today, since all that matters is performance, understanding is deemed irrelevant. But, it's not. Consider the earlier example of converting fractions to decimals. All of my college-level physics students can perform this task using a calculator. However, each year I encounter many students who, given a problem such as $3/(6 \times 4)$, will neglect to enter the parentheses into their calculators and tell me that the answer is 2 instead of 0.125. When I ask them how the result can possibly be greater than 1, given that 6×4 is clearly greater than 3, they are confused by my question. They have no understanding of what a fraction actually is—that it represents a relationship between two numbers.

Driving from my house in Baltimore County to my parents' house in upstate New York is an observable measureable action. If I were teaching driving I could formulate an SLO for this task. I could write: "The student should be able to navigate the car to a relative's house located more than 300 miles away." It would be an easily measureable outcome. But there are many ways to understand the task. When I navigate I think in terms of spatial relationships. I am always aware of my orientation in space with respect to north, south, east, and west. My wife has a phenomenal memory of place and uses landmarks. My children, who are now all old enough to drive, use the GPS applications on their smartphones. Each of our navigation methods has advantages and limitations. My method works well in unfamiliar rural environments without remembered landmarks or a strong phone signal. My wife always knows exactly how to get to any place that she has been before, no matter how complex the environment, without my need to read signage. My children can get around confusing urban environments where the shortest time between two points is often not the shortest distance much better than I can. Clearly, our different ways of understanding navigation are not irrelevant.

Do Robots Understand?

In Kasparov's match with Deep Blue, he became convinced that its programmers were cheating [4]. As his anger built, he could no longer focus and played terribly in the final decisive game of the match. He felt that the Deep Blue's operators were intervening at crucial points in the games and getting outside help from actual human grandmasters. The reason for his anger was that the computer was playing moves that he believed only a human could find. Deep Blue appeared to understand chess.

Prior to the match many predicted that Kasparov would win easily by simply playing "anti-computer" chess. In the morality play that unfolds on the chessboard, computers had always been notorious for willful ignorance and for succumbing to the sins of materialism and greed. Grandmasters dazzle their audiences with the aesthetic elements of chess, but these concepts were beyond the grasp of computers because of their limited ability to quantify aesthetics. Material, which is simply the number of chess pieces the player controls, can always be quantified and computers are good at counting. For the early chess computers, the grandmaster could always win by sacrificing material for other kinds of positional advantages—more active pieces or more control of the board—advantages in chess that the computer could not quantify but the human could intuit.

Computers also suffered from an inability to plan. They could only project the future through calculation, but that calculation, of necessity, must terminate at some finite number of moves in the future—the computer's "event horizon." If a computer could find a sequence of moves that would postpone a looming problem beyond its event horizon, it would play them regardless of the consequences—even if those consequences would eventually prove catastrophic in comparison to the problem it was trying to avoid. This is essentially willful ignorance on the part of the computer, and a grandmaster could always exploit it. Grandmasters cannot calculate all possibilities 15 to 20 moves into the future, but they can certainly plan that far ahead. They know the kinds of long-range problems and advantages that lurk in a given position without the need to calculate at all.

But Deep Blue was apparently finding human-like moves. Kasparov did not believe that it could because he felt that the computer would need to understand chess in order to do so. The secretive behavior of the research team operating the computer, including grandmasters providing advice to the programmers on chess strategy, fueled his belief that he was being duped. His anger continued to build until he could no longer focus on playing chess.

The "Turing Test"

Twenty years later, computers play strong chess because they can find very "human-like" moves. In the realm of chess, it can be said that computers have passed what has come to be known as the "Turing test." In 1950, the mathematician and philosopher, Alan Turing, whose work laid much of the foundation for modern digital computing, addressed the question of whether machines could think in what has become a widely cited paper "Computing Machinery and Intelligence," published in the philosophical journal *Mind*. In it Turing described what he calls "The Imitation Game." [5]

The imitation game is "played with three people, a man (A), a woman (B), and an interrogator (C) who may be of either sex." The interrogator stays in a room apart from the other two and asks A and B questions, in writing, so that there exists no sensory contact—visual or voice communication—between them. The object of the game for the interrogator is to determine which is the man and which is the woman. A and B are obligated to answer the questions, but have different goals. For A, the man, the object of the game is to trick the interrogator into making the wrong identification. For B, the woman, the object is to help the interrogator make the correct identification. At the end of the game, the interrogator must state which person is the man, who is trying to deceive, and which person is the woman, who is trying to help. Turing then imagines replacing person A, the man who is trying to deceive, with a machine. Will the interrogator make the wrong identification with a machine in the role of A, as often as with a human male in the role of A? Turing proposes that this question replace the question: "Can machines think?" This thought experiment has come to be known as the "Turing test."

Therefore, to pass the "Turing test" and be said to have intelligence and thought, the computer only needs to perform in a measurable, observable way—much like meeting the SLOs in the modern classroom. Unobservable actions, such as understanding or appreciating, are not relevant outcomes. But it is interesting that Deep Blue's designer, Feng-Hsiung Hsu, while acknowledging that Kasparov's cheating allegations "confirmed that Deep Blue passed the chess version of the Turing test," did not view the machine as intelligent at all. To him it was a "finely crafted tool" and he saw the contest as "between men in two different roles: man as performer and man as toolmaker." [6]

Hsu, the toolmaker, prevailed in the contest against Kasparov, the performer, because he built a much better tool (computer) than his predecessors.

His computer was much faster, had much more processing power, could analyze many more positions, and eventually through sheer force of calculation could avoid moves with long-range negative consequences that a grandmaster knows are bad without the need for analysis. In other words, Deep Blue won because it became better at doing what computers do. It found more "human-like" moves by operating in a less human manner. Deep Blue could go through the process of playing high-level chess, but it did not in anyway start mimicking human thought processes, or develop any understanding of chess. It did not analyze the game as a human would.

A Return to the "Chinese Room"

In Chapter 4, I claimed that we are turning grade-school math classes into real-life versions of Searle's "Chinese rooms" in which students process inputs by following a rigid set of rules, but never understand the problems they are solving or the reasons for doing so. But now imagine two human occupants of the Chinese room. They both flawlessly perform the same task, writing in Chinese according to a pre-defined set of rules. In an educational setting they would both be meeting the SLO's. However, in this thought experiment there is one important difference between the two humans: one is completely ignorant of Chinese; the other is completely fluent.

Of course both humans would be aware of their respective understandings of Chinese. For the person fluent in Chinese the tasks performed might be tedious, but they would have meaning and purpose. He would be *communicating* in Chinese. For the other person it would be all tedium. He would simply be *copying* Chinese. Moreover, if these two occupants of the Chinese room were transported to China, one would have an immense social, cultural, and economic advantage over the other. They might both meet the same educational SLOs in terms of performance, but actually understanding Chinese matters. People are not robots.

Without going into the extensive philosophical literature surrounding Turing's or Searle's papers, I will assert that as artificial intelligence evolves, which it will, that intelligence will be very different than human intelligence—like the unimaginable differences between dogs and humans discussed in Chapter 5. The AI of the future will be an alien form of intelligence that humans will not be able to emulate, nor would they want to. Therefore creating "Chinese rooms" in our schools and using assessments that amount to a kind of "Turing test" are not serving our children or our society well.

Willful Ignorance in the Classroom

In fact, the ability to understand and not just perform is so powerful that it threatens the entire concept of using SLOs to measure student achievement. This has caused education reformers to purposely introduce willful ignorance into classrooms in order to inhibit understanding. Consider an instructor guide for the "Common Core Unit: A Close Reading of Lincoln's Gettysburg Address." [7] It provides instructors with classroom activities that are entirely "text-dependent," meaning that students are not to be provided with the actual historical context that makes this speech so important. The guide explicitly states:

> "Refrain from giving background context or substantial instructional guidance at the outset. … This close reading approach forces students to rely exclusively on the text instead of privileging background knowledge, and levels the playing field for all students as they seek to comprehend Lincoln's address."

To further emphasize the text-only approach an appendix gives examples of "erroneous guiding questions," and the reasons why these questions are "misguided." Examples given of "misguided" questions:

- "Have you ever been to a funeral?"
- "Lincoln says that the nation is dedicated to the proposition that "all men are created equal." Why is equality an important value to promote?"

The reasons given for the misguidedness:

> "The overarching problem with these questions is that they require no familiarity at all with Lincoln's speech in order to answer them. Both seek to elicit a personal response that relies on individual experience and opinion, and answering them will not move students one inch closer to understanding the 'Gettysburg Address.'"

But it is clear from the recommended activities that "understanding" in the context of this lesson refers only to knowing definitions of the difficult and arcane vocabulary Lincoln used and following the structures and methodologies of his rhetorical arguments. To develop this kind of "understanding" any random piece of writing would suffice.

But the Gettysburg Address is not just a brief random sample of political oration. It magnificently and succinctly presents a sweeping vision of what it means to be American. Its impact on American history ranks close in importance to the Declaration of Independence and the Constitution. Pretending that history doesn't exist will not level the classroom playing field. Stripping the historical context from this speech erases its meaning and willfully ignores its relationship to events preceeding and following the Civil War.

Relationships across time matter because it is important for each one of us to understand how we came to be and how the circumstances we live in and with arose. Consigning these relationships to an Orwellian memory hole removes the motivations for learning history. And conveniently for the ruling class, makes it difficult to question the political and economic dysfunction of the present.

You might wonder what kind of writing assignments can be created from this kind of a lesson. The guide does provide an essay prompt for students:

> "In the last paragraph of the "Gettysburg Address," Lincoln shifts the focus of his speech away from what he says is its purpose at the end of the second paragraph. What reasons does he give for the shift in focus? What does Lincoln think is the task left to those listening to his speech? Use evidence from the text to support your analysis."

In other words, all students are being asked to do is parse the text for keywords and phrases; they are not being asked to perform any real literary analysis.

Reading Stripped of Context

Of course, this kind of context-free, text-dependent only, formulaic analysis could be performed on any reading excerpt; it doesn't have to be the Gettysburg Address—it could be the user manual for your automobile. And indeed, the Common Core publishes a "Complete Guide to Creating Text-Dependent Questions" that suggests students perform tasks that parse documents at the word and sentence level without any regards to the intended purpose of the writing [8]. Suggestions include:

- Analyze paragraphs on a sentence-by-sentence basis and sentences on a word-by-word basis to determine the role played by individual paragraphs, sentences, phrases, or words
- Investigate how meaning can be altered by changing key words and why an author may have chosen one word over another
- Probe each argument in persuasive text, each idea in informational text, each key detail in literary text, and observe how these build to a whole

These kinds of assignments turn reading and writing into a robotic activity that would certainly *not* motivate instructors and students. The fact is *all* published writing exists within a larger context because otherwise the activities of writing and publishing would have no point. Stripping that context away removes any sense of purpose for learning as one reads. This is a technique used to dismember reading assignments, as I described in Chapter 6, in order to avoid facing actual truths.

Text-dependent analysis essentially treats written language as a dataset to be mined for information rather than as a means of communicating human relatedness. One of its chief proponents is David Coleman, the lead architect of the Common Core English Language Arts (ELA) standards, who in 2012 was appointed President and CEO of the College Board—the organization that implements the SAT and Advanced Placement (AP) exams for college-bound high school students. Coleman has never taught high school English and lacks the academic credentials needed for serious literary analysis, but he is an expert on data analysis. Prior to his work on the Common Core standards he co-founded the Grow Network, a company that analyzed test scores for large school districts and was eventually sold to the textbook publisher McGraw-Hill.

In talks that Coleman has given on his vision for education, he displays obsessions with universal standards, assessments aligned to them, and mining the data from the assessments for information on what *he thinks* that students should be learning [9, 10]. He explains his standards-based approach to text-dependent analysis in an essay with a title that reeks of Orwellian double-speak, "Cultivating Wonder." [11] In this essay, Coleman analyzes short passages from several great works of literature that include the Gettysburg Address, Shakespeare's *Hamlet* and Twain's *The Adventures of Huckleberry Finn*. From his analysis, you will learn a great deal about word usage and sentence and scene structures. But if you are wondering, for example, why *Hamlet* is considered one of the greatest works ever written in the English language, you will get no inkling of those reasons from his kind of analysis. Ironically, Coleman is a strong advocate for standards that require the use of great works of literature in the classroom. But somehow he seems to think that it is the words themselves that make these works of literature "great" rather than the timeless truths about human relatedness that the words convey.

It is tempting to speculate on the motivation for this unwilling-to-see-the-forest-for-the-trees approach to reading instruction. A possibility that comes immediately to my mind (and others have also pointed out [12]) is that it better enables computerized grading of student essays. Grading writing is time-consuming; for the organization that Coleman heads, it is also a major expense, as "graders" must be hired for the SAT and AP essay components. Like the third-grade math class I observed, these outside evaluators prefer clear-cut means of evaluation. Making it easy for a computer to do the work would be even better. I strongly suspect that stripping context from reading as a way of "leveling the playing field" for all students really means putting all students at the same level as computerized grading programs.

Robotic Grading and Writing

For example, instructors can already purchase software that automatically grades written essay assignments. The company ExamSoft has a commercially available program *Rubrics* that can scan essays and "run data-driven reports to quantify student learning." [13] It is marketed with the tag line "Objective evaluation of subjective assignments." Educational Testing Service (ETS), the company that actually administers the SAT along with many other standardized tests has developed robotic readers to grade essays. Their *e-rater*® scoring engine is already in use to grade the essay portions of the Graduate Record Exam (GRE) and Test of English as a Foreign Language (TOEFL) tests that ETS also administers [14]. It seems to be just a matter of time before the writing portion of the SAT is graded using this technology. All that needs to be done is to "align" the SAT test with the Common Core standards, which is one of Coleman's goals as President of the College Board [15].

Of course, if a computer can extract data from formulaic writing, the process can also be reversed—data can easily be folded into computer-generated formulaic writing. There are products on the market that perform this task. The programs *Wordsmith* sold by Automated Insights [16] and *Quill* from Narrative Sciences [17] will take data in the form of sports statistics or corporate earnings reports and generate natural language narratives describing sporting events, or stock market reports suitable for publication. Already wire services such as the Associated Press generate some of their news stories using this technology in place of actual human journalists. Given the typical technical savvy of the average young person, it is easy to imagine a future in which students complete text-dependent essay assignments using robo-writing programs that are then evaluated by instructor-operated robo-grading programs.

By the way, experiments with the automated grading programs used by ETS show that Lincoln would have received a poor grade on the Gettysburg Address [18]. I suspect that part of the problem with the Gettysburg Address is that Lincoln is not giving us an evidence-based analysis of a text; rather he is giving us his *opinion* on the American experiment in self-government.

An opinion is not something a computer program can have. But David Coleman is very clear that students are not to have opinions either; he clearly sees them as robots to be programmed. In one of his most revealing comments he disparages high school writing assignments that ask students to express a personal opinion or provide a narrative on a personal experience. The reason he gives, in his own words:

> "As you grow up in this world you realize people really don't give a shit about what you feel or what you think." [19]
> --David Coleman at NY State Department of Education presentation, April 2011

Relatedness

What makes understanding an activity so fundamentally different than just performing the activity? Let's return to chess and examine why a chess-educated human can compete at all against a computer, given all the advantages that the computer has. This requires *understanding* the game of chess. Fundamentally chess is a game of resource management. At the start of the game, the two players are allotted the same resources: equal numbers of chess pieces, with equal mobility, arranged in the same way on opposite sides of the playing space, the chessboard, on which all squares are identical in spacing. The player of white pieces is given a slight advantage by being allowed to act first. That first move breaks the perfect symmetry on White's terms, but after that initial action, the players alternate turns and the advantage of moving first can quickly dissipate.

To obtain a winning advantage in a game that begins in a condition of near perfect symmetry and equality a player must use his or her allotted resources more efficiently than his or her opponent. In chess this requires planning strategic objectives and then commanding one's pieces to act in a coordinated and cooperative manner to achieve them. High-level chess players do not see individual pieces; rather, they see the evolving relationships between pieces as the game progresses. Grandmasters can take in the entire position at a glance and instantly know the relationships between the pieces. Moreover, they can understand how that position relates to other positions that have arisen in the centuries-long history of chess, a history well documented in a rich and evolving literature on the game.

Maintaining cooperation between the chess pieces and commanding them so that they act efficiently in achieving strategic goals is essential to winning.

Long-term thinking is also crucial, not so much in calculating ahead, but in planning ahead. There is a difference: calculating is an algorithm, while planning is based on meaning. Humans are really, really good at discerning patterns and relationships because humans seek meaning. Meaning always comes through relationships.

The ability of the grandmaster to at a glance see the entire chess position as a whole, and at the same time discern the meaning of the multitude of relationships within, is why a winning computer program needs a high-speed processor that can examine many trillions of positions per second. The human versus computer chess experiments actually show that computer and human intelligences are incomparably different. While the SLO might be the same—play chess at a grandmaster-level—the understandings that humans bring to the task are vastly different than a computer. AI is a form of intelligence that humans can never hope to emulate, nor should that even be a human goal.

Are we turning our children into unconscious robots that we command, or autonomous agents with lives that have real meaning? We don't need children who are better robots, who can perform tricks on our command. We need children who are better at what makes us human.

Authentic Education

As I stated in the preface, education may be a difficult undertaking, but the process itself is not mysterious. Plenty of legitimate science exists on human development and best practices in education, as well as rich and evolving, scientifically valid, peer-reviewed literature on effective teaching and learning methodologies. Numerous people with experience and authentic expertise could potentially advise policymakers and school districts on the *actions* that need to be taken and the *resources* that need to be allocated to remediate poor educational outcomes.

If you want to know what works in education you can delve into that literature, or you could find out in an even simpler way. Do an Internet-search for the expensive private schools in your area—the ones with tuitions exceeding the cost of some colleges. Then visit the websites for these schools and explore their offerings.

In the Baltimore-Washington area in which I live, families that can afford high-priced tuitions can select among dozens of private schools. A random sampling of my findings: Park School of Baltimore, Friends School of Baltimore, St. Albans School in Washington DC, and Sidwell Friends School in Washington, DC. When I visit their websites, I cannot find anything about test scores in reading and math, or much in the way of data at all. What I do find are well thought-out statements on mission and education philosophies, lots of information on arts, sports, and science experiments, numerous photos showing students engaged in activities, and a great deal of emphasis on teamwork and relationship building in their curricula. Some examples:

- Sidewell Friends' philosophy statement includes: "We seek to promote an environment that emphasizes fair play, integrity, sportsmanship, learning, and overall health and wellness for a purposeful life." [20]
- Park School promotes experiential learning: "Park students learn and do. Science … is not just information gathering; it is an ongoing process involving investigating, questioning, reasoning, predicting, discovery, and problem-solving." [21]
- Friends School of Baltimore's philosophy includes: "Friends School cultivates the intellectual, emotional, social, physical, artistic, and spiritual development of the students. Our program balances academics, athletics, and the arts." [22]
- St. Alban's Welcome Statement includes: "St. Albans students thrive thanks to close relationships with their teachers and fellow students, cultivated in chapel, on the sidelines, in small seminars, and during daily family-style lunches." [23]

In Chapter 8, I cited recent research showing that a strong predictor of whether students from impoverished urban environments would succeed as students is the presence of "Identity Projects," activities that youth commit themselves to that forge relationships with adult mentors and provide a strong sense of meaning and purpose. That research could not explain why some youth developed Identity Projects and others did not because these projects appeared to arise from random encounters, often in an extracurricular activity that piqued a particular interest.

It is clear from visiting the websites of these private schools that the formation of Identity Projects for their students is not left to chance. Providing an environment to explore and find one's identity and then have it nurtured is essentially what these schools are about. As St. Alban's Welcome Statement puts it: "… sports and arts are not extracurricular activities here; they are essential elements of our course of study." [23] Articulating the concept of Identity Projects for at-risk urban youth might be new, but forming identities through activities and relationship building is what the schools for the elite have essentially been doing all along.

The wealthy patrons of private schools would never subject their children to a standards-based education with data-driven testing and accountability metrics focused only on reading and math, and devoid or arts and athletics. They know better.

The Use of Pseudoscience in Education

But what if authentic education were not my goal? What if I wanted to design an education system to serve purposes that were political and corporate? What if I wanted to ...

- Maintain an existing, entrenched and corrupt political class?
- Transfer public wealth to private corporations?
- Exacerbate income inequality?
- Create a "Brave New World" kind of underclass to serve the elites?
- Keep masses of people so busy and distracted that they never question the Orwellian pronouncements issued on a daily basis by their leaders?
- Subvert the founders' vision of self-government?
- Undermine the societal institutions essential for maintaining American democracy?

How would I achieve those goals?

Freire's "Banking Model"

There is actually a literature on the educational practices used to further these purposes. A widely influential book by Brazilian education theorist Paulo Freire—*Pedagogy of the Oppressed*—published in 1968 describes what he calls the "banking model" of education [24]. These are educational practices that treat students' intellects as empty "bank accounts" in which knowledge is "deposited" by their teachers. In this model students are the recipients of an education, objects to be acted upon, rather than active participants. Students are taught not to think for themselves, question others, or voice opinions.

Freire argues that banking education enables an oppressive society because it trains people to be manageable and adaptive beings who don't critically question and intervene in the world. A student-teacher relationship in which students accept and believe what they are told prepares students for the submissive roles that they will have as adults. He wrote: "The more the oppressed can be led to adapt to that situation the more easily they can be dominated." [24, p. 74] In prescient observations that foreshadowed the current philanthropies that fund the "school choice" and privatization movements, Freire wrote: "The oppressors use their 'humanitarianism' to preserve a profitable situation." and "The 'humanism' of the banking approach masks the effort to turn women and men into automatons—the very negation of their ontological vocation to be more fully human." [24, p. 73].

Of course Freire's book was not an endorsement of these practices, but an exposé of them and a call for their abolishment. He argued that the "banking model," because it enables oppression, is dehumanizing to both students and their teachers. In its place he argued for "problem-posing" education, which he defined as "posing of the problems of human beings in their relations with the world."[24, p. 79] In problem-posing education students and teachers enter into a dialog and "become jointly responsible for a process in which all grow." [24, p. 80] In Freire's model students are no longer passive listeners to the teacher, but active co-investigators with the teacher. Because the problems posed concern the students' relationships in and with the world, they will feel increasingly challenged and rise to those challenges.

The problem-posing model of education is entirely consistent with the change-focused approach I advocated in the last chapter—a mutual relationship between students and teachers that focuses on overall human development rather than standards, and produces optimal engagement in learning. Freire wrote *Pedagogy of the Oppressed* during the infancy of the digital age, before the advent of "big data," before the automation that enables mass testing and grading, and before reams of computer-generated spreadsheets and charts that display "progress" towards meeting various accountability metrics.

Using Pseudoscience to Rebrand the "Banking Model"

Unfortunately, Freire's exposé of the "banking model" did not kill it. Instead it has been rebranded as the standards and accountability movement and dressed up using pseudoscience. In the modern era, pseudoscience is the perfect con because most people trust science but few understand it. All cons work using the same formula—gain victims' trust and then using that trust, entice them to willingly abet the con artist. As shown in Chapter 5, many schools do a poor job of teaching authentic science, which makes it difficult for their graduates to spot pseudoscience and easier to gain their trust.

Pseudoscience is prevalent once I leave the websites for the elite private schools in Baltimore and Washington and instead visit the websites for the public school districts in these cities [25, 26]. The differences are striking. Instead of succinct mission and philosophy statements I find elaborate five-year strategic plans couched in business jargon and laden with quantifiable goals and extensive details on the metrics that will be used to assess them [27, 28]. It is clear from the language in these documents that the leadership considers these institutions businesses, not schools. They are certainly not scientific enterprises because there is no meaningful context given for all the data that they go on to present.

For example, the Baltimore City School District has a Mission Statement so trite that it borders on being a tautology: "Excellence in education for every child at every level by focusing on quality instruction, managing systems efficiently, and sustaining a culture of excellence." [29] When I go to the "School Effectiveness and Achievement" page I can choose to look at a multitude of data summaries that include school surveys, profiles, performance plans, and report cards [30]. Under school profiles I can select for any one of the dozens of schools in the district and examine a full-color report filled with tables and charts showing data on teacher qualifications, enrollments, student demographics and suspensions, climate surveys, and PARCC assessment results [31]. I click on one particular school's performance plan and find a document with 35 pages of charts that present the school's goals, strategies and results indicators [32]. But I cannot find any explanation of how all this data would fit into a valid *predictive* model for improving education outcomes.

I can't find a Mission Statement for the Washington DC public schools, but in the strategic plan I find a list of "Stakeholder Commitments" that consist of equally vacuous statements that no one would argue with. The commitment to children is to "ensure the opportunity to attend a great school," which is defined as "one that you love and that prepares you for success in life." [28] I can also look at individual school profiles that consist of pages of color-coded charts illustrating data for various metrics for progress, performance, and PARCC assessment results [33]. There is even an interactive feature on this webpage that allows me to easily make statistical comparisons between schools, much like the comparison charts of features on automobile models. Am I shopping for a basic, midrange, or luxury model? As a parent, what features do I want my robot—I mean child—to have after graduating from school?

For the DC schools the achievement goals are expressed in terms of numbers pulled out of thin air. The DC Strategic Plan states that in five years the goal will be to increase reading and math proficiency from 43% to 70%. Where did the 70% figure come from? Have they used all this amassed data to build a predictive model that shows that if specific actions are taken over the next five years, reading and math scores will increase by that much, or did 70% sound like a good number to use when writing the plan?

It might be argued that comparing elite private schools to public schools in the same urban areas is unfair because the former select their student bodies while the latter must educate everyone. But the kinds of educations offered in private schools that focus on personal development and relationship building should be just as desirable in the public schools. I also find it ironic that the private schools put some effort into remedying their greatest deficiency—a lack of diversity—while the public schools, by aspiring to universal standards, are essentially trying to erase diversity.

Enormous investments of time and money have been made in producing these massive data-dumps. But while the elaborate color-coded graphs, charts, and tables might lend a veneer of scientific authority to these documents, many of the essential elements of science that I listed in Chapter 1 are missing. I cannot find any discussions of controlled experiments that establish chains of causation and enable the construction of predictive models to improve education outcomes. As a result of these omissions, the educational strategies and plans presented are based on pseudoscience, and pseudoscience is always destructive because it diverts scarce resources away from critical actions that need to be taken.

The Real Crisis

"We are drowning in information, while starving for wisdom. The world henceforth will be run by synthesizers, people able to put together the right information at the right time, think critically about it, and make important choices wisely."

E. O. Wilson

While the digital age has enabled the creation of the standards and accountability movement by making it practical to collect and process massive amounts of data, it has also rendered the movement obsolete. Pocket-sized smartphones have already obviated the need for rote memorization. Now if educational writing standards, like those in the Common Core, are at the same level as the output from robotic writing programs, students are not learning a useful skill. It is easy to see going forward that all tasks that are formulaic and repetitive—which include many of the tasks found in lists of mandated education standards—will eventually be automated. An education system designed to train people to be better computers has no point. A computer will always be better than a person at being a computer.

It is ironic that motivations for the automation of repetitive work include more than just increased economic efficiency and enhancement of corporate profits; automation is also intended to free people's time and attention for more meaningful pursuits. But people did find meaning from repetitive, rote tasks, so long as they served a greater purpose. With those tasks now offloaded to machines, people need to find alternative sources of meaning. This will be possible with an authentic education that guides people through the journey of discovering meaningful relationships.

However, what we have seen throughout this book are pseudoscientific practices and policies that deliberately corrode our relatedness. We have seen:

- Testing metrics used arbitrarily to bully students, teachers, and schools rather than to identify actual causes of academic failure.
- Math and science reduced to tools of corporate profitability rather than as a means to understand our relationship with the natural world.
- Narratives constructed to poison public discourse with false choices rather than to bring people together to solve communal problems.
- Market forces allowed to produce extreme levels of economic inequality rather than managed in a way to serve the basic needs of the collective.
- Education focused on "college and career readiness" rather than as an ongoing process that enhances one's quality of life.

The crisis we have in education is misunderstood and our fears are misplaced. The crisis is not test scores and our standing on lists of international rankings. It is not lack of preparedness for college and career. It is not economic competitiveness in an age of globalization. The crisis in education is a breakdown at a very human level of our relatedness with one another, with our institutions, with our environment, with our past, and with our future—and this extends well beyond the classrooms and schools. Education is suffering because of this crisis. However, education can be the solution. In fact education must be the solution.

A Call to Action

The founders of the United States understood that for their plan for self-government to succeed universal education must be available because democracy can only function if there is an educated populace. Thomas Jefferson wrote:

> "If a nation expects to be ignorant and free, in a state of civilization, it expects what never was and never will be."
>
> --Thomas Jefferson to Charles Yancey, 1816.

It was also realized that universal education would require public funding. John Adams advocated in 1785:

> "The whole people must take upon themselves the education of the whole people and be willing to bear the expenses of it. There should not be a district of one mile square, without a school in it, not founded by a charitable individual, but maintained at the public expense of the people themselves."
>
> -- John Adams

The nineteenth century education reformers that followed, such as Horace Mann, promoted a system of universal public education as a means to preserve the American experiment with democracy.

> "Education is our only political Safety. Outside of this ark all is deluge."
>
> -- Horace Mann

Using pseudoscience to undermine education, especially public education, is an attack on our democracy that we must defend against.

The founders of the United States embraced both libertarian and socialist ideals. The soaring language of the Declaration of Independence boldly asserts inalienable individual rights: "Life, Liberty, and pursuit of Happiness." Yet the Declaration continues with a list of shared grievances and ends with a commitment to collective action: "we mutually pledge to each other our Lives, our Fortunes and our sacred Honor." The Constitution of the United States is in many ways a libertarian document in that it sets limits on the power and scope of the government and its executives, and provides a list of individual rights on which the government may not infringe. Yet, the preamble to the Constitution is a call to collective action that states:

> "We the People of the United States, in Order to form a more perfect Union, establish Justice, insure domestic Tranquility, provide for the common defense, promote the general Welfare, and secure the Blessings of Liberty to ourselves and our Posterity, do ordain and establish this Constitution for the United States of America."

The founders had a profound sense of purpose and a keen awareness of their moment in time. In crafting their government, they looked to the distant past—the experiences of the classical Greeks and Romans—and also to their immediate predecessors—the 17th and 18th century philosophers of the enlightenment. But the founders also felt a moral obligation to work for the betterment of an unimagined future that would exist beyond their lifetimes.

While the founders were products of their time, steeped in what today we would call racism, classism, and sexism, they understood that progress in human understanding would continue and moral standards would evolve long into the future. The founders deliberately created a democracy that would be an ongoing process of balancing individual rights with the evolving needs and mores of the collective. The government that they established is still in use today, over 200 years later, because it was designed to be flexible and adaptive. The founders themselves forged difficult and painful compromises in order achieve their goals. While they had sincere beliefs and convictions that differed from each other, they did not succumb to the paralysis of false choice.

As Americans, we take an oath to these political ideals—"to preserve, protect, and defend the Constitution"—not to any person, ethnicity, race or religion.

We the people must embrace our history and commit to a purposeful and meaningful future for our posterity.

We must reject the pseudoscientific belief in numbers and data stripped of any meaningful context.

We must reject the manipulation of the scientific method in order to advance narrow self-interests.

We must reject the paralysis brought on by false choices imposed by narrow and rigid ideologies.

We must reject the religious devotion to the amoral forces of markets.

We must not tolerate the willful ignorance displayed by many of our leaders and their overt intellectual dishonesty.

We must not be deterred from acting by the incessant fear mongering and aversion to risk echoed throughout the government and media.

We must reject the culture of unending trivialities and amusement, and its distraction from forming meaningful relationships with the people around us.

Most importantly, what we must do is to become involved. At the very least we must participate in our democracy by informed voting. But we must also get out and take part in organizations that further our personal sense of meaning, whether it is in our communities, churches, schools, or government. Our involvement must not be in a condescending, feel-good, self-promoting way, but in a way that builds authentic relationships with our fellow citizens from all walks of life. Those people fortunate enough to be educated have a duty and responsibility to become involved.

The purpose of education is to empower people to live more meaningful lives because the process of education strengthens and enriches our relationships with one another. Education allows us to become a part of something larger than just ourselves—to transcend our finiteness and contribute to the greater good in the present and for the future. Yes, there is an economic benefit to that enhanced relatedness, but more importantly, it radically improves our quality of life because the education process enables us to become more fully human. It connects us to each other, to our shared history, to our environment and guides us as we build a better future—one in which *all* lives have meaning and purpose.

How will we *know* when we have arrived at a place that we have never seen before? The bonds we forge with others don't happen when we arrive. Our connectedness with each other is woven by the shared struggle of the journey.

References

1. "The Brain's Last Stand," *Newsweek Magazine*, May 5, 1997.
2. Mona Kheiry, and Terri Tarr, "Writing Student Learning Outcomes," IUPUI Center for Teaching and Learning, accessed May 1, 2018, https://ctl.iupui.edu/Resources/Preparing-to-Teach/Writing-and-Assessing-Student-Learning-Outcomes.
3. Lindsay Coco, and Ashley Jordan, "The Basics of Writing Student Learning Outcomes," Center for Teaching and Learning, University of Georgia, accessed May 1, 2018, https://www.ctl.uga.edu/pages/writing-slos.
4. Vikram Jayanti, director, *Game Over: Kasparov and the Machine*, video, 1:30:00 (Toronto: Alliance Atlantis Communications and National Film Board of Canada, 2003).
5. A. M. Turing, "Computing Machinery and Intelligence," *Mind* 59 (1950): 433–460.
6. Feng-Hsiung Hsu, *Behind Deep Blue: Building the Computer That Defeated the World Chess Champion*, (Princeton: Princeton University Press, 2002), ix-x.
7. "Common Core Unit: A Close Reading of Lincoln's Gettysburg Address," Student Achievement Partners, accessed May 1, 2018, http://achievethecore.org/page/35/the-gettysburg-address-by-abraham-lincoln.
8. "Complete Guide to Creating Text-Dependent Questions," Student Achievement Partners, accessed May 1, 2018, http://achievethecore.org/page/46/complete-guide-to-creating-text-dependent-questions.
9. David Coleman, "From the Classroom to the Boardroom: Analytics for Strategy & Performance," filmed at Strategic Data Project (SDP) Convening, Center for Education Policy Research at Harvard University, Boston, MA, May 2013, video, 58:25, accessed May 1, 2018, https://www.youtube.com/watch?v=IPoUmSfTTNI.
10. David Coleman, "Assessments that Support the Goals of the Common Core State Standards," filmed at the Institute on "Assessment in the Era of the Common Core" at the International Reading Association, April 19, 2013, San Antonio,

TX, video, 33:58, accessed May 1, 2018, https://www.youtube.com/watch?v=VLba9mBFmbY.

11. David Coleman, "Cultivating Wonder," (New York: The College Board, 2013). Accessed May 1, 2018, http://simplebooklet.com/userFiles/a/4/1/0/7/6/RglFZX37Iaup7i97hzLAJw/63g92LeZ.pdf.

12. Nicholas Tampio, "David Coleman's Plan to Ruin Education," Aljezeera America, December 5, 2014, http://america.aljazeera.com/opinions/2014/12/common-core-collegeboardeducation.html.

13. *Rubrics*, ExamSoft, accessed May 1, 2018, http://learn.examsoft.com/exam-software-products/rubrics-from-examsoft.

14. *Wordsmith*, Automated Insights Inc., accessed May 1, 2018, https://automatedinsights.com.

15. *Quill*, Narrative Sciences, accessed May 1, 2018, https://narrativescience.com.

16. "About the e-rater scoring engine," Education Testing Service, accessed May 1, 2018, https://www.ets.org/erater/about/.

17. Abby Jackson, "There is a surprising explanation for why the SAT is changing its format," *Business Insider*, June 29, 2015, http://www.businessinsider.com/the-sat-is-getting-a-format-change-to-align-to-the-common-core-2015-6.

18. Scott Jaschik, "Can you trust automated grading?" *Inside Higher Education*, February 21, 2011, https://www.insidehighered.com/news/2011/02/21/debate_over_reliability_of_automated_essay_grading.

19. David Coleman, filmed at NY State Department of Education presentation, April 2011, video, 00:42, accessed May 1, 2018,https://www.youtube.com/watch?v=ua4240ddDaI.

20. "Program and Philosophy," Sidewell Friends, Washington, DC, accessed May 1, 2017, http://www.sidwell.edu/athletics/program-philosophy.

21. "Topics to Explore: Experiential Learning," The Park School, Baltimore, MD, accessed July 24, 2017, http://www.parkschool.net.

22. "Our Mission," Friends School, Baltimore, MD, accessed May 1, 2018, https://www.friendsbalt.org/page/about/our-mission.

23. Vance Wilson, "Welcome," St. Albans School, Washington, DC, accessed May 1, 2018, https://www.stalbansschool.org/page/about/welcome.

24. Paulo Freire, *Pedagogy of the Oppressed*, originally published in Portuguese in 1968, trans. by Myra Bergman Ramos (New York:Continuum, 2007).

25. Baltimore City Public Schools, accessed May 1, 2018, http://www.baltimorecityschools.org.

26. Washington DC Public Schools, accessed May 1, 2018, https://dcps.dc.gov.

27. "Baltimore City Public Schools' Five-Year Strategic Plan 2016–2020," Baltimore City Board of School Commissioners, (December 2015), http://www.baltimorecityschools.org/cms/lib/MD01001351/Centricity/Domain/10215/2015StrategicPlan_Final.pdf.

28. "A Capital Commitment: 2017 Strategic Plan,"District of Columbia Public Schools, accessed May 1, 2018, https://dcps.dc.gov/sites/default/files/dc/sites/dcps/publication/attachments/DCPS-Capital-Commitment-Strategic-Plan-April-2012.pdf.
29. "Board of School Commissioners: Mission, Vision, Goals and Priorities," Baltimore City Schools, accessed May 1, 2018, http://www.baltimorecityschools.org/Page/24786.
30. "School Effectiveness and Achievement." Baltimore City Public Schools, accessed May 1, 2018, http://www.baltimorecityschools.org/schools/school_effectiveness.
31. "School Effectiveness and Achievement: School Profiles," Baltimore City Public Schools, accessed May 1, 2018,http://www.baltimorecityschools.org/Page/30346.
32. "School Performance Plan for Bay-Brook Elementary/Middle School," Baltimore City Public Schools, accessed May 1, 2018, http://www.baltimorecityschools.org/cms/lib/MD01001351/Centricity/domain/8783/performanceplans/2017/20170207_Bay-Brook_Elementary_Middle_School_Performance_Plan.pdf.
33. "School Profiles Home," District of Columbia Public Schools, accessed May 1, 2018, http://profiles.dcps.dc.gov.

Index

0-9, AND SYMBOLS

1984, 144, 147

A

Abeles, V., 214, 215, 218
Accuplacer test, 72
Adams, J., 242
Adequate yearly progress (AYP), 23, 46, 105, 171, 215
Advanced placement (AP), 48, 232, 233
AIG, 212
Alabama, 174, 175
Algebra, xiii, 48, 49, 69, 76, 83, 86–88
American Association of School Administrators, 27
American Federation of Teachers, 60, 164
Amusing Ourselves to Death, 145
Anthropic principle, 117
AP, *see* Advanced placement (AP)
Apollo Education Group, 160
Apple Computer, 174, 178
Arizona, 59, 60
Arizona Association of School Administrators, 59
Arizona Department of Education, 59

Arizona Republic, 59
Artificial intelligence (AI), 87, 229, 230, 235
Assessment
    colleges, 37, 203
    educational, 201
    math, 85, 86
    measurable, 16, 117, 226, 228
    metrics, 154, 239
    narrative, 40
    PARCC, 81, 85, 239
    teachers, 226
    tests, 189
Atlanta, 27
Atlanta Journal Constitution, 27
Autism, 109
Automated Insights, 233
AYP, *see* Adequate yearly progress (AYP)

B

Baltimore
    City School District, 60, 138, 239
    County, 58, 129, 139, 226
    eastern, 197
    Filipino teachers, 60, 61
    Patterson High School, 197

Baltimore (*cont.*,)
   public housing, 216, 218
   schools, 60, 129, 138, 197, 236,
      238–239
Baltimore Sun, 15, 137, 197, 211
Banking model, 237–240
Baton Rouge, 61
Behavioral economics, 86, 170
Behavioral psychology, 154, 170
Behaviorism, 154, 170, 171
Bernier, M., 92
Bloomberg Business, 91, 122
Bloom's Taxonomy, 79, 191
Borowy, D., 138, 139
Bowie, L., 197, 198
BP, *see* British Petroleum (BP)
Brave New World, 145, 147, 237
British Petroleum (BP), 110, 111, 122
Bush, G.W., 210
Bush, J., 122
Business Insider, 92
Business model, 26, 27, 151, 154, 161,
    170, 175, 200

C

Calculators, 26, 69, 88, 226
Calculus, 48, 74, 77, 78, 88, 119, 141
California, 72, 178, 196
Campbell, D.T., 27
Cashing in on Kids, 167
Casinos, 136, 137
Cassano, J., 212
Center for Education Reform, 165
Center for Public Education, 165
Centers for Disease Control, 110, 131
Ceresney, A.J., 162
Change-focused education, 194, 200, 203
Charlotte Danielson: The Framework
   for Teaching Evaluation
   Instrument, 54
Charter schools, 164–168

Chess
   computer, 222, 223, 227, 228, 235
   skill, xiii, 50, 63, 79–80, 113, 187,
      194, 200, 202, 203, 206, 209,
      222, 223, 229, 234
   tournaments, 50, 78, 222
   understanding, 8, 37, 70, 76, 77
   world chess champion, 221, 223
Chicago, 8, 9, 164
Chinese rooms, 87, 229, 230
Christians, 6, 116, 117, 152, 158
Clampet-Lundquist, S., 216
Classical economics, 170–172
Cleveland Plain Dealer, 72
Climate change, xv, 97, 108, 122
Climate change denial, 108
Colbert Report, 142, 143
Coleman, D., 232–234
College
   admissions, 29–31, 171, 215
   annual rankings, 30
   assessment, 37, 40, 72, 81
   college and career readiness, viii,
      200, 203, 204, 215, 241
   college math, 69–78
   college-level physics, 226
   degrees, 30, 32, 36, 94, 160
   experiences, 36, 40, 160, 178, 203
   for-profit, 160–165, 167
   gender gap, 115
   going to college, 99, 203, 205
   majors, 31, 91, 96
   return on investment, 152, 216
   students, 32, 39, 92–94, 132,
      142, 190
College Board, 232
Columbine, 130, 138, 139
Colvin, G., 206
Coming of Age in the Other America, 216
Common Core, 30, 82, 98, 140, 144,
    188–191, 193, 194, 198,
    230–233, 240

Confessions of a Bad Teacher, 51
Congress, 131, 141, 179
Constitution, 27, 133, 231, 242, 243
Continental Resources, 122
Corinthian Colleges, 160–162
Countrywide, 212
Cramer, J., 143
Crawford, J. III., 134
Creationism, 11, 108, 117, 122
CREDO, *see* Stanford Center for
        Research on Education Outcomes
        (CREDO)
Csikzentmihalyi, M., 194, 210

D

Daily Show, 142, 143
Dallas, 27
Däniken, E. von, 109
Data-driven, viii, x, xii, 3, 9, 10, 12,
        16, 37, 151, 218, 233, 237
Davis, A., 197, 198
Declaration of Independence, 231, 242
Deep Blue, 221–223, 227–229
Deficit models, 188, 192, 196
Deficit thinking, 192
DeLuca, S., 216
Democratic, 137, 142
Department of Education
        Arizona, 59
        New York State, 51
        U. S. Department of Education, 38,
            71, 162, 163, 174
Deresiewicz, W., 215–218
Detroit, 27
Dictionary.com, 100
Dintersmith, T., 180
*Dismantling Contemporary Deficit
        Thinking*, 192
District of Columbia (Washington,
        DC), 175
Dogs, 119, 170, 229
Dunn, A.H., 61
Duvall, D., 59

E

Economics
        behavioral, 86, 170
        classical, 170–172
        home, 100
        market, 151, 154
Edin, K., 216
Education Management Corporation,
        161, 163
Education reform
        business model, 26, 27, 151,
            154–155, 170–176, 200–203
        Common Core, 30, 81–82, 98, 140,
            144, 188–191, 193, 194, 198,
            230–232, 240
        data-driven, 12
        pseudoscience, viii, x, 12, 40
        Race to the Top, 174, 175
        school choice, 151–181, 238
Education Trust Fund (ETF),
        136, 138
Educational Testing Service (ETS),
        233, 234
Einstein, A., xxii, 54, 95, 104, 107
Ellenberg, J., 70, 86
Emmanuel, R., 143
Enron, 27, 174
ETF, *see* Education Trust Fund (ETF)
ETS, *see* Educational Testing Service
        (ETS)
Evolution, 95, 101–103, 108, 110,
        111, 117, 119
Ewing, J., 20
ExamSoft, 233
Expectations, 23, 46–48, 55, 56,
        58–64, 72–74, 96, 106, 167,
        173, 177, 190, 191, 194, 197,
        198, 207–211, 214, 224

F

Fallacy, 53, 154, 168, 173
False choices, ix, xi, xiv, xv, 11, 79, 81,
        147, 168, 169, 241, 243

Feynman, R., 75, 87, 112
Filipino teachers, 60–62
Financial crisis, 27, 136, 211–213
Financial literacy, 86, 211, 212
First Amendment, 135
Flow, 163, 194, 210
Fogal, R.M., 15
Fortunes, 91, 177, 242
Fowler, S., 172
Franchot, P., 211–213
Free markets, 151–155, 157, 176
Freire, P., 237–238
Friends School of Baltimore, 236
Fuld, D., 212

G

Gambling, 135–137, 146
Genesis, 116
Georgetown University, 59, 91
Georgia, 27
Georgia Bureau of Investigation, 27
Gettysburg Address, 230–232
Gibran, K., 78
Gladden, R. Jr., 129, 132, 138, 139
Global warming, 111, 122
God, 6, 116–118, 120, 152, 153
Google, 87, 178
Gospels, 152, 158
Grades, vii, x, xiii, xvi, xix–xxii,
    6, 7, 9, 15–17, 20, 23, 25, 31,
    34, 39, 40, 46, 49–51, 53,
    58, 71–74, 76, 77, 82–84,
    104, 106, 109, 133, 142–144,
    171, 189, 192, 196, 197, 199,
    201, 208, 209, 214–216, 229,
    233, 234
Graduate Record Exam (GRE), 233
Grandmasters, 80, 222, 223, 227–229,
    235
Greenspan, A., 179, 180
Gulen, 164
Gulf oil spill, 110

H

Haertel, E., 19
Hall, B., 27
Hall, P., 129, 132, 138, 139
Hamm, H., 122
Hawking, S., 116–118
Higher education, 26, 30, 33, 39, 143,
    160–163, 167, 169, 203
High school
    curriculum, 72
    developmentally appropriate,
        xiii, xv, 76, 77, 191
    diploma, 162
    dropping out, 164
    grades, 15, 84, 109
    Hall, P., 129, 132, 138, 139
    math, 71, 73, 74
    Mission High, 195–197,
        200, 203
    Patterson Park, 203
    science, 114
    students, 30, 31, 48, 71, 232
    teachers, 50
Homeopathy, 4, 11
Homo sapiens, 53, 119
Horseshoe casino, 138
Houston, 27
How Not To Be Wrong, 70
Hsu, F.-H., 196, 228
Human development, xiii, xv, 10, 39,
    191, 200, 213, 235, 238
Human trafficking, 61
Huxley, A., 145–147
Hypothesis, 4, 6, 7, 11, 17, 24, 101,
    102, 106, 109, 116, 119,
    152–153, 155, 163

I

IBM, 221, 222
Identity Projects, 216, 217, 236
Imitation Game, The, 228
Income inequality, xii, 179, 180, 237

In Search of Ancient Astronauts, 109
Intelligent design (ID), 101, 102,
    108, 111
ITT Educational Services, 160, 162

J

Jefferson, T., 241
Jesus, 153, 158
Jobs, S., 174
Justice Department (U.S. Justice
    Department), 61, 163

K

K-12
    curriculum, x, 10, 191
    education, 30, 136, 203
    schools, 30, 38, 105, 167
Kansas, 101, 102, 122
Kansas State Board of Education, 101,
    122
Kaplan, 29
Kasparov, G., 221, 222, 227–229
Kenntnis, 114, 115
Kindergarten, xiii, 93, 189–191
KIPP, 164
Kohn, A., 171

L

Lagrange, J.-L., 116
Lang, A., 45
LaPierre, W., 135
Laplace, P.-S., 116
Large Hadron Collider (LHC), 97
LA Times, 20
Lehman Brothers, 212
Liberal arts, ix, 36, 93, 122, 123, 202,
    203, 205–207, 209
Libertarianism, 159
Libertarians, 136, 145, 156, 157,
    159, 242

Limbaugh, R., 143
Lincoln, 230, 231, 234
Livio, M., 107
Los Angeles, 20, 61
Los Angeles Unified School
    District, 20
Louisiana, 61
Loyola University Maryland,
    15, 29, 74, 98

M

Mann, H., 242
Marciano, P.L., 172
Market(s)
    definition, 181
    free markets, 151–155,
        157, 158, 176
    fundamentalism, 158
    gambling, 136–138, 146
    job market, 15, 30, 31
    market-based solutions, 158
    market share, 97, 160
    moral limits, 159
    stock market, 8, 233
    tautology of the market, 181
Maryland
    Baltimore, 60, 137, 197, 211
    Baltimore County, 129,
        139, 226
    charter schools, 166
    Common Core standards, 188
    comptroller, 211
    governor, 137
    high school curriculum, 72
    kindergarten, 189, 190
    legalized gambling, 136, 156
    Loyola University, 15, 29, 74, 98
    Prince Georges County, 61
    private schools, 17, 164
    public schools, 17, 27, 60,
        164–166, 197, 240
Massachusetts, 174, 175

Math
    applying, 70, 79, 81
    assessments, 85, 86
    classes, x, xvi, xix, 7, 25, 48, 70, 72,
        73, 82, 104, 212, 229, 233
    college, 71–78
    curriculum, 8, 10, 78–81
    education, 71, 79, 87, 151, 226
    expectations, 73–74
    expertise, 85
    high school, 71, 73, 74
    remedial, 71, 72, 74, 75
    scores, 9, 31, 166, 240
    standards, 73, 88
    students, 48, 57
    third grade, xiii, xvi, xix–xxii, 6, 7, 104
*Mathematical Methods in the Physical
    Sciences*, 73
Mathews, J., 215
McCarthy, J., 110
McCrory, P., 92
Middle States Commission on Higher
    Education, 33–34
Miller, K., 117
Milwaukee Journal Sentinel, 72
Mission High, 195–197, 200
Mississippi, 174, 175
Mizeur, H., 137, 138
Mlodinow, L., 116–118
Mnookin, S., 110
Mobile, A., 110
Moral hazards, 153, 163, 164, 167
Mozilo, A., 212
M-theory, 117, 118
Murphy, S., 172

N

Napoleon, 116
Narrative Sciences, 233
Nation at Risk, A, 38
National Commission on Excellence in
    Education, 38

National Mathematics Advisory
    Council, 71
National Rifle Association
    (NRA), 133, 135
NCLB, *see* No Child Left Behind
    (NCLB)
New Teacher Project, The, 46, 53
Newton, I., 4, 35, 100
New York City
    schools, 18, 51, 52
New York State, 51
New York Times, 18, 94, 95
Nicene Creed, 116
No Child Left Behind (NCLB),
    23–25, 71, 192
North Carolina, 92, 122

O

Obama administration, 92, 162, 174
Obama, B., 92, 141, 162, 174
Objectivism, 158
Ohio, 72, 134, 165
Oklahoma, 72, 122
Oklahoman, 72
Omni Consortium, 61
O'Neil, C., 23
Open Carry Texas, 130
Opinions, 33, 112, 190, 230,
    234, 237
Oprah, 110
Orwell, G., 145–147
Orwellian, 146, 231, 232, 237
Over-fitting, 5, 8–10, 21, 35, 52, 53
Owens, J., 51–54, 58, 62, 63

P

Palin, S., 143
Panic Virus, The, 110
PARCC, *see* Partnership for Assessment
    of Readiness for College and
    Careers (PARCC)

Parents, xxi, xxii, 37, 40, 46, 49, 63, 73, 98, 113, 151, 152, 164, 166, 169, 190, 197, 198, 200, 207–209, 211, 215, 216, 224, 226, 239

Park School of Baltimore, 236

Partnership for Assessment of Readiness for College and Careers (PARCC), 81, 82, 85, 239

Patterson High (Patterson), 197–198, 203

PCAST, *see* President's Council of Advisors on Science and Technology (PCAST)

Pedagogy of the Oppressed, 237, 238

Philippines, 60

Philosophiæ Naturalis Principia Mathematica, 100

Philosophy, 32, 55, 100, 115, 116, 158, 206, 208, 225, 236, 239

Physics, 9, 63, 69, 73, 99, 103, 112, 113, 117, 119, 141, 178, 226

Pink, D., 172, 206

Pledge to America, 141

Postman, N., 145

President's Council of Advisors on Science and Technology (PCAST), 94, 112, 120

Press-Register, 110

Prince Georges County, 61

Princeton Review, 29, 30

Private schools, 17, 23, 92, 152, 160, 164, 235–238, 240

Pseudoscience
  attributes of, x, 56, 108, 191
  data-driven, x, xii, 40, 218
  debunking, 20, 110
  deficit thinking, 192
  education reform, viii, 40
  magical thinking, 11
  narratives, x, xi, 147
  use in education, viii, x, xxi, 12, 40, 147, 237–240

Psychology, 49, 50, 154, 170, 194

Public schools, 17, 23, 27, 38, 51, 53, 60, 122, 164–166, 169, 178, 197, 239, 240

Punished by Rewards, 171

Q

Quantitative literacy, 16, 86, 88

Quill, 233

R

Race to Nowhere, 214, 215

Race to the Top, 174, 175

Rand, A., 158

Ravitch, D., 38, 167

Regan, President, 38

Reign of Error, 167

Religions, 109, 115, 158, 243

Republicans, 11, 92, 141, 143, 157

Rhee, M., 45, 46, 62

Rice, T., 134

Rivoli, P., 157

Rizga, K., 195, 196, 198, 200

Roberts, R., 107

Rothstein, R., 19

Rubrics, 51, 233

S

Sandy Hook, 130, 138, 139

San Francisco, 178, 195–197

Santa Clara, 178

SAT, *see* Scholastic Aptitude Test (SAT)

Satz, D., 159

Sax, L., 114

Scholastic Aptitude Test (SAT), 29, 39, 203, 232, 233

School choice, 181, 238

Science
  definition, 100, 101
  distorting, 112
  essential elements, 4–10, 16, 131, 240
  experiments, 236
  limits, 94, 97, 120, 180, 181
  skills, 16, 112
  teaching, 98, 104
  understanding, 35, 37, 54, 63,
    93, 102
Scopes Trial, 122
Scott, R., 92, 122
Searle, J., 87
Second Amendment, 133, 135
Securities and Exchange Commission
  (SEC), 162
Senate, 135, 137, 142, 161
Shanker, A., 164, 165
Sidwell Friends School, 236
SLO(s), *see* Student Learning Outcome
  (SLOs)
Smartest Guys in the Room, The, 174
Smartphones, 4, 12, 82, 145, 177, 187,
  224, 226, 240
Smeeding, T., 179
Smith, A., 180
Smoking, 7, 47, 212, 213
Socialist, 242
Space shuttle Challenger, 112
St. Albans School, 236
Stanford Center for Research on
  Education Outcomes (CREDO),
  166, 167
Starbucks, 130, 134, 135
Statistics, viii, x, 8, 9, 11, 18, 30, 45,
  71, 72, 95, 132, 162, 217, 233
STEM
  careers, 95, 120
  education, ix, 120, 121
  majors, 31, 32, 92, 94
Sterling, R., 109
Stewart, J., 143
St. Louis, 27

Stock market, 8, 233
Strayer Education, 160
*Student Learning Assessment: Options
  and Resources*, 34
Student learning outcome(s) (SLO(s)),
  6, 36, 47, 225–230, 235

T
Target, 130, 146
Tautological, xi, 22, 115, 117, 118, 169
Tautologies, 6, 40, 94, 115, 118, 192
Tautology, xi, 6, 20, 21, 24, 46, 47,
  53, 101, 116, 117, 151–181,
  192, 239
Teachers Without Borders?, 61
Teaching Goals Inventory (TGI), 34, 35
Teaching-to-the-test, 25
Tennessee, 122
Test of English as a Foreign Language
  (TOEFL), 233
Texas, 61, 130, 157
Theory of Everything, 118, 119
*Travels of a T-shirt in the Global
  Economy*, 157
Trigger warnings, 146
Turing test, 228–230
Turing, A., 228
Twilight Zone, 109

U
UnderstandingScience.org, 107
United States, xx, 16, 24, 30, 38, 60,
  62, 72, 94, 111, 114, 120,
  134–136, 146, 147, 153, 157,
  158, 175, 179, 180, 201, 202,
  212, 241, 242
University of Oklahoma, 122
University of Phoenix, 160
U. S. Census Bureau, 40, 179
U. S. Department of Justice
  (Justice Department), 61

U. S. Department of Labor, 40, 61, 62
U. S. News & World Report, 30, 174, 175
U. S. State Department, 195
U. S. Surgeon General, 212

V

Vaccines, 109, 110
Valencia, R.R., 192
Value-added models (VAMs), 21, 22, 24
VAMs, *see* Value-added models (VAMs)
Virginia Tech, 130, 138

W

Wagner, T., 180, 202, 203
Waiting for Superman, 38
Wall Street, 160, 163, 180

Wall Street Journal, 91
Walmart, O., 134
Washington, DC (District of
    Columbia), 45, 239
Wasmer, J., 139
Wealth of Nations, 180
Weapons of Math Destruction, 23
White Hat Management, 164
*Why Some Things Should
    Not Be For Sale*, 159
Wilson, E.O., 240
Wissenschaft, 114, 115
Wordsmith, 233

Z

Zakaria, F., 206
Zhao, Y., 200–202, 207

CPSIA information can be obtained
at www.ICGtesting.com
Printed in the USA
LVHW02s2109020918
588942LV00005B/45/P

9 783319 778594